LIES
Have Ruined the World

LIES
Have Ruined the World

How the lies of religion,
government and the courts have invaded every
corner of our lives, enslaving billions on the globe.
And the solutions that will give us back our Freedoms.

DENNIS RICHARD PROUX

Copyright © Dennis Richard Proux.

All rights reserved. No part of this book may be reproduced in any form or by any electronic or mechanical means, including information storage and retrieval systems, without permission in writing from the publisher, except by reviewers, who may quote brief passages in a review.

ISBN: 978-1-63684-564-7   (Paperback Edition)
ISBN: 978-1-63684-565-4   (Hardcover Edition)
ISBN: 978-1-63684-563-0   (E-book Edition)

Book Ordering Information

Phone Number: 315 288-7939 ext. 1000 or 347-901-4920
Email: info@globalsummithouse.com
Global Summit House
www.globalsummithouse.com

Printed in the United States of America

CONTENTS

Foreword ix
Introduction xvii

Chapter 1: THE Biggest LIE of all: RELIGION 1
Chapter 2: Mass Murder, Rape, and Genocide: A Love Story 31
Chapter 3: Lies, Myths, and Fabrications 39
Chapter 4: Religious Realities 43
Chapter 5: If Religion Were True 48
Chapter 6: The God Quiz 52
Chapter 7: Religious Outcomes from Lying Liars 54
Chapter 8: Religious Reactions to New Scientific Discoveries
throughout History 66
Chapter 9: The Age of the Earth 69
Chapter 10: Lies and Fraud derived from the greatest lie of all:
RELIGION 72
Chapter 11: Gods are nothing New 79
Chapter 12: A Short Quiz 88
Chapter 13: Every Religionist is a LIAR (about religion and
usually much more) 91
Chapter 14: Religion vs. Reality: No Match 96
Chapter 15: Contract on A Scarica 103
Chapter 16: Liars Who Have Impacted My Life and Community ... 108
Chapter 17: A Lie Begins the Loss of Freedom 136
Chapter 18: Elected Officials have all been influenced by MONEY. 139
Chapter 19: If you see an 'EXPERT', you have been fooled. 155
Chapter 20: All Lawyers are SCUM 160
Chapter 21: The LIE of Race, Gender, Ethnicity, and Nationality ... 180

Chapter 22: Truth is Truth A Lie is A Lie Hypocrisy is
             Hypocrisy Debauchery is Debauchery 185
Chapter 23: The United States Personal Income Tax System
             isn't FAIR 189
Chapter 24: Lies Told by Your State 201
Chapter 25: The Big LIE of Wall Street 212
Chapter 26: The Lie of the Self-made Man 219
Chapter 27: Institutions of Higher Learning have become a LIE 224

Bibliography 233

DEDICATED

to
ADDIE AND WILLIAM
An Oasis of Sanity in a
schizophrenic world.

And to

MY DAUGHTERS
Who have always encouraged and inspired me.
For we know that the search for truth and compassion
is a never ending journey in life.

FOREWORD

FACTS have created this wonderful and progressive world in which we live. Facts are the basis for every great medical breakthrough. Facts are behind every single one of the trillions of components, which make up our world of computers. Facts have led us to breakthroughs in biogenetics and bioengineering. Facts have opened up to us the vastness of space, and a greater understanding of our universe. Facts are the reality of 'what is' and science is the process for getting there. Facts are always verifiable. If something cannot be falsified, then it is meaningless. Facts are everywhere and can be discovered by anyone.

Every statement that a person makes is either true, or it is a lie.

So that's where I began. Can you imagine what it would be like to wake up one day and realize that everything you once believed was actually all a lie? For me, the realization did not arrive all on one day. The process was gradual and involved a lot of reading, living, and agonizing. I felt alone, and I remained in deep denial in the face of facts and evidence at every turn.

Death is real and permanent.

If I accepted the fact that my religion had been one lie after another, then there could be no Heaven. If there was no Heaven, I would never again see my most beloved sister, Deanna, who died as a child. That was an extremely difficult hurdle on my way to discovering truths about the world.

Patriotism must always be rational.

I would have to accept that my country was responsible for many heinous crimes through its history. The unfettered pride I felt in my supposed nationality would have to be tempered by a greater sense of humility and an onerous obligation to repay the wrongs. Those wrongs, which had enabled me to experience such great opportunities for wealth and personal expression, had harmed countless others.

Rights are different from wrongs.

It would mean that I could no longer take for granted a Justice system that gave me rights, but stole freedoms, dignity and opportunity from the majority of our citizens.

Some might call it a loss of innocence, but, in fact, my entire past had been a product of the religious, social and community lies that were instilled in everything that I did. I had become the lie myself.

Surrounded by FACT and truth, everything else was now just the noise of unverifiable gibberish used by religionists, dishonorable politicians, unconscionable health quacks, incompetent judges, and millions of superstitious liars.

Discovery of a whole new world.

The first fact-based book I read was *Ascent of Man* by Jacob Bronowski. There it was, the beauty of taking life on its own terms. A marvelous world opened up to me, as though I had been blind all my life. The next book I read that changed my thinking was *Flim Flam* by James Randi (whom I believe to be one of the greatest human beings to have ever lived). He taught me that knowledge is about facts, not just claims, but verifiable, testable, repeatable data. He helped me to see that "extraordinary claims, require extraordinary proof." I was an ordained Christian minister at the time and began to wonder if any of the claims of religion had been subjected to this vigorous standard of verifiable truth. I soon realized that everything about religion, the doctrines, the rites, the edicts, were all anecdotal, unproven, unjustified, unsubstantiated and actually quite cruel when exposed to the naked light of truth.

I couldn't get enough. I wanted to challenge everything. I read Bertrand Russell's *Why I am not a Christian*. I got a subscription to the *Skeptical Inquirer*. I devoured every issue. I read every book that they recommended—and there were hundreds. I read the works of Martin Gardner, Paul Kurtz, more James Randi, and probably half of the wonderful catalogue of Prometheus Books at the time. Then I read *The Voyage of the Beagle* by Charles Darwin, and I knew that I was a liar, a teller of the lies, which I had been taught. Everything smashed me against a giant mirror. I was forced to face the fact that I would either lead a meaningless life or live a life open to truth in all that I did.

Truth is a long-time comin'.

It took me twenty-three years to cast off my indoctrinated past. It was gut-wrenching. One of the toughest realities, which I knew I would have to face, was the fact that people whom I care for very much, would probably hate these changes in me. My very existence would now be a direct challenge to the lies of their lives. My caring for them has not changed, but I will no longer allow the fear of the loss of their affection to keep me enslaved to the lies of our lives.

It has become easier over time. I never saw any of the truth-tellers in church (none of the great authors, whom I had been exposed to, would ever be found in church) and I never found believers willing to work with facts, instead of myths. Fairy tales, subjective experiences and outlandish claims were the basis for their own beliefs. I came to realize that Lies have ruined the wisdom of the world, and lies are on constant attack against science and truth, in all its wonderful forms.

An Open Invitation.

I invite you to spend time with my new friends: Charles Darwin, James Randi, Richard Dawkins, Christopher Hitchens, Martin Gardner, Paul Kurtz, Thomas Paine, Bertrand Russell, Ibn Warriq, Carl Sagan, Randel

Helms, Joe Nickell, Robert Ingersoll, Mark Twain, Harry Houdini, Matt Taibbi, Graeme Donald, William Stiebing, Mark Perakh, Gavin Menzies, R. Joseph Hoffman, Gerd Ludemann, Neil Shubin, C. Dennis McKinsey, Kancha Illaiah, and more than two thousand other authors. Many of them will be listed in the Bibliography at the end of this book. Don't be surprised if you can't find most of these books at your local library, because the shelves are probably already packed with religious devotionals, cook books and the latest diet gimmicks. I was actually able to find very few of them locally.

The truth and the facts will begin to overwhelm you. You will learn to sniff out the lies. You will no longer be comfortable living with the lies of society, nor the fools who will try to steal away your new freedoms.

A challenge to my students.

For one of the graduate-level classes that I taught, I asked my students to make out a list of ten things, which they knew to be absolutely true, and to return to class the next week with the list. At the start of the next class, I asked them to place their lists in a pile at the front of the room and pick out one list, not their own. I then asked them to look at the list and decide which item on the list might not be defensible with facts. (As you can imagine many of the students listed religious ideas, national historical events, the Ten Commandments, clichés, and so on). They put a star by that item, and then, handed the paper back to the original student. The next assignment was for the students to write a five page paper defending the factuality of the starred item on their paper. When they came back to class, the papers were again piled at the front of the class, and again, the students came forward, chose a paper, not their own, and graded that paper on how successful the student had been at making their case. Most had had no experience in defending the fact-based truth of what they held dear. It was a business class and I wanted my students to realize that we live in a world which quite often has no factual basis whatsoever. Businesses have to run on facts. Personal lives have to be run on facts. Personal health and hygiene must be based on factual information. To live on lies has serious consequences. To try to run a business on fallacious information is asking for disaster.

As a consultant to major corporations, I was often concerned that their business was being conducted on unwarranted assumptions. Anyone who asks the wrong questions, will necessarily go in the wrong direction, no matter how good their answers will be. Many strategic plans have failed exactly for this reason. Facts are everywhere, but they are useless unless they are acquired and put to use. If a person can read, but doesn't, then he has no advantage over an illiterate. If a person can afford healthy food, but doesn't eat healthy, then he has no advantage over the poorest of citizens. If a person can walk, but doesn't exercise, then he has no advantage over a paraplegic.

Everything you need is all around you.

We live in a natural world. Everything we need to know can be obtained through observation, experimentation and education. There is NO unnatural world. There have never been miracles, or the suspension of the laws of nature for, or by, anyone. Visions, resurrection of the dead, ESP, fortune-telling, cosmic omens, the supernatural, and reincarnation, are all nonsense. Proponents of these phenomenon are easily proven to be nonsensical by quite natural means. In fact, I have personally investigated hundreds of claims. These events were all shown to be lies or delusions.

When I studied archaeology under Dr. George Mendenhall and Dr. Paul Orlin at the University of Michigan, we participated in a project in Israel under Dr. Yigael Yadin. At the site, it became obvious that some were only there to prove what they already believed to be the truth of their religions. Unfortunately for them, the evidence showed just the opposite. What they expected to find, was not there. The facts, the evidence, pointed 180 degrees away from their preconceived beliefs. The strong evidence of a major habitation of early Israelites just could not be confirmed in any way at the site where we were digging near the Negev Desert.

Truth is never schizophrenic.

During my naval service in the early 70's I worked as a Russian linguist with a Top Secret Cryptographic Clearance for the United States. Our objective was to find the 'truth' about Russian movements and intentions. Anything short of absolute, objective, provable data was unacceptable.

There was no room for compartmentalized thinking: rational thinking at work, and irrational belief systems in our personal lives. But I did just that, and so did most of my comrades. We were mostly practicing religionists and undoubtedly patriotic in an unquestioning way.

History is made by writers, not by people who lived it.

History is not made by the people who lived events, but by the people who *wrote* about those events. All history accounts are distortions, or lies, to a greater or lesser extent. Please read *1421* by Menzies (where the true discoverers of the New World are confirmed to be the Chinese and not Christopher Columbus). It will change everything that the western world has ever thought about its own history. There is more knowledge regarding these historical events available to us today than what the original authors could possibly have known. What we find is that too often the chroniclers had very personal agendas in how they related their so-called histories. They may not have even cared to capture history in the factual sense that is so important to modern people. When we look at the writings about religious history, we can be fairly certain that the writers were not trying to capture 'events' as they happened, but more likely, to reinforce a different theology, of a totally different era. The many, many writers who tried to capture the events of Jesus's life and death were so totally removed from the events and eye-witnesses that their accounts are clearly a presentation of their own agendas, not a faithful exposition of any religious movement. The chasm of disagreement among these writers, factual errors, and superstitious beliefs (astrology, omens, fortune-telling) are all clear indicators that the real events are now lost to history. Just for fun, on this point, read: *What They Never Told You in History Class* by Kush. When I read his book it was so refreshing to discover the fascination of history written for discovery and not with a hidden agenda in mind. The historical characters end up being very human and very approachable.

Billions of people will hate that they have been proven wrong.

There are over six billion people in the world who will never be open to hearing these words. Their minds are made up and *closed*. But I am not writing these words for them. I am writing them for you. If you are diligent about the journey to truth, then you will certainly be set free. As a result of releasing yourself from these lies, your children will live free and the world will have a beacon of light that cannot be extinguished.

Facts, facts, and more facts. I intend to excoriate the lies and the liars. So fasten your seat belt, it's going to be a bumpy ride.

INTRODUCTION

For twenty-three years I have avoided writing this book because I had hoped that someone else would have done it. But sadly it has not been done.

I am writing this book because I believe that all humans yearn to be free in every way. They want to discover their own worlds, to realize their own full potential. The enemies of these desires are the very institutions, which must be challenged with a massive assault of TRUTH. Truth will expose their lies, and the ultimate damage that those lies have wreaked upon the earth.

Author Disclaimer.

I am not a writer, and that will probably become painfully obvious. I have lived a life that exposed me to enough experiences that will validate my conclusions, however. I am not writing this exposé on our world because I am exempt from the consequences of being untruthful. My hands aren't clean. And I have shown cowardice in confronting the LIES that I will expose in these pages. I cannot expose the lies without a level of harshness towards us liars that will seem cruel to many. However, I know that the lies are so deeply entrenched in our world, that simple defense mechanisms and denial will otherwise quickly kick-in and soften the blow of being singled out as liars. We are frauds and hypocrites who have contributed to mass murder, hate and destruction. My finger is pointing directly at YOU, but I am painfully aware that four fingers are pointing harshly right back at ME. I have been a Christian minister, a non-questioning patriot who was more than willing to kill for my country, a sexist, a bigot, a compromiser of others' freedoms, and a coward! The few individuals, who will find common cause with me, will be greatly outnumbered by those who would like to shut me up permanently. I have already experienced that a thousand times in casual conversations throughout my life.

I was very young, when I realized that everyone was lying. They were lying not just about personal protective information, but about universal, community realities, which had a great effect on how the world would progress or regress.

At age ten I heard a sermon about how women, who worked outside of the home, were destroying the family unit, and could be justly compared to whores. That was a lie and everyone knew it was a lie, but no one said anything. All the nurses at the hospital were women. All my teachers were women. All the clerks at the grocery store were women. All the cleaning people, who cleaned after hours, were women. All the secretaries were women. Even the minister (who gave the sermon) had a wife who was a teacher. This man was a hypocrite, but he was highly respected and used the Bible to substantiate his outrageous claims. It seems so foreign now, but people used to argue about whether or not women should be allowed in the workplace or get equal pay. It was debated whether women could attend law or medical school or be allowed to join the local country club. It was expected that women, and women alone, would be primary caregiver for the children in the home. The rich phrase 'chauvinist pig' hadn't even been invented yet, but it would have been a good start. All these lies have been protected by a male-dominated society with determination to keep it that way.

My hometown Melting Pot.

I lived in a city, which was divided right down the middle by a river. Whites lived on one side of the river and blacks lived, only, on the other side. I asked several people why this was so and got the reply that 'sometimes things are better off left just the way they are.' In fact, I was told that it was not wise to challenge why God did things the way he did. Mixing of the races was clearly not a wise thing to do and considered 'ungodly', because

God himself separated the races in order to keep the faith of his chosen people pristine. That advice came from religious and civic leaders. It was a lie, but everyone believed it, and even retold it. We were taught that there was a 'natural' order to things and it was best to just accept them. In some states, when I was growing up, it was illegal for persons of different races to associate, date or marry. In Virginia, it could even lead to the punishment of death. I played on all-white sports teams from ten years old all the way through high school. Often our leagues wouldn't even allow the black teams in, so that we wouldn't have to play on the other side of the river. Was all this sick? Was it all a lie, even then? Was it a lie that the WHOLE COMMUNITY conspired to tell and to live? I can tell you that we lived it, and we were afraid to confront it.

Our schools faithfully taught us the lies.

The athletic managers and coaches were not the only authority figures who believed and perpetuated these lies. The lies came in many forms. Many through education. My Middle School English teacher believed that the earth was flat. She said that the Bible was very clear on this point. She told us she had served in the military, traveled extensively, and had never encountered the earth as 'curved'! Yet she kept a globe of the earth on her desk! But when my seventh grade science teacher started talking about evolution, as a fairly firmly supported theory of the human race, one of his students (a fundamentalist) went home and told his parents. They registered a complaint and had the teacher sanctioned for teaching lies and corrupting his students. We all knew that the parents were lying. We all knew that the school board was wrong. But none of us said anything. The teacher acquiesced and removed all material from the walls that referred to Darwin's theory. He was told that his job was in jeopardy and that 'corrupting youth' would be a difficult charge to live down for a teacher. I would not be exposed to this rich material again, until choosing my own personal reading selections, long after I had completed Graduate School in business. But I knew that they were all lying. I just wasn't brave enough to lead the parade in the right direction.

Social pressure can stop even the fastest train.

It was startlingly obvious, that when anyone stood up to any of these lies, they were branded as radicals, atheists, communists, destroyers of youth, and were ostracized from the community. When people tried to challenge lies, they became the target of gossip, which had nothing to do with what they were challenging.

Always tell the truth.

I was taught that a person should always tell the truth. Adults said, 'Honesty is the best policy,' but they did just the opposite. My parents lied. Religious leaders lied. Civic leaders lied. I was not exempt from this play it safe telling of lies. It was just easier to go along. Don't rock the boat. No matter how many minorities, females, foreigners, scientists, or courageous people get hurt. It's just too dangerous to challenge these powerful influences.

When the first heart transplant took place in South Africa, the remarkable event was denounced as opposing God's law. Religionists said that the recipient would be consigned to Hell for taking another man's soul. It was a lie, but brought shame on progressive doctors, scientists and health professionals. Blood transfusions were not practiced in the United States until the middle of the Twentieth Century, even though the first ones took place in the Seventeenth Century. The Catholic Church stopped the practice dead in its tracks and drove the scientist, who engineered the practice, out of town and out of hope! The Church caused fear, where hope and encouragement should have been the reaction. It took years to overcome the fear of retribution generated by so-called leaders with this patent garbage. A physician at Cleveland Clinic told me about all the Catholics who had denounced this scientific breakthrough, and had bypass or transplant surgery at the Clinic. Even the Bishop, who was still "bothered by the ethical concerns of such procedures", had a by-pass done, as well.

The Curse on Eve.

For centuries the world was taught that women should experience excruciating pain in child-birth. This was God's way, and was the result of Eve's sinful act in the Garden of Eden. I was taught this in the 1950's. Of course, it was a lie. In fact, it was used to keep women down (in their place!) by male religious leaders and ignorant male chauvinists. These same liars had for over a century preached against the work done on germs, viruses and bacteria, because they were all used as agents of God to punish evil, and should not be interfered with! Women and children were most often the victims of this anti-scientific attack upon the vagaries of life. More lies from the very leaders of our communities. But they had the Apostle Paul to thank for his great insight into the "world being demon possessed until the return of the Messiah."

We were all taught that a fetus in the womb did not become 'ensouled' until it experienced quickening at birth. "Quickening" was the act of a newborn baby breathing on its own after the Holy Spirit entered the birthing process. If the fetus was aborted before quickening, it would be consigned to Limbo for all eternity. It would never experience normal sadness or joy, but it could never go to heaven. If a fetus made it to birth, it could go to Purgatory, where it could work off the effects of 'original sin' and work its way to Heaven. That's what we were all taught. But things changed drastically, when the churches realized that they had a real winner on their hands (you know, fuller offering plates to support the work of the righteous Pro-Lifers), if they changed the time of becoming fully human to conception! That way they could pander to the anti-abortion crowd by pretending to be protectors of life. What a lie!

If Adam and Eve obtained the gift of knowledge, they sure didn't pass it on to religionists.

The problem lies even deeper for religionists. The doctrine of 'original' sin is a total historical lie. Again, Adam and Eve, the Fall, the onset of death as a result of mankind's grievous error of offending the Creator, never happened. The attempt to protect this doctrine by hundreds of theologians, scholars and popes with encyclicals and documents, was just to reinforce the foolishness of the entire enterprise. Even Augustine was willing to consign 'unborns' to the torments of Hell, in order to protect this specious doctrine (Original Sin) of his church. There is no 'moral' ground to stand on, to defend something that has no basis in history, or, in fact. It is science that taught the apologists of religion about what actually went on inside of the womb, not the 'visions'of ascetic irrationalists through the centuries. Besides, their doctrinal position on Limbo, Purgatory, fetuses, 'ensoulment', and quickening have changed so often, through the centuries, that you need a special program just to identify the players.

Check their catechisms to verify these blatant lies and deceptions.

You might have to get a key, for the lock, on the door, in the basement, of the Vatican!

We all knew that they were lying, but no one said anything. They could now have even stronger power over women because only women have abortions and only women, who have abortions, go to Hell for it.

The Church has changed its mind many times before. One example is when the Catholic Church got rid of Saint Christopher. It seems that this 'saint' never existed. Most of my friends wore ST. C's medals around their neck; in fact, I would say it would have been probably 100 to 1 over those who actually wore a crucifix around their neck. It was preached that St. C healed thousands, St. C kept people safe on airplanes, and in battles in war, St. C won basketball, baseball, football and tennis matches for the wearers, and St. C kept pre-pubescent teens from getting acne, St. C was a lie and we all knew it! Do you know anyone, who still wears a St. C medal, anymore? How on earth could millions of medals just disappear, when we had the 'fact' (strongly promoted by the Roman Catholic Church) of St. C rammed down our throats, as true, when we were growing up? It was a Lie.

What happened to that other fallacious doctrine of the religionists? You know, the one about the dead, who are all waiting for the Day of Resurrection? It seems, that there are an awful lot of people, who have been comforted by their religious leaders, with the notion that 'junior is looking down from heaven on us, right now.' 'Why, they're all up there singing in the choir.' Too bad their own holy books paint a totally different reality about the state of 'death' and this time of waiting for the resurrection. Again, St. Paul makes it very clear that there will be a Day of Judgment when ALL the dead will be raised on the same day, some to eternal life and some to eternal damnation. So, how come, everyone is up there watching right now?

During my lifetime Mary went from simple 'virgin' (not many early believers believed this), to 'Ever virgin' (no one knew this at all), to 'Immortal virgin' (nothing in scripture even alludes to this), to 'Mother of God' virgin (had to wait a very long time for this designation). And in the same period I got to witness Mary's own mother go from a local 'nobody' to sinless carrier of the mother of god. They said she never died. And for hundreds of thousands of years not a single person in the entire world knew that, until Pope Pius XII realized that all Christian churches were beginning to look a lot alike - and the possession of this specialized Mary would certainly be a benefit to the church which possessed her. Maybe he was still exhausted from having all the Franciscan brothers slaughter a million non-catholics during WWII in Serbia/Croatia (while he was hiding in the Vatican basement). Eye-witnesses said that the dead/ beheaded bodies were so thick on the lakes, that you could have walked to the other side of the lake on dead bodies, and not gotten your shoes wet. With the funny glasses he wore he probably couldn't have seen beyond this grand play for Mariolatry. Of course it was a lie, but a lie that was needed to further drive the dividing stake between religions and sanity. Send your Peter's pence to the Pope and don't forget St. Bingo night is every Tuesday. Please don't bring your St. C medal for luck, it is just so darn embarrassing.

All these institutions were lying. Government leaders, religious leaders and community leaders all playing to their own advantage with lies. And we knew it. They kept passing endless laws to discriminate, deprive and destroy the fabric of society. The freedoms of billions of people have been affected by laws, which made females not equal to males, which made whites more free than blacks, which made gays invisible, which made all foreigners a danger to our way of life. Whites could not marry blacks. Women could only own a small portion of the family estate. If gays were killed, everyone looked the other way. All lies, but the stink and the garbage have not gone away. Leaders still pander and lies still are the culture that we live in, and support, and are willing to kill and ostracize for.

No safety in calling on our historical heritage.

I looked at history to see, if perhaps, we had just lost our way. Maybe there was a better time, when persons, with high ideals, told the truth, and were willing to devote their lives to the truths, which make us all free. Sadly, I found that there never has been a time of truth and honor.

Thomas Jefferson wrote so glowingly about the right of everyone to be free, yet excluded women, landless persons, the poor and slaves. Jefferson himself kept slaves. Not just kept, but raped. When a person is in chains, living in the barn, and is not free to ever leave, that person cannot have consensual sex, with the Massa, EVER. The Founding Fathers might have thought that a justification for this activity might have been that everyone was doing it, but I'm sure it was never expressed, just silently agreed to. Slaves were a source of free labor, 'not gonna let them go'. He let them go after he died (it became a means to settle bankruptcies). He was a despicable liar, a hypocrite, and one of our great Founding Fathers of the Lie. Do you think that everyone knew that he was lying about these things while all this was going on? Of course, they did. Some were just protecting their own lies. Most had no power to do anything. The lie lived on for centuries, after good old Thomas had left the scene. And the lie lived on because historians continued to lie to us about what had really happened. It was not until the last two decades that the truth about these things finally came out. Still there are masses of people with blinders on, who willingly denigrate anyone who publishes such truths.

What is there to be said about good ole' George Washington? He fought for freedom, that is, the freedom of commercial wealth for wealthy landowners, and he did quite well for himself. He had slaves—free labor to create more wealth. And we now have convincing evidence that his slaves didn't even get to eat the food, which they produced from the Massa's huge estates. They scrounged for food out of the local creeks! He was a liar and delusional about the so-called great service he was providing for humanity. After all, didn't he allow the slaves to fight alongside whites in the Great War to bring freedom? When it was all said and done, women were no better off. Slaves certainly were no better off. Poor farmers got nothing, except amputated feet from the freezing, icy snow. And then of course, old George went right up to the cathedrals of the religious leaders to thank them for the victory, which God had delivered into his hands.

Freedom? For whom?

Please read: *In Her Place: A Documentary History of Prejudice Against Women* by Joshi. Well worth your time. It is tragic how many respected leaders, writers and columnists have written demeaning articles about the role of women in the world. This collection of articles should certainly sober up anyone who thinks that the work of freedom and equality is anywhere near to being accomplished.

Our government was supposed to be established on the basis of the right of the people to be governed, *only*, based upon their consent. When did women consent to being discriminated against, and not voting for centuries? When did slaves consent to being enslaved by the government? When did Native Americans consent to having their land confiscated, and their lives destroyed? Consent was never given. It was stolen by slick liars, who stole this great land for themselves and their own personal pleasure. They called it Divine Right of Kings, or Rule of Law, or the right to enact laws to enforce their whims. All lies. These lies were exposed by Thomas Paine (*Common Sense*), but he was quickly dispatched to irrelevance by the religious and the wealthy, who never did buy into his crazy notions of 'freedom' for all. Well these powdered Whigs have never left New England wealth, nor the halls of government. The lies they have told have only multiplied.

Let justice fall like rain.

Were we able to turn to the high courts of the land to find truth and justice? Hardly. Centuries of discrimination, injustice and destruction of opportunities, for the great majority of our citizens, were the result of the societal lies, which were written in stone, by small-minded men, in black robes (or was it white hoods and sheets?).

On one occasion, when I was in graduate school, I was asked by a friend to help him out at a local private country club. He asked me to be attentive to a group of men sitting around a large table. Mostly I was just delivering to them fresh alcoholic drinks. One of the men was an elderly person, whom I recognized as a local judge (he was decidedly drunk, already). One of the others (all lawyers) told the judge that he 'owed' him one and the judge consented to help him 'win' his case. It was not about justice. It was about 'horse trading'. The lawyer then reminded him that his client was wealthy, and that the judge should allow the case to be dragged out for a couple of years to build up fees. I asked my friend if I had heard them correctly. He told me that this went on all the time. Anyone who goes to court thinking that the courts are about justice are just suckers that the system will eat alive. He warned me, that if I told anyone what I had heard, that there would be 'hell' to pay. I wondered how much of the justice system in America was just a total lie. Over my lifetime I have, unfortunately, seen very honorable people destroyed by lying judges and lawyers.

Everyone needs a safe harbor away from the storm.

We had a local priest, in my hometown of Saginaw, who liked to bring in young girls from El Salvador to serve as housekeepers for his Manse. They almost never spoke English, and they never went anywhere (including shopping). It was clear that they were used for sexual favors by the priest. Many, many people talked about how the priests had to sacrifice so much of their lives to be priests, that it was OK, if they got this little bit of 'service'. Since these young girls were often returned to Central America, in the middle of the night, and most likely pregnant, the scandals were mostly abated. All too often, the local 'policia' (in our wonderful diocese in Saginaw) fully protected the church from any potential scandals.

I had a friend confide in me that he had been repeatedly raped by a priest, when he was a young man. The priest had been a counselor for sexually abused children, and was considered to be a 'specialist' in his field. This priest also ran a 'special' camp for young boys in a retreat setting in Upper Canada. My friend described to me, in great detail, what this priest had done on many occasions. He described an especially disturbing time, when the priest, in polka dot briefs, greeted him in his office, and proceeded to rape him anally, with a broom stick.

I reported this to the local sheriff. I reported it to the State Police. I reported it to the Bishop of the local Diocese. What happened? My life was threatened. My house was broken into. A local Monsignor called to remind me, that I had attacked the church, which was also known as the 'church of the Mob'. "Capice?!" I did follow-up. I was told that I had never made any such report! The priest is still in the parish. He still goes to Canada, with little children, each year. My friend has attempted suicide, on several occasions, and his life has never been 'normal', even after years and years of counseling.

Kennedy, Johnson, Nixon, Clinton, Bush…

In my lifetime, political leaders have blatantly lied to the people they were elected to protect. Is it about debauchery, sending young citizens off to die in a war, which was unjust and uncalled for, or is it about 'laws be damned', I have power! How 'bout congenital liars, debauched lives and massive efforts towards concealing the truth for decades. That doesn't say much for the Key Man theory of history, where the right leaders supposedly came along, at the right time, to lead the nation. We have experienced too many horrible presidents to buy into that theory anymore.

I ask again, why is everyone lying? And what impact does it ultimately have on the real truth being found?

No government, no religion, no society has a right to lie, to manipulate, to deceive, or to enslave. But all have done it. Every religion has denigrated women (and still does). Every religion has been complicit in slavery. Every society has excluded the 'other'. Every religious group has stood firmly behind the wars of their nation. All based on lies, superstitions, and hate. These lies lead down one road: to the destruction of personal freedoms. Governments, religions, and societies create endless laws to discriminate, deprive and destroy hopes for freedom of billions of people. When the very fabric of society insinuates that women are not equal, that minorities are less than, that foreigners will pollute the good things that we have, then the lies have become the culture, the standard, the derangement.

Who will finally expose these lies? Not religion, not government, not societies. They all have a vested interest, wealth, and leverage to maintain. So they glorify the lies, which they have been entrusted with! No System is *ever* self-correcting. Resistance to change is just too great, and usually stands firmly on the side of the LIE.

So how do we do it?

I am well aware that a fish in water knows no other environment. His surroundings are his natural world. To have the courage to challenge the lies, which have infected all of the institutions of the world, which we live in, is to step into the 'unnatural' world of being attacked, hated, despised and gasping for air. I love my country, but I am not so foolish to ever say again 'my country right or wrong, but my country'. If the love of country is greater than the love of truth, then both are irretrievably lost! I love life. I love the endless opportunities for discovery and growth. I think that life, with all its complexity, is beautiful and worth the journey. I love the promise, which was solidly affirmed at the beginning of our country, that all mankind is created equal and, by right, should be free. People should never be governed, by any entity, without each person's consent. In our quest for true freedom, we must annihilate all royalty, all autocracies, all isms, all slavery, all LIES, all coercion from societal and communal hypocrisies, and all non representative systems. For this to happen, we will need to expose ALL the lies, which prevent us from experiencing the absolute joy of total self-determination, and the passive slothfulness of being chained to the wall of community slavery. If the comfort of living a LIE, is more enticing than the aspiration to live in a world of equality free from constraints with the opportunity to fulfill one's potential, then please pass this book on to that non-religious, friend of yours.

I will expose what I believe to be the greatest lies in the world today, and I will suggest healthy alternatives.

Number one: Every religion is a LIE. They are based on lies and they are passed on by liars.

I am woefully aware of Jonathan Swift's warning: "It's difficult to reason someone out of something that they've never been reasoned into."

But here goes.

CHAPTER 1

THE Biggest LIE of all: RELIGION

All western religions (Judaism, Christianity, Islam, and all their derivations) are based on the premise that Judaism is true. If Judaism can be proven to be false, a fabrication, then all the other western religions will fall like a house of cards. Christianity is totally dependent upon the prophecies which state that a messiah will come out of the ranks of Judaism. The very foundation of the Christian religion is a recitation of genealogies from the Old Testament and predictions from the prophets. Islam is a cornucopia of quotes from the Old Testament, and the Koran shows the early workings of substantial Jewish input. Mohamed clearly views the history of Judaism and the leadership of Jesus as essential to the foundation of Islam.

The Jewish religion is based on the belief that all sin came into the world through an act, directly counter to God's commands, committed by Adam and Eve. God created death as a consequence of this act. The punishment was to be final and irrevocable for all of God's creation (this included all humans, all plant life, all animal life, all viruses, all bacteria, i.e. all life).

Judaism: First attempts at 'green' gardening don't work out.

Yet, the Garden of Eden never existed. **Adam and Eve never existed.** Without Adam and Eve, the fall from grace could not have happened. The world was not created 6,000 years ago. Timelines, which have been heavily supported by Jewish scholars and Christian apologists over the centuries, are totally unsupportable by their own chronologies. Their stories and characters can no longer fit into what we know, scientifically, about ages, eras, and confirmed data. Unfortunately for the creative liars who wrote about these made-up events, the world has uncovered DNA, mitochondrial DNA, and paleoanthropological artifacts, among hundreds of other scientific discoveries. The mitochondrial DNA (the genetic information which is passed on from mother to daughter) had already spread around the world hundreds and thousands of years before these supposed events took place. This genetic material was spread thousands of miles, and thousands of years, away from the Middle East by the time period that Judaism describes.

Thus, no cosmic 'sin' event could have occurred. At least, not by the fictional characters of Adam and Eve, who were created out of pagan myths. Death has been a natural part of existence for every living creature on the earth for billions of years. Death did not come as a result of one 'apple-cruncher'; it is as normal and common as the sun rising. Unfortunately for those who enjoy feeling worthless without groveling, there was no "sin" and no casus belli for death.

The whole structure and foundation for Judaism is thus wiped away. It is totally based on the disobedience of two humans and the consequent suffering and death of all humanity and life. The sacrificial systems, the laws, the history all are now seen to be completely meaningless.

It logically follows: Jesus could not have been the fulfillment of these lies. He wasn't the answer to any intelligent question. In the Christians' own theology "by one man sin entered into the world and by one man it was redeemed." However, there was nothing to be redeemed from. Humans were just humans. People are flawed, yes, but are certainly not horrible creatures that deserved to be tortured and killed for one single act. How did all the babies, who apparently also were consigned to eternal damnation, deserve such a fate? Only in the minds of some fairly primitive sadists and masochists could these horrible conclusions have been feasible. It was the delusion of Jesus and his followers that he and he alone was the solution to that age old problem of sin and death. To be fair, we can't even be sure that Jesus himself believed his own stories. A reading of the events after his earthly departure confirms that almost all of the stories about Jesus were invented. The writers are unknown or unknowable and likely held greatly varying agendas.

Therefore, **Judaism is built on LIES.** The creation of a murderous, tyrannical god (modeled from pagans) and their tradition of sacrifices are documented as human fabrications.

Without Judaism being factual, there could be **NO** Christianity. Where did Judaism get all these horrific stories about human sacrifice and sacrifice of animals by the millions? They borrowed heavily from the pagan myths that they experienced all around them. That was what they knew, but it was not based on reality. It was not based on any observation of the natural world all around them. It was not based on any healthy mental calculations on how human beings could learn to live together. The founding of Christianity had the same problems. They were surrounded by Judaism and pagan mythologies. They knew nothing else. So they re-wrote the ending of the story of Judaism, threw in lots of pagan ideas, and there you had it. A brand new religion that was ninety-nine percent borrowed from lots of made up stories, again, none of them based on reality, or history, or facts, just the desires of lots of local religionists to make sense of their worlds. It didn't work, even for them. They were still building on ancient myths that couldn't be so easily explained in their world.

The justification for the existence of Christianity was to present an escape from the angry god of the Old Testament, but the grounding for such an agenda does not exist. Christianity tried to present Jesus as the ultimate faithful Jew, a keeper of the law. But even Paul tried to present him as one who was above the law and the destroyer of its consequences, including death. It sounds confusing, because it is. There is no basis established for a 'savior' being needed to undo the damage caused by the mythological acts of the first two humans. And there is certainly no rational explanation for why the horrendous death of one human being would equate to the billions of humans committing trillions of acts of sin. Jesus was not the ultimate pagan sacrificial lamb, the scapegoat for the first chapter of Genesis.

So it follows, without the myths of Judaism and Christianity, there could be NO Roman Catholics—1.3 billion people adhere to this particular brand of lies, and NO Protestants, and NO Orthodox Christians, and NO Baptists, and NO Pentecostals, and NO Jehovah Witnesses, No Seventh Day Adventists, and No Lutherans, and No Anglicans, and NO Mormons. **These religions vanish because all were based on human fabrications.** And everything that they have created out of these fictitious myths are just lies, upon lies, upon lies. It's all gone now because all were based on a religion, which was a total human fabrication.

Jesus died…after that everything else is made up. The lie of Judaism. The lie of Christianity stops here. So the Orthodox Church and its icons and ceremonies and rites and appearances and miracles and saints are all lies. Lies created by people who were stuck in a time-warp of irrelevance. The Roman Catholic Church and its statues and stigmata and visions and demon possessions and infallible messages from space and its Lourdes and its Fatima and its never-ending Marian pop-ups around the world are all made up. By a steady stream of liars, many of whom are the most despicable kinds of humans.

The Roman Catholic rites, the hocus-pocus ceremonies used to bind followers in fear and dread are just pathetic expressions of losers who never grew up historically. The poor Protestants who have tried to re-invent themselves in so many ways to escape the lies of Catholicism, but have tragically failed. Snake-handlers, life-deniers, grumpy stoics, medical fools, social mutants, racial purists, end-timers, angel-morony-ists, right day-wrong god crowd, dress-up group, no dancing crowd, sex sends you to hell crowd, were you dunked or only sprinkled crowd, can you speak in tongues crowd, and ad infinitum. It couldn't get any crazier and it was all based on lies that have no foundation in history.

Islam dies a harder death. You see, Islam could very well have been just another sect of Judaism, if not for the maniacal tendencies of its founder. The Koran is chocked full of writings stolen from Jewish scholars. The followers of Islam just love all these myths (Adam and Eve, Abraham, Noah, Jonah), which have been proven false. Today the believers of these myths kill innocent women and children based on this psychotic notion of religious beginnings.

There were some great passages in the Myth about Adam and Eve naming all of the animals on earth. Apparently after 'horsie' and 'duckie', we lost the list naming the other millions of creatures, which existed by the time this duo arrived in the Garden.

If there is no list naming every creature on Earth, how could Noah have saved them all? Yet he collected bears, lions, jackals, pandas, butterflies, amoebas, staphylococcus, and six million varieties of flowers. Millions and millions of species were loaded onto the ultimate water craft, designed and built by that wunderkind Noah. Take a moment here and reflect on what the first day on this craft must have been like. There were over a million predatory animals just straining on the leash to get at their prey. I would put my money on the mastodon and the saber-toothed tiger. One writer says 'two' of each animal, while another writer says 'seven' of each animal. This is good though, because it means that they weren't peeking at each other's work.

Adam and Eve sinned. Everybody dies! Is this a story about redemption and forgiveness? I guess I'll have to go back and read between the lines.

The importance of the Flood story for those who wrote the Torah was to emphasize that their Cosmic Bastard would take no prisoners. They wanted us to feel the full impact of his wrath toward anyone and everyone who refused to believe their fairy tales and lies. When the Flood waters began to rise, the real suffering began. Screaming babies were ripped away from their mothers' arms. Handicapped children were defenseless against the destructive force of the waves. The elderly, too feeble to rise from their cots, were left to fend for themselves. People screamed in horror and chaos reigned everywhere. Their Cosmic Bastard would get them all! Swat them like flies. Crush them like ants. Eviscerate them like slaughtered pigs. Create more agony than the world had ever known. And so many 'innocents' were utterly destroyed. **The fabricators of Judaism were more than pleased to present this image of their god to the world.**

We're Number One, and if you don't obey our god, then this is what is going to happen to you. How pleasant. Believe in the Cosmic Bastard, or else! Not to be outdone, the Christians and Moslems went even further in creating a permanent HELL where all infidels will go. Their god of compassion and love had limits. Only the chosen few will exist in peace; all others will suffer for trillions of years with never-ending pain. Believers will be able to see the suffering of others, and be glad, because unbelievers deserve what they get. God won't intercede like he did with Noah and his family, saving them from the deluge. The time of grace is over.

Had this flood actually occurred, the keepers of the Guinness Book of World Records would have had to record **THE LARGEST MASS SLAUGHTER OF THIRD-TRIMESTER FETUSES IN THE HISTORY OF THE WORLD.** Brought to you by the Cosmic Bastard himself.

Since no human can be sinless (anywhere in the universe), and since the Cosmic Bastard had to have Junior killed in order to save what was left of his handiwork, and since there are literally billions and billions of galaxies, with billions and billions of stars, and likely billions and billions of planets in the universe, then the Cosmic Bastard would have to have sent Junior to live and die, on every one of these planets. Talk about having your work cut out for you.

The Great Escape from Egypt: Only requires one flashlight and five snacks.

What about the Exodus and those millions of people wandering in the wilderness for over forty years? **It never happened.** These religionists have claimed for centuries that their writings about the Exodus are the true and *inerrant* Word, directly from God. Yet there has never been any physical proof of this large community's time spent in the desert. Just the 'scat' (fecal matter) produced by millions of people, in one day, could not be hidden forever. Someone would have come upon evidence of all this human excrement. Multiply the bowel movements taken by millions of people in one day by 365 days over forty years and you have a problem. A problem, which New York City hasn't been able to solve with modern technology. On top of that, there would be artifacts, shoes, jewelry, bones of the dead, bones of animals, monuments which would be there for someone to discover. Yet, not one single sandal has been found. **It didn't happen.** Think of the logistical problem of feeding millions of people in the desert, every day, for over 40 years! Modern armies with the greatest logistical support are often stymied by much simpler tasks. Don't be fooled. Jewish scholars, over the centuries, have whittled this number of people down considerably. Now some are saying that the "millions" were only a couple dozen. They now claim that the cataclysms weren't quite so dramatic, that the people weren't really all originally Jewish (maybe Canaanite or 'apiru). In fact, the foundations of their religion could have come from a small semi-nomadic group to the south of the Negev. Maybe the Conquest of the Holy Land was also total mythology. And maybe, and maybe, and maybe! It will become extremely difficult to continue to rescue these lies in the future as education envelopes the world.

There are a lot of problems with this Exodus story. We are told by the writers of the Torah—and we don't really know who these liars were since they forged their writings and many versions were melded into the final product—that their god created *all things* in heaven and earth in just one week. Nothing was created after that. So the Office of Angel of Death existed before there was even a need for it. If their god knew that his human creation would need the ultimate sanction of death before he even created them, then he is absolutely responsible for this massive design flaw. He made the mistake and then punished his flawed human creatures for being flawed.

Furthermore, angels and demons weren't even around during the supposed events of the Exodus. These ideas were stolen from the Mesopotamians during the Jews' overnight stay as 'guest' workers there. This would have been 600 to 700 years after the Egypt lies, and there is no trace of angelology in their language before that time.

Can you imagine how all this must have taken place? "Please have Harold the angel come to my office immediately." "Harold, I want you to fill the position of Angel of Death on my new Cabinet." "What's death? And what's human?" "Never mind, but I've got a lot of work for you to do. I'm talking billions and billions and billions. That's why I appointed you. Don't worry, it's going to be a lot of fun. And, from now on, call me by my preferred name 'El Cosmic Bastard – the Mass Murderer of the Ages!"

"Oi vay, you're gonna love the project I have for you in Egypt! You get to kill 500,000 to one million kids in just one night. It will be the largest mass murder of its kind in history. Just imagine smashing the heads of newborns, slicing teens in half, crushing little pretty boys, who are the pride of their parents. I get perfectly orgasmic, just thinking about it! I'd do it myself, but that's my bowling night."

"And before you get there, we're going to kill about one million sheep, so that we can spread blood on the doorposts, so that you can skip those houses. I can't figure it out either, it's just something those crazy priests came up with, but we'll finish them off later in the desert."

I wish I could make this summary of their history less sarcastic and disgusting, but it is clearly the story that they have been telling for three thousand years, or so. It is their argument to the world for why they are better than the rest of humanity.

Of course, none of this nonsense ever took place. The fact that these people wanted to memorialize such an horrific event is where the problem lies. They write about mass murder, the Cosmic Bastard behind it, and the fact that the Bastard did it all for them. To this very day, they celebrate these mass murders as just another of their very special holidays.

Jewish genocide was not invented in the Twentieth Century by Hitler. The act of mass slaughter of others because they are different, worship another god, look differently, or speak a different language was memorialized by a people, who cry '*foul*' at the slightest act of discrimination, but live lives of separation and arrogance. The haughtiness of victim and victimizer in the same skin!

So light your candles. Tell your lies. Rehearse your role as the victim in the play of life while justifying the victimization of others. It's all fantasy anyway—make-believe. But science and historical knowledge have now convicted you of being liars, deceivers, and unworthy of serious conversation about any topic. As the number of religionists tumble worldwide, all that remains are a few fools who shame others for abandoning traditions, which were meaningless three thousand years ago.

Jews are in De-Nile: The Blood Gift that Just Keeps on Going and Going and Going.

Wait a minute, what about the Blood in the Nile? Go ahead, say something about that. This is what the idiots, who fabricated the Jewish religion, had to say about that subject. To show the Egyptians that they were messing with the Cosmic Bastard, and that he had circus tricks that would blow them away, he said the following:

"Take your staff and stretch out your hand over the waters of Egypt – over the streams and canals, over the ponds and all the reservoirs – and they will turn to blood. Blood will be everywhere in Egypt, even in the wooden buckets and stone jars." "…and he struck the water of the Nile, and all the water was changed into blood. The fish in the Nile died, and the river smelled so bad, that the Egyptians could not drink its water."

Over *seventy-four trillion* cubic feet of water turned into blood! And today there is not a single piece of evidence in the layers of silt in the Nile, that any such event ever took place. There is no documentation, by any other source, that this cataclysmic event ever happened. Here's where some of the problems lie. There was no water for millions of Egyptians still living there. You have to figure that for these millions to go without water for four days would kill them all. But this didn't happen! All the fish died. When and how were they replenished? What of the wildlife? They would have been decimated. Fish don't spontaneously regenerate. Their parents were all dead. Except that this event never happened. The Nile was a fast moving body of water, and seventy-four trillion cubic feet of blood would have been spotted by sailors in the Mediterranean Sea, and there is not a single notation of this anywhere. Remember that the blood just kept coming because all the streams, canals, buckets, jars, and every other conceivable container were all turned to blood. If you have ever cleaned up after your dog did the 'diarrhea dance' on your patio, you will know what a mess this must have been. This event could only have taken place in the delusional minds of these buffoonish liars who wrote the Torah—possibly six hundred years after the supposed event! Was this even feasible? They also didn't consider how many decades, or centuries, it would have taken to replace the flora and fauna, which would have been destroyed. **FACTS AND SCIENCE ARE DETRIMENTS TO FABRICATORS OF RELIGIOUS LIES!**

Lego Experiment in Egypt goes Wacky in Israel.

Another debunked lie: The Jews didn't build the pyramids. There is not *ONE SINGLE* clue that the Jews got anywhere near the Pyramids until a travel group from Tel Aviv left a lunch box there in 1978. If they were so clever in master minding the building of the pyramids, then why didn't they take this Masonic knowledge into the Promised Land when they started building their own structures? Juvenile 'rock pilers' could have done better! Four-room adobe squats—what archaeologists found from the period of early Israel—are not remotely equivalent to the chambers of the Pharaohs' burial tombs.

You can Run, but you can't Hide all the Documentation that would have been spawned by these events.

What about writings and linguistics? Silence, and a total vacuum of any confirming recording of these events, even by the Israelites in the succeeding seven hundred year period are what we have. Remember that all of the first-born children of Egypt were killed by the Angel of Death the very night that the slaves escaped. Yet not a single writer, in the whole world, made note of this event? That is really strange since we have far less crucial events recorded in many forms throughout the known world at the time. We have even found laundry lists on steles. It didn't happen. There is not even any trace of any linguistic influence of Hebrew in Egyptian writings, and that's over a 400 year period of supposed captivity in Egypt. It didn't happen. Slaves in America, and other places, have had significant linguistic impact upon the languages of their masters. Why not in Egypt? Simply stated: The enslavement and exodus NEVER HAPPENED. Now there would have been stories of people being taken into servitude by conquering peoples. Conquest and enslavement have been common themes throughout history. Perhaps some of these myths were borrowed and just embellished, but it is extremely clear that the events written about in the Torah are completely fictional. And even worse, they have been used to justify the most despicable acts.

Can you imagine all the people of New York City leaving the city in the middle of the night and never returning? Do you think that they would have left any trace of their existence during the 400 years that they lived there? Do you think anyone would have noticed? Do you think that anyone would have made a record of the event? This whole story is so undocumented and grotesquely exaggerated that it strains credulity to believe that anyone would ever have the 'hutzpah' to repeat it.

The audience for these religious lies must have been either naïve or ignorant. Apparently, they still are both naïve *and* ignorant. They still slaughter an innocent lamb each year to celebrate these non-events. They still denigrate women. They still condemn their neighbors who refuse to believe their patent lies. They still glorify the rape of infidels, as just something that their Cosmic Bastard did to demonstrate that he was not to be fooled with. Why else would they continue to honor this filthy 'Torah' and retell the stories of mass slaughter with such awe?

Christians and Moslems also recognize, and celebrate, these events as a part of their rich heritage.

Who were these people who wrote these religious lies? They were apparently Habiru—semi-nomadic people who used their war powers to destroy and steal established cities for their own use. Even this point is now in doubt. They weren't very talented. They left no significant architecture. There were no discoveries of math or science that came from these nomads. They didn't forge iron or philosophize about the world. They did one thing; they created a god who was a lot like themselves: a ruthless killer. They went from town to town killing their half-brothers and half-sisters. Then they created the god who they said delivered these enemies into their hands.

They could have fabricated a god who was compassionate and loving to all human beings. They could have made him inclusive. But they made him into a ruthless, narrow-minded hater who only loved them. "You are my chosen people" To perdition with everyone else. Kill them and their children so they will know that I am not to be ignored.

If there had been Copyright Laws back in those Days: the Jews never could have stolen all this Rich Material from their Pagan Neighbors. And there would be no Dreidel.

Christians and Moslems found these ways of being in the world well-suited to their needs as well. They weren't even smart enough to create their own myths. They simply stole them from other people and made the endings more horrific. Noah's Ark, that piece of glorious power and slaughter, was taken from the story of Utnapishtim in pagan theology. It would be as if I stole the entire Harry Potter series of books and just retitled them Harry Totter and claimed originality. That is exactly what the writers of the Torah did to poor Utnapishtim. Judaism needed to steal this story because they had to reinforce the great damage that had been done to God's creation by Adam and Eve. There had to be devastation, consequences and death. What has become a children's story is a lie, of course, but reveals a lot about the god whom they fabricated. It seems that the Cosmic Bastard got really miffed about how some of his self-made toys were malfunctioning. He was so angry, that he decided to break all of his toys and start over. But there was one toy that could still toot and work, so he decided to give that toy one more chance. And so he saved Utnapishtim and his family. Oh, I'm sorry. I meant he saved Noah and his family. Well, you get the idea.

One doesn't have to go into the foolishness of a little boat containing the millions of species, which would have to be gathered, boarded and fed. It's just a story. And it's a story that undergirds the truly gruesome revenge capabilities of the supposed Author of their religion.

Judaism was designed from day one to show the full impact of the Cosmic Bastard and his wrath toward anyone who refused to believe this series of fairy-tales and lies.

You can't really tell a Sin without a Program: The Program – Everything is Dirty.

This all leads us to the Ten Commandments—or as Catholics like to say, "The Ten Suggestions." Of course, the events leading up to the receiving of the TC's never happened. The story goes like this. Moses was invited to go, all by himself, up to the top of a mountain, to talk face to face with the Cosmic Bastard. How convenient that even their Cosmic Bastard always seems to want no witnesses (this is a common approach by all religions). Moses descends from this hike with a face glowing like a 1,000 Watt bulb. Thus, proof that he really did meet with the Cosmic Bastard. Oh well, let's not belabor the point. There was no trip up the mountain to get the goodies from the Cosmic Bastard. Picture in your mind: Moses coming down the mountain with these two tablets of granite, each probably weighing about 350 pounds. This is where Hebrew started to be such a guttural language, but that's another story. This was also the first 200 pound hernia ever recorded in history. These events were written about by Moses who coincidentally also wrote about his own death, after the fact. We now know, for an absolute fact, that Moses never wrote anything. Actually, no one has ever discovered any evidence of the existence of these TCs in the 400 year period following the supposed Exodus events.

The Ten Commandments really do follow nicely with the rest of the depraved religion created around this Cosmic Bastard. I'm not saying that laws aren't important for an orderly society. There are many wonderful examples of 'community' created and oriented laws around the world. The laws of Judaism also appear to be an attempt to bring order to their emerging society. Unfortunately, these laws point to a very defective, psychologically needy diety.

Number 1: I am the Cosmic Bastard and you better know it! Capice?! (A little narcissistic, don't you think.) It's hard for me to even conceive of a 'god' who is so insecure that he has to demand that someone love him. I've tried it, it doesn't work.

Number 2: Be careful how you use my name, because I get angered, fairly easily, and my Mudder says that I am a sensitive guy. Thanks Ma! Again, no free speech. You must act like a robot, and say and do what is required in a very 'un-free' state. When I read the TC's my mind very quickly reverts to *1984* and Big Brother (Orwell was attacking the Anglican Church in England for this very same garbage).

Number 3: Saturday is Grovel Day. Be there or be dead! (No RSVP needed!) This actually became very freeing for most religionists, because the requirement was reduced to one day of the week. Then along came the Moslems and the Christian fundamentalists, who started getting crazy about 'five a days' and week night interference with preferred programming on TV.

Number 4: Parents are my tools to indoctrinate you little losers. So don't question anything they say. If your mother says she's a virgin, don't laugh, you little sinner! If you are going to create robots and loyalists, parents become an essential tool. In the small communities in the Middle East this might have even been useful. In the modern world we have come to realize that most parenting is an amateur sport and the requirement turns out to be quite cruel.

Number 5: If anyone is going to kill anyone around here, I will do it. Occasionally, I will recruit you. Stand by for instructions. Murder was the first and most useful tool of religionists throughout history. You would think that this commandment would have been a good thing. But it was very rapidly converted to 'it's not murder if you kill an infidel', or 'it's not murder if it is done in a justified war', or 'it's not murder if you are defending the honor of your family'. There you have it, all the bases are covered.

Number 6: Don't diddle other women. That's for the rabbis, priests, kings and prophets. Give me a list of the 1,000 people in our society who 'rail' against promiscuous sex. I will choose ten at random and prove to you that this commandment has had absolutely no effect, whatsoever, on the affairs of mankind.

Number 7: Don't steal. I can't stand competition! Didn't I take the land from all those losers in the Middle East and give it to you. Don't go cheap on the sacrificial lambs anymore either! You little thief, study for Wall Street on your own time! Give me a list of the most recent imprisonments of thieves who have stolen more than one million dollars and I will guarantee to you that every one of them will have a very strong religious affiliation. Madoff and Abramoff are just poster children for a degeneracy which has infected the financial worlds we are victimized by.

Number 8: If you gotta lie, you gotta lie. In the oath when you get to my name, just mumble, like Greenspan! Lying is so common in our society, that the courts don't even pursue obvious cases of perjury. All of our words are supposed to be true. When we wear a religious label attached to our names, the assumption is that we are speaking as representatives of the god behind our identity and those words. That notion died thousands of years ago. And the writers of this dribble are perfect examples of the hypocrisy of making it one of their ten biggest laws to be recorded. Nobody could compete with King David for lying and personal treachery.

Number 9 and 10: Wives are property, and so are slaves. Don't be a schmuck. Just borrow them back and forth like you would a garden rake or shovel. Oi vay, you gonna have problems with women and slaves your whole life. Why do you think I'm a Cosmic Bastard?! Just call Gov. Spitzer (212-867-3475), he'll tell you! It is not a protection for women to have listed them as property. It is an unbelievable lost opportunity to have not mentioned that no one should be enslaved under this new religious movement and gracious god. And so, it took enlightened societies thousands of years later to recognize the value of women and persons. You would have thought that the god of the universe might have said something a little more in tune with reality and decency.

When you hear about how your religious friends are fighting to have the Ten Commandments displayed in public places, please remember that the following offenses are also listed as capital (death penalty) cases under these commands: heresy, non-intact hymen at time of marriage, working on Saturday, cursing parents, gay sex, fortune-telling, loving your pet too much, saying God's name, et al.

THIS WAS THE ONLY ARTIFACT IN HISTORY WHICH CAME DIRECTLY FROM THE COSMIC BASTARD, WRITTEN IN HIS OWN HAND.

What did they do with this irreplaceable piece of evidence? **THEY LOST IT!**

We would have had the proof in CB's own handwriting! I'm sure it would have been distinctive. Truth is that it was probably just chock full of Persian idioms. But they lost it. The only other potentially compelling artifact would have been a pile of human excrement from the desert, which could have been carbon dated to the Exodus. Those darned Palestinians, probably went out and removed all the crap that they could find out there, just to tick-off the Israelis.

The lies didn't get any better as the so-called history of the Jews progressed. Joshua never defeated the towns, which they said he did. Ai had ceased to exist a thousand years before Joshua was even born. Jericho sits on top of a Fault-Line and has been destroyed many times by earthquakes 'with the walls falling in and out.' Jonah has always been a fishy story, even to the Jews. Balaam's talking ass was really his son-in-law. Daniel was fantastic at predicting events, which had already happened two hundred years before he predicted that they would eventually happen in the future. The Profits, yes that's the way it was originally spelled, sold shares in stolen cities courtesy of the Cosmic Bastard. The original Temple Mount was Bathsheba and Solomon tried to get Wednesday (Hump Day) to replace Saturday as the Sabbath. When Solomon was told that he couldn't 'work it' on the Sabbath, he decided to leave it on Saturday. If you are not already steeped in these nonsensical stories from the Old Testament, don't waste your time reading them. They are just pathetic attempts to undergird a religion that is irrational and foolish, on so many levels.

Cafeterias, Not Just for Lunch Anymore: They work for Religions as Well.

History that is based on lies doesn't get any better with age. Neither does false religion. Judaism now comes in several varieties to appease the sensitivities of its various adherents around the globe. There's Ultra-Orthodox, Orthodox, Conservative, Reformed and Free-Lance. The lies in the Torah are all told differently by each of these different persuasions. Most of them hate and distrust all the others. Who are the real keepers of the LIES in our modern world? If no one ever challenges the lies, then the lies will have an ongoing life of their own, further infecting the progress of truth in the world. One of my dearest friends (and a great business partner) had members of his family in each one of these branches of his religion. None of them could even stand to be in the same room at the same time. I experienced the violation of many of their own commandments in casual conversations that they had about each other.

Judaism is a lie. Christianity is a lie. Islam is a lie. Those who follow the lies become liars themselves! No one can *DISCOVER* religion. They must be *indoctrinated* into it. That's why so few people ever change major religions during their lifetimes. They've been indoctrinated. Worse still, they are only practitioners of those religions because of the accidents of birth, place of birth, parentage, and cultural influence. They are not religious by choice, they are religious by default. Ninety-nine percent of religionists have never really thought about what their religion teaches and they don't really care. It works because everyone else is doing it and it's just too hard to think about these matters in a way that might cause any discomfort. As a result we live in a world where it is acceptable to kill people of other religions because 'god' will eventually destroy them anyway.

Positive Proof: Jews were not first Vegans!

Further indoctrinating their followers, the leaders of Judaism made it clear that the Cosmic Bastard was easily bothered by human behavior. So they set up a system, whereby they could constantly appease his irritable nature. They created—out of whole cloth—a system of animal sacrifices for any offense against the Cosmic Bastard, whether minor or major. They would slit the throats of millions of innocent animals and burn them on the altar so the Cosmic Bastard could get his 'count to ten' moment finished! Even this didn't always work. The Cosmic Bastard knew his meat! Don't just burn any old animal (a pin sized mark behind the ear of a lamb could get the animal disqualified), that could get you killed, or worse, get your whole family, whole clan, whole tribe or whole nation annihilated. When there were thousands of animals sacrificed—the writers of the Torah tell us—the Cosmic Bastard would get the smell of the burning flesh in his nostrils and it would please him. He would actually forgive the penitent just this once. Records show that there were actually thousands of things that made the Cosmic Bastard so angry that they required animal sacrifice to stop the ire.

Even today, every CHRISTIAN church has one of these sacrificial altars in the middle of their church, which hearken back to the good ole days of mass slaughter, a vicious Cosmic Bastard, and the joys of groveling.

It could have been so easy for this people to have created a religion that would have stood the test of time. Love and peace everywhere. The welcoming of strangers. The inquisitiveness of mind that almost certainly always leads to a more wonderful and expansive world. But the Israelites didn't stand on every corner telling of the wonderful love of their Number One. They just killed everyone who disagreed with them by the orders of the Cosmic Bastard. And so the world was introduced to xenophobia, hate, war, and murder.

Jesus and Mohamed picked right up where the dispersed nation of Israel left off. It really is a great sadness that all this nonsense has brought us to the state of the world that is cursed, even today, trying to undo the damage of thousands of years of accumulated lies.

You shall know the truth and the truth will set you free to live a life free from this mass of garbage! We were promised that the truth would set us free. But the truth cannot do its work when it is couched so deeply in lies.

Christianity: Something old, something new, something made up just for you.

By the time the fabricators of the Christian religion got around to their task of creating a foundation for their version of the Jewish myth, they realized that they could not have Jesus be a stand-alone. They had to plant him firmly in a prognosticated past, which he would be the fulfillment of. Thus, their mad dash to find Jesus under every rock of their former Jewish neighbors. They were not unlike the crazies of today, who occasionally pull out their Nostradamus to find the predictions of Kennedy's assassination, the destruction of the Twin Towers on 9-11, the tsunami in Indonesia, the introduction of the new Ford Focus and the decline in the sales of Twinkies. It's all there; you just have to look hard enough and take everything with a grain of salt and a massive amount of gullibility!

The Jesus' boys (some variation of the supposed twelve) didn't even think that their religion was important enough to put into the 'book' until over 300 years later. It is truly amazing that not a single one of the original followers even wrote down these world-changing events for their own families, if not for others. The equivalent in today's terms would mean that we would not even have a copy of the Declaration of Independence and the Constitution until the year 2076 AD. Worse still, by that time, there would have been hundreds of different versions with differing stories about the original writers. How would we know what to believe and what to discard? There were hundreds of versions of the Jesus' myth, written by thousands of unknown writers, from communities far away, who had no exposure to Jesus or any of his original followers. Some of the garbage which they started writing was becoming a problem. For instance, the time that Jesus struck down a classmate dead on the playground at school, just because he could. That was a problem. What about the version that has Jesus and his local gansta Judas plotting to fool the Romans and deceive the Jews by pretending to die and then starting a revolution, which would throw out both? That was a problem. What about all the predictions that some of Jesus followers would never die before the End came. That meant a time soon after Jesus left. At some point everyone who believed in that 'promise' were all dead and in their graves. Over three hundred years had passed from the time of those promises. So they did what all good fabricators do: they called a meeting. Over a thousand reps came and they brought copies of the 'books' which they insisted be included in the true and inerrant version of their scriptures (written and inspired by their 'god', no less). After all was said and done, they finished their work, and a vote was taken on the 'new' book. The vote was 568 to 563 (actually). Then the killing began. Anyone, whose writings were not included, were now heretics and so the true religionists slaughtered them, their children, and their communities.

It helps to remember that these writers of the New Testament were simpletons who lived completely in the context of their own times and did not have a clue of the wider world, science, or the future ability to read through their made-up schemes! What seemed reasonable to them is now completely laughable. They got the Bethlehem/Herod shtick all wrong! It didn't happen, because their little Jesus was born after Herod would already have been dead. They were really torn. Some needed to prove that Jesus was really human, so they made up 'birth' narratives to get him to earth (not all these narratives even agree). Some also wanted to prove that he was really a god, so they included elements of the story that clearly broke all the laws of nature which we experience universally in our daily lives. What you get is a very confusing amalgamation of 'is' and 'is not'. Also, do you think that the Romans would have been dumb enough to have over a million angry Jews (who hated them just slightly) on the 'move' around the country to go to their home districts for the purpose of a census? Why don't we just count all the illegal aliens in this country by having them come to NY to be counted? They used astrologers (pseudo-scientists) to discover their 'messiah' (the manger was a nice humble touch to undergird his human origins). However, they got the genealogy all wrong. See, Joseph did not have a sexual relationship with Mary—according to their writings—the big Holy Spirit did. For non-religionists this gets a little confusing. Let me make it very understandable to the novice. A third of God had sex with the human Mary and produced a third of himself, who was one hundred percent human and one hundred percent God. OK, got it? And that means Jesus was not descended from David through Joseph. Genealogies appropriately understood are about true parentage and true ancestors. Today we have DNA, etc., but back then they had to rely on astrologers (don't be cruel, they did the best that they could with the tools that they had). Why, that means that everything else that they said about Jesus was also a lie. He was not Cosmic Bastard Jr. He was just an unemployed day-laborer, making a living off of money from people whom he swindled with religious palaver! Tragically in our own day it has led to other religious swindlers: Anal Roberts, Billy GrahamCracker, Jimmy Swagart it Both Ways, and Jimmy Baker License Plate Maker.

In order to cover all possibilities, the writers of the NT included two *COMPLETELY DIFFERENT* genealogies, so that future readers would get to pick and choose how the 'holy' one got here. I'm kind of fond of the Luke one, because it includes adulterers, murderers, thieves, genocidal experts (you know the kind of genealogy we all have, now don't we!). And John tops them all by stealing directly from the Greeks the notion of 'The Word'. Before everything else, there was 'The Word', and that word became flesh, and appeared on Broadway in Springtime for Hitler. You got a better meaning for this nonsense! The problem for the writers of the New Testament was that at different times the 'humanity' and the 'divinity' of Jesus took greater or lesser prominence. Even they struggled with the notion that he could be both at the same time, and yet be one hundred percent true to his true nature. See, you can't really be a 'sacrificial' lamb for humanity if you really know that it is all a game and that you can't really die. Not really anyway. Confused? Religious leaders are just so confident that all this stuff rings so true and that you will gladly give them all your money just so they can continue to explain.

The 'miracle' stories seem so important to Jesus's present day followers. But look, Luddites, every one of them is an exact 'copy' of a 'miracle' stolen directly from the Old Testament. Even today, Third Graders don't get credit for turning in another student's paper. He must create his own and it must not be a replica of anyone else's. Worse still, these miracles are stolen from the Septuagint, which is a Greek version of the original Hebrew texts. Some of the words used in the Hebrew telling of the miracle are critical to the event. When the event is translated into Greek, the meaning changes because the Greek words may not match the event exactly. The people, who wrote these lies, were probably living in Greek communities, and would not have realized that they put words into Jesus' mouth that he couldn't have known and certainly would never have said. There are even Christian doctrines today that are based on Greek words, supposedly spoken by Jesus. Splangnistheis. Don't worry it's not dirty, just pathetically hypocritical to have stolen its meaning from others, and given it to the 'historical' Jesus. All his stories (so-called parables) had *ALL* been told by rabbis for hundreds of years before he started LaLeche with Mary. Again, the 'slight' changes in the parables, the new twists, were in GREEK (but stolen non-the-less). What about the multiplication of 'fish and bread' miracles. Replicas of all of these were done before by Profits in the Old Testament. The school for modern televangelists is still conducted on Mt. Carmel in Haifa, on a quarterly basis, to continue these 'magical' ways (James Randi would call them 'slight of hand'). I don't recall Jesus ever sawing an assistant in half, but his followers would still be talking about that one if he had. The writers of Jesus' myths just couldn't hold back from urinating in their pants over these writings, they made sure that Jesus always did the Profits one fish and one loaf better!

Bedtime Stories: Now let's all suspend our sense of discernment Forever.

Jesus celebrated the Passover Meal with his followers, but he—the diviner of all knowledge and all wisdom, the seer of the ages—forgot to tell them that the Angel of Death in Egypt was all made up. It never happened— *unless Jesus himself didn't know that historical fact*. Oh, how blasphemous to think that Jesus wasn't prescient of all events in history. Why, that would make him just another low-life liar and cheat. Draw your own conclusions! This was a group of thirteen guys, who traveled everywhere together, slept together, went 'boating' together and whenever the 'broads' came around they were always 'shooing' them away. Even Jesus own mom got the 'bum's treatment' for challenging their fun together. "Who are my mother and brothers?" "It's you babe, you're the one I love!" Were they ascetics? Were they anti-disestablishmentarians? Were they communists? Were they socialists? Were they anti-Jewish? What was the purpose of all these collected, very loosely connected stories of their 'adventures'? And then, they all just disappear and leave the creation of their new religion to others hundreds of years later. It does appear that Jesus was, at least, a little more sensitive to the plight of women (the Jews said that he was a drunk and a whoremonger), but his future churches have pretty much wiped out that sensitivity. Gays, of course, have always gotten the short end of any religious breakthrough. Too bad the Jews keep trying to cover over King David just gushing over his orgasmic events with his lover Jonathan. The priestly order fixed that later when they ordered the stoning death of all homosexuals.

Celibate Masochism: The Norm for Buddhists, becomes Standard for Catholics

The writers of the Jesus myth use the Jonah story as support for their resurrection theme but got it all wrong. First, it never happened. Then they got the timing all wrong. 'Three days' and quit playing games with the clock to prove your lie. Count them using the Jewish notion of days. I know that this is a minor technicality, but the religionists claim that their whole book is inerrant, so it makes commas, historical facts and verifiable artifacts extremely important. New day starts at sundown. So we got Saturday, Sunday, then, Monday: three days! It must have been on a Monday that he arose from the dead, which makes you wonder why people hate Mondays so much. 'And after three days, just like Jonah, you will see me again.' Apparently smelling a little fishy from being in the 'big fish's intestines' (whales are mammals) or being in the tomb without embalming fluid. The smell comes from the telling of this story to gullible religionists who just want to gush with amazement at the events. Instead we blush with embarrassment that there are human beings who are so stupid that they have bought into all of this! Nothing that they wrote about Jesus can be proven historically; in fact, quite the opposite. Whoever Jesus was, he was a product of his environment, and he was totally ignorant of the facts of history, science and the true complexities of the real world.

Every single supposed miracle of Jesus was just borrowed whole cloth from others in history. Here's what they wanted us to believe: Jesus suspended the laws of nature—under which we are all cursed—in order to prove that he could win our unquestioned awe, fear, and adoration. When you suspend the laws of nature to pull the rabbit out of the hat for one person but then allow billions of others to suffer from the same maladies, then you are not a magical holy figure. You are a bastard who raised expectations that you would intercede for others universally. Besides, feeding the thousands with a few loaves of bread is no big deal. Smoke and mirrors have been employed by governments, businesses, entertainers, and others, for a very long time to claim the same out-comes.

It is interesting how the writers of the Jesus' myth never want their Jesus to refer to all the mass murders in Jewish history as somehow redemptive acts, and clearly, what he came to justify. This is CB's son. He wants to fulfill all the kinder, gentler points of light of the OT. Be a do-gooder. Extend a helping hand. Occasionally curse a no-good fruit tree that was barren when you were really hungry. Get your *goon* squad to go over, dig it up, and burn it! And don't miss the opportunity when you pass the place where they throw all the dead bodies of the poor (Gehenna) to say a little word of kindness for these misbegotten few. "This is what eternal punishment will be like in hell, forever, for everyone who doesn't bow the knee to me." So the true nature of CB, Sr. occasionally seeps through, even into the 'kinder, gentler' dialogue. Jesus was a little early with that one, however, but I'm sure that Hallmark would certainly have wanted to use that one on one of their thank you notes!

Christianity 102: A Brand New Course for Freshman and Lunatics.

Still, the whole Christian experience had a hard time getting off the ground. It seems that this odd-ball named Paul or Saul or whatever, came along and really needed to start his own religion. He wasn't accepted by any of the other religions and for good reason: he was short, fat, bald, ugly, covered in pock-marks (probably from venereal disease), couldn't express himself well, and loved to have young boys travel with him. He was one messed-up, ego-centric dude. That just didn't make him welcome anywhere he went. So when he heard about this new religion, he decided to make it his own. He would finally be accepted just for himself, as he was. Problem came when James—the younger brother of Jesus, who never got the same amount of love that his older brother did but was hatched from a virgin himself—wasn't going to allow someone else to take his place in the sun! Besides, this Paul guy was changing all the rules. It all had to do with the *Dick*! Now James, who was a dick himself, told Paul that the only way that a person could be a genuine follower of his brother Jesus was to undergo circumcision. That was the problem. Paul could almost get people to listen to him, but then he threw in the part about getting their dick cut and they just walked away. Paul had a lot of young boys, who would partner with him on his travels, but they would all eventually tell him that they wanted to go back home to mommy. Well, Paul just wouldn't stop making up all these lies about Jesus and denying the fables that James was spreading, so James insisted that Paul meet him in Jerusalem. James set about to have Paul castrated by the Romans! And it worked. Paul was killed by Caesar but got the last laugh because his version of Jesus' lies became the NEW religion even though he really didn't believe in, almost all, of the fantasies that James was teaching! In fact, you could say that Paul stole Jesus from the Jews and gave him to the Greeks. Now that's true.

YOU WERE HOPING THAT CHRISTIANITY WOULD HAVE BECOME THE INCLUSIVE RELIGION OF LOVE, PEACE, AND UNDERSTANDING FOR ALL, BUT COSMIC BASTARD JR. PROVED TO BE JUST A CONTINUATION OF COSMIC BASTARD SR.

The killings began immediately and they have never stopped. How could anyone take seriously the supposed message of the Gospels and still set out to kill everyone who disagreed in any way? But they did. Maybe that is really the true message of religion: mass murder, rape, and genocide.

OVER 700,000,000 PEOPLE KILLED BY CHRISTIANS

That number represents about half of all people who had ever lived on the earth by that time! These people were trained, proficient killers. Start with heretics, work your way to Jews, proceed to pagans and don't forget to annihilate all the men, women and children. That was just like the Cosmic Bastard did in the pornographic Torah of the Jews. Work your way up to other Christian sects, then any Muslim and native or aboriginal populations. Don't forget to plant the cross, like Columbus did, before wiping out over 10,000,000 indigenous people. DeSoto, Pizzaro, Cortez – all Christians, who just had to murder, rape and massacre those pagan natives to clear the way for little Jesus to take his place in the New World. They actually had people kneel down and in the name of their Savior, Jesus Christ, they executed them.

Don't forget about those Puritans in New England who found ingenious ways to burn natives to death, after the natives showed them how to survive in the new wilderness. Preacher Jonathan Edwards jumped up and down at the sight of Indians—the Pequot tribe who had befriended the settlers—being burned alive. You can still buy copies of Edwards' sermons on forgiveness and living the moral life. Even more atrocities were to come. Texas Christians slaughtered the Mexicans and Indians in Jesus name. Brigham Young massacred every last Indian in the whole territory. The Mormon Church honored this murderer by naming a university after him and then built it on the land that was saturated with Native American blood.

At least one hundred schools in the United States have a 'Crusader' as their mascot. Yet these monsters were responsible for the mass slaughter of several hundred thousands of innocent men, women, and children. This blood-letting continued for a couple of hundred years. The Crusaders would go to the Pope's Office and get his special instructions and blessing. I hope these schools don't have the same bounty system where if they cut off the ears or testicles of the opposing team it gets them a special reward!

At least the followers of Judaism were given a chance to convert during the Inquisition, but those Jews just couldn't let go of the ole mezuzah. That's not what you think. A couple hundred thousand at the end of the knife, or the middle of the bonfire, and I think that we got their attention. The bishop would burn a Jew at the stake as a gift to the new confirmands (these were seven year olds who had just graduated and were now welcome into drinking the blood and eating the flesh of the dead Jesus). Torture and kill a dozen Jews, at one time, and you're talking a pretty big gift to the Bishop for all of his important work.

Catholics killed protestants. Protestants killed catholics. Everyone killed pagans, atheists, gypsies, teachers, heretics. Protestants killed protestants. Anglicans killed Methodists and Puritans. All the villages in Europe participated in some sort of annihilation of their neighbors over religion, at one time, or another.

Bewitched, Roasted and Bewildered: The Welcome Wagon comes to Religion.

Did I mention witches? Now this was a special case because even today you occasionally hear someone say "Oh, she's a real witch!" Just two hundred years ago, and those words were a death sentence. A couple hundred thousand corpses and it saved millions on digging up coal, because they had all this charcoal left over from the burnings at the stake. You could always spot a witch: unkempt hair, long fingernails, blood-shot eyes, broom, a passé hat, bad credit rating. There was no hiding them. It was Christians, who were doing all the killing!

"What did you do today Minister Goodbar, daddy dear?" "You know that neighbor, who always ticked me off? Well, it turns out that she was a witch, so we killed her and her daughters, just to be safe! I feel a lot better knowing that Jesus Christ is my personal savior, and that I have a guardian angel to watch over me and my family. It kind of makes me feel sad for all those infidels out there, who don't have the same confident faith and assurance, that if I died today, I would go directly to heaven."

I'm sure glad that things were different when the Cosmic Bastard Jr. came along, after the terrorism, slaughter and cruelty of the Cosmic Bastard Sr. years.

"With the Cross of Jesus going on before." A hymn that was sung after the slaughter.

Washington slaughtered the Iroquois. Jackson slaughtered the Indians. Salem burned the witches. The Dutch slaughtered the Indonesians. The British slaughtered the Maori, Aborigines, Zulus, Hutus, India Indians, and Chinese. The Croats slaughtered the Serbs. The Serbs slaughtered the Muslims. The Italians slaughtered the Libyans and Ethiopians. The Turks slaughtered the Greeks. The Holy Roman Empire slaughtered everyone. The French slaughtered the Haitians and Jamaicans. The Portuguese slaughtered everything that was moving. The British slaughtered the Irish. The Norwegians slaughtered the Swedes.

And Jesus was always there. His Holy Book was carried. His Cross was always planted. His ordained representatives were always blessing.

Religious wars, persecutions, mass murder, rape, genocide, cruelty... Converts to Jesus were sometimes spared the shooting, burning, beheading, impaling and di-section, that comes to all Infidels!

Why is it that there is not a single Christian sect, in the entire world, which has not willingly and happily participated in the slaughter of their neighbors? Maybe religion is just a fraud. Maybe the degenerate writers of the Torah actually got it right. Their God really is just a Cosmic Bastard and Mass Murderer! And CB Jr., was all that too.

Arabian Sand Trap Produces Very Angry Golfer: The Life Story of a Brand New Prophet.

Mohamed—who formed his religion based on Judaism, Christianity and special revelations, which were given just to him —didn't even know that someday all this religion would be proven to be pure fraud. Didn't Joseph Smith try this same con after being arrested for starting several other religions? Joseph Smith – Mr. Mormon - even got special revelations from the Ether which enabled him to molest little girls. But wait a minute, Mohamed was molesting children long before Joseph Smith. He married his six year old niece but waited until she was nine before he showed her the joys of having sex with a shriveled-up, old man. The 'age of consent' in Moslem countries is apparently some few days after a female child is able to say 'dada'.

And Mohamed just couldn't wait to get into the Mass Murder business. You see, he lied a lot. Well, that's obvious. But the Jewish businessmen in Medina didn't have much choice in the matter. You see, Mohamed, the congenital liar, told the Jews that if they gave him all their money, that he would let them live. They resisted, but finally gave Mohamed all their money. Then Mohamed followed the path of the Cosmic Bastard (or should I say the Bastard Allah Mode). He killed them all. One by one on the town square and then buried them all in a great big ditch in the center of town. While committing this act, he referred to Deuteronomy 20, which also happens to be a favorite verse quoted by USA military clergy.

Let's see, we have a new religion, founded by a polygamist, a pedophile, a mass murderer, a genocidal maniac, a liar, a deceiver, a deluded egotist, one who sees invisible creatures, one who plagiarizes material, which he claims is 'original' from an angel – that only he can see, a person who converts more archaic myths into supposed religious rituals (Mecca, Kaaba, Abraham, initiation rites of running the hills…) Oh, you get the idea. He was a fraud and a degenerate. No wonder he wanted to follow in the footsteps of CB Sr. and CB Jr. He made it all up, and the mass killing began and hasn't stopped to this very day. They want us to believe that this is a religion of PEACE.

Enough of the killing and mass slaughter, already! Nope. I want you to have a firm grasp of how deep these religions are into presenting their 'holy books' as justification for terrorism in the world. The next chapter should cause you to go to your religious leaders, and ask them, if this is really what they want to present to the world as the basis for their religion: mass murder, rape and genocide.

These are all FACTS. As I told you, I will present you with facts, but you must do your own diligent work to discover what absolute nonsense all religions are. I don't want you to just trust me. That is the trap that religious leaders use. I want you to prove me wrong, but I want you to do it with verifiable evidence.

So, here are some excellent resources to get you started:

Lies, Damned Lies and History by Donald.
Mythology's Last Gods: Yahweh and Jesus by Harwood.
Gospel Fictions by Helms.
The Bible Against Itself by Helms.
Biblical Errancy by McKinsey.
The God Delusion by Dawkins.
Jesus Outside the Gospels by Hoffman.
Why I am Not a Muslim by Ibn Warraq.
Out of the Desert? Archaeology and the Exodus/Conquest Narratives by Stiebing.
Did Jesus Exist? by Wells.
What the Bible Really Says by Smith.
Deconstructing Jesus by Price.
The Great Deception: And What Jesus Really Said and Did by Ludemann.
Paul: The Founder of Christianity by Ludemann.
In the Name of Heaven: 3000 Years of Religious Persecution by Engh.

CHAPTER 2

Mass Murder, Rape, and Genocide: A Love Story

"Whenever we read the obscene stories, the voluptuous debaucheries, the cruel and tortuous executions, the unrelenting vindictiveness with which more than half the Bible is filled, it would be more consistent that we call it the word of a demon than the word of God. It is a history of wickedness that has served to corrupt and brutalize humankind" (Thomas Paine).

The Bible is nothing more than a catalogue of Mass Murder, Rape and, Genocide that even a cursory list of these horrifying tales will serve to demonstrate that fact.

The Flood. Every human on earth died. And God did it.

The Passover/Angel of Death killing the Firstborn. God's personal representative killed more people in one night than have ever been killed on one night in the history of the world. And God did it.

King David slaughters friend and foe alike. I Chronicles 20:3. No 'white flag' surrender! They were all slaughtered after they surrendered!

Moses kills his own! Numbers 25: 3-4. And then mutilates the bodies in public! "Take all the leaders of the people and hurl them down to their death before the Lord in the full light of day, that the fury of my anger may turn away from Israel."

Gideon kills thousands! Judges 6-9. He tore off their flesh and made jewelry out of their skin.

The sadistic Cosmic Bastard has people buried alive, including innocent children and their pets! Numbers 16. "The earth opened its mouth and swallowed them and their homes…They went down into Sheol with all that they had, the earth closed over them; and they vanished from the assembly."

In the Old Testament accounts alone, the Cosmic Bastard Mass Murdered, Raped and Committed Genocide against more human beings (percentage wise) than Hitler, Stalin and Attila the Hun combined. You go girl, some things are just really worth bragging about!

Seventy thousand died at the hands of Cosmic Bastard's (heretofore referred to as CB) special agent 'the destroying angel'. I Chronicles 21.

CB kills Ethiopians in mass numbers. II Chronicles 14. This act justifies future abuse of minorities, and is often cited by members of the Ku Klux Klan as they continue to murder in the name of god.

The blood of those killed by CB will be so deep that the victors will be able to 'bathe' their feet in the enemy's blood! Psalm 68. "The Lord says, 'I will fetch them back from Bashan, I shall fetch them from the depths of the sea; that you may bathe your feet in blood, while the tongues of your dogs are eager for it."

50,070 murdered, just for looking at the Ark of the Covenant. I Samuel 6.

If you think that this was just evidence of an ancient depraved population, you would be grossly mistaken. Religionists continue to cite the Bible as justification for their actions against INFIDELS to this very day!

Lies Have Ruined the World

You can't trust anyone. Religionists are told: If your own children fall from the faith, you must kill them. If your wife, or any family member falls from the faith, you must kill them. Does this sound familiar? That's what people still do today with FULL JUSTIFICATION from quoting scripture! Deuteronomy 13. "If your brother, your father's son or your mother's son, or your son or daughter, your beloved wife, or your dearest friend should entice you secretly to go and serve other gods…put them to death, your own hand raised against them…stone them to death." Are we overly cautious to be concerned about these leftover remnants from their cave-dwelling ancestors? Or, is this a real and present danger, which menaces our modern world every day?

I can see killing the innocent little children, and even raping the women as booty from war, but killing their innocent pets is just the most despicable thing that I have ever heard of! Take the pussy, but don't kill little pussy! Hamsters have a name you know! They're not just some little stuffed toy! I could never believe in a Cosmic Bastard that would do this. I want an apology! I'm sorry, I just can't take all this nonsense seriously. But this is the record that the religionists have given to us and the record that they demand 'seals the deal' for why we should all believe them, and believe in their fabricated god. Here's the verse from their holy, inerrant Scriptures, if you would like to look it up.

"[A]nd utterly destroy all that they have, and spare them not, but slay both man and woman, infant and suckling, ox and sheep, camel and ass" (I Samuel 15:2-3).

KILL, KILL, KILL, and again, I say, KILL, KILL, KILL and then KILL again! Who needs an Ark. I can defoliate the earth, even without the use of Agent Orange! Because I AM. *I AM THE COSMIC BASTARD* and I will be obeyed, because I love you, yes I do, I really, really do…Junior, will you tell these sinners that I really do love them…oh, God, where's that whore Mary, is she ready to go yet?! No, Mary, anal is NOT sex! You are still a virgin! 'Jesus Christ, it seemed like such a simple concept.' Would somebody please get Mary a cue card, or pope or saint or something!

HOLOCAUST, HOLOCAUST, HOLOCAUST, HOLOCAUST,.... WARNING!

King David builds the FIRST OVEN to burn his enemies *ALIVE!*

That's II Samuel 12:31 for all you feckless religionists! They had to build the brick ovens themselves for their own destruction.

"[K]ill every male among the little ones, and kill every woman that hath known man by lying with him. But all the young girls, who have not known man by lying with him, keep alive for yourselves" (Numbers 31:16-18).

How sweet, the Cosmic Bastard has provided little four year old girls to be 'molested' by his faithful followers for a job well done! You want to know where the Moslems picked up on this sadistic practice of violating children for their own pleasure. You want to know why religionists sodomize little boys, and don't consider it wrong, or sex! It's in their HOLY BOOKS, their fabricated Torah, their make-believe Koran, their fairy-tale New Testament. How many thousands of little boys will be molested by Catholic priests before you will see rioting amongst Catholic parishioners to stop the slaughter? The 'silence' of the sheep is as repulsive as the 'acts'!

Moses killed about 100,000 men and 68,000 women. They came right into their homes on Main Street, under a Full Moon. Hacked the women and boys to death, and then dragged off the little baby girls to be molested in every orifice on their little bodies. And the Cosmic Bastard saw that it was GOOD, so he did it again and again so future generations would know that it was not a mistake. It was who he is and always will be because the Cosmic Bastard is changeless—the same yesterday, today, and tomorrow until the end of time! (the writer of Deuteronomy, supposedly Moses, brags about it).

"Their children also shall be dashed to pieces before their eyes, their houses shall be spoiled, and their wives ravished" (Isaiah 13:15-16).

Isaiah is the prophet who brought us the prediction that the savior to come would be born of a virgin (actually 'young maiden' from the Hebrew 'almah'). Actually, it was amazing that there would be any left, after the Cosmic Bastard had them all raped by his followers! After the Cosmic Bastard had everyone else raped, he wanted us to know that no one would be allowed to 'touch' his chosen Mary! 'The first time she spreads her legs, my little peapod will pop out and her hymen will still be intact. "No magician ever reveals his tricks, but I am going to tell Pope Pius XII how I did it. Maybe we can get a Nobel!" So Pius spoke Ex Cathedra and created the myth of Mary and her immortal ways. No Nobel Prize, however. The Swedes are Protestants you know.

Remember, Mohamed married a nine-year-old girl and Paul had a fourteen-year-old boy. Twenty-three thousand priests had an assortment of little boys. Remember also, that these activities have never stopped since the time of Moses! It's just the way the Cosmic Bastard wanted it and his faithful religionist followers have 'trumped him in spades!'

"[U]tterly destroyed the men, and the women, and the little ones, of every city, we left none to remain" (Deuteronomy 2:34).

"...and the little ones..." It's so sweet, when they describe their murders in this way, smashing in their "little" heads. This is the basis for morality which will stand the test of time? I can condemn my worthless neighbor for his stance on abortion. I can bury my family members, without tears, because I know that they are going to a better place. I can secretly smile, because I know that everyone who differs from my beliefs will be punished in torment forever. I can torch ACLU buildings, kill abortion doctors, and be proved right.

Numbers 5, I Samuel 15, Psalm 1 "...put them all to death."

When I served in the military, during Vietnam, we had a chaplain who was big on justifying our killings by referencing the Bible. War is honorable, and it has always been a tool for God to do his work on earth. To die in battle is to guarantee your place in the afterlife. To kill, even children, (and he cited dozens of OT passages) is NOT wrong in God's eyes. You can hate the enemy because God does too. Again, Deuteronomy 20 "Then when fighting impends, the priest must come forward and address the army in these words: ...The Lord your God accompanies you to fight for you against your enemy and give you the victory." In other words, God is on our side, no matter what we do. That means that killing innocent children has already been approved by God's own history.

Here are a few more biblical references just to point out that militaristic murders are not a random way of doing business with religionists:

Deuteronomy 3, 7, 12, 20, 25, Joshua 6, 8, 10, Judges 21, II Chronicles 20, Numbers 21, 31, I Kings 20-42, I Samuel 15, Isaiah 11, 13, 15, Jeremiah 12, Daniel 11, Amos 9, Hosea 13.

"Slay utterly old *and* young, both maids, and little children, and women: but come not near any man upon whom *is* the mark; and begin at my sanctuary" (Ezekiel 9:5-6).

If a person tells you that they believe that every word of their Bible is true….RUN LIKE HELL. Get away from those morons! They can justify murder, rape, genocide and bad hygiene!

New Testament 'kinder, gentler' anyone? How about Revelation 9 and 14? Going be a whole lot of dead bodies lying around, just like in the Old Testament. And please read very closely what it actually says. These are not Christians who will be saved! It will be 144,000 from the TRIBES of ISRAEL. Those are Jews! They pulled a fast one. They had this last book written by a little Jewish community, on an island off the coast. And yes, the Cosmic Bastard will again be killing "…all the little ones." Man, he just doesn't stop with the shiv! So the New Testament religion was not really a departure from the depraved slaughter of the Old Testament, maybe just a breather until they recognized who they really were.

"I cannot imagine a God who rewards and punishes the objects of his creation, whose purposes are modeled after our own—a God, in short, who is but a reflection of human frailty. Neither can I believe that the individual survives the death of his body, although feeble souls harbor such thoughts through fear or ridiculous egotism" (Albert Einstein).

This was the 'god' who the anti-abortionists want to use as the Poster Child for their campaign to protect the unborn. Sorry anti-abortionists, better hurry, at the rate that this world class murderer is going, there won't be anyone to save. Please stop talking about the sacredness of life which you have supposedly discovered by reading your Bible.

Was all this true? Was this what the Jews, Christians and Muslims really wanted the world to think that their god was like? The next chapter outlines a fall-back strategy. 'We were just kidding about all the mass killings!' 'We were only joking about all the rapes and beheadings.' 'We were just having fun with you with all those stories about how we sliced up all the children'. 'Can't you take a joke?!' 'We just made up all those stories to get your attention. Haven't you ever heard of 'myth' before?!' What else is there for them to say?

A reading for your reflection:

When the Christians conquered Alexandria, they destroyed the greatest library that the world had ever known. It was a repository of knowledge from all over the known world. And the Christians sought out Hypatia, who was known as the wisest, most intelligent person in the world. They skinned her alive, tortured and raped her. And then they burned her. Just to teach her that a new 'morality' had entered the world, one that modern societies could base their very lives on.

Hypatia of Alexandria: Mathematician and Martyr by Deakin.

Your argument is not with me. It is *your* Torah, *your* Old Testatment, *your* New Testament, *your* Koran. *Your* mass murderer.

The LIE of religion is the **Big Elephant**
in the room.

And everyone pretends that it is *invisible*.

But it is there. In every conversation – in every political speech – in every legislative session – in every international crisis – in every war – in every law that is passed – in every political campaign – in every societal concern – in every courtroom – in every media broadcast – in every newspaper – in every terrorist act – in every social taboo – in every masochistic sanction against freewill – in every boycott of scientific breakthrough.

Silently it commands a huge presence in everything that happens in our world.

And so our leaders just lift up the 'tail' and step over the 'poop' to get to the mundane issues that will never solve anything.

And a baby cries. Not just over the 'religion-caused' death of his mother, but at the total loss of any hope for the future.

CHAPTER 3

Lies, Myths, and Fabrications

I met a professor of religion in Israel during our work on an archaeological site. In our discussions of the many factual errors, inaccuracies, and outright lies in the 'holy books', he made a startling disclosure. "Yes, the Bible is full of lies, myths and fabrications, but they are written to reveal much deeper, more profound truths about the universe." I told him that made absolutely no sense to me. Is there another world beyond the physical, observable, and testable? He told me that his 'truths' could only really be discovered on a much more spiritual level!

Religionists have been on the defensive now for almost one hundred years. Science, history and new methods of understanding documents from the past have totally obliterated the religionists' sacred, unchallengeable books. So now we know that they are all lies. But religionists must still find a way to justify commitments that they have internalized in their own indoctrinations. I sensed a 'crisis' mentality in Israel. If their religion were proved to be based totally on lies, then the country's existence could not be justified on any level. It also meant that their number one source of income, religious tourists, would most surely dry up over time. I told the professor that a crisis on his part did not necessarily create an emergency on my part. I was there to find the truth, but let's take a look at logical conclusions.

Let's see how his way of understanding the world would work in our daily lives.

Imagine a doctor telling his patient that his diagnosis is based on lies, myths, and fabrications, and that he had decided to remove the patient's heart, lungs, kidneys and liver in order to create a higher state of health for the patient.

Imagine an accountant telling shareholders that his audit of the corporation is based on lies, myths, and fabrications which will clearly raise the share value for all investors.

Imagine a lawyer telling a judge in court that his case is based on lies, myths, and fabrications which will demonstrate the innocence of his client.

Imagine a teacher telling her students that everything she will teach them will be based on lies, myths, and fabrications, but if they listen closely they will discover the great truths of the universe.

Imagine a car salesman telling a customer that everything he will tell him is based on lies, myths, and fabrications… wait a minute, that's already happening!

Imagine parents telling their children about the absolute importance of always being truthful, but that the parents reserve the right to use lies, myths, and fabrications.

Imagine police officers using lies, myths, and fabrications in their testimony in court.

Imagine pharmaceutical companies using lies, myths, and fabrications to sell their products to an unsuspecting public because they have the greater health of individuals at heart.

Imagine peace treaties between warring nations being based on lies, myths, and fabrications because it is impossible to trust the other side. That was probably the basis of the conflict in the first place.

Imagine the FDA using lies, myths, and fabrications in regards to food safety because research is expensive and commerce is more important than the life of any one individual.

Imagine the world banking system being based on lies, myths, and fabrications. People could work hard all of their lives and have it all stolen from them by the actions of just a few of these treacherous fiends.

Imagine the FAA being based on lies, myths, and fabrications so that more flights could take off and arrive on schedule. So that passengers could be processed more quickly. So that all involved could make much higher profits!

Imagine hospital safety being based on lies, myths, and fabrications so that patient stays could be shortened, insurance profits maximized, and hospital staffs downsized and marginalized.

Imagine car safety, as determined by the auto manufacturers, as being based on lies, myths, and fabrications, all in the name of profits.

Imagine your most intimate relationships being based on lies, myths, and fabrications so each partner can make himself or herself more desirable to the other.

Imagine your insurance policies (car, home, belongings, liability) being based on lies, myths, and fabrications, which are only discovered after the fact of disaster.

Imagine your dentist basing his diagnosis, not on X-rays, but on lies, myths, and fabrications. He then proceeds to remove twelve of your front teeth.

Imagine that everything in your life is really based on lies, myths, and fabrications. It would not take very long for you to go insane!

WHY IS IT THAT WE ALLOW RELIGION TO BE BASED ON LIES, MYTHS, AND FABRICATIONS? (Adam and Eve, Noah, Jonah, Moses, age of the earth, fallacious miracles, mass murders, strained history, the Exodus, etc.). It is because we have never rationally thought about the garbage into which we have been indoctrinated.

Religion is the last, greatest curse and cause of slavery on the earth!

People who are religious are already insane in a significant way. They have managed to accept the lies, myths, and fabrications as true for their own lives. While at the same time, absolutely insisting that everyone and everything else must adhere to a more universal standard of truth. The two don't meet in reality. To live their daily lives without going insane trying to navigate through a constant barrage of liars, manipulators, and the most untrustworthy examples of human degenerates, they are forced to 'compartmentalize' their whole existence.

In the next chapter we see what the outcomes are when people try to live a 'rational' existence at work and an 'irrational' existence in their 'religious' lives. They make a mockery of everything.

Some suggested reading:

The Acts of the Apostles: What Really Happened in the Earliest Days of the Church? by Ludemann.
Atheism: The Case Against God by Smith.
God the Failed Hypothesis, How Science Shows That God Does Not Exist by Stenger.
This is the Place: Brigham Young and the New Zion by Taves.
Christian Science by Twain.
God is Not Great: How Religion Poisons Everything by Hitchens.
Sources of the Jesus Tradition: Separating History from Myth by Hoffman.

CHAPTER 4

Religious Realities

One of the strongest arguments that religionists put forward for the importance of religion, is that if we didn't have religion, then there would be no basis for morality. They truly believe that all would be chaos. Now there is not a single example in the world where this is consistently true. There are hundreds of countries where less than ten percent of the population is religious in any way. They seem to do just fine. There are, however, many examples of 'religious' nations where lives of millions of persons are destroyed daily by the enforcement of 'religious' morality.

Quite often parents will teach morals to their children that even they do not follow. It may even be a desire, on the part of parents, to have their children live more moral lives than the parents have. At any rate, it becomes very confusing as children age and discover the real circumstances of the lapses of adults around them. And so:

Indoctrinating children into religion is nothing short of child abuse.

Religious Education is an Oxymoron. No group has tried to disparage and destroy the advances of education and science more than religious groups. Come with me to Catholic CCD classes, or Koranic rote sessions, or Hebrew School and you will clearly see that this is an absolutely true statement.

If ignorance is bliss, then religionists must be in a constant state of euphoria (fundamentalist Christians, Moslems and Hindus can look this word up in their dictionary).

Religionists are cowards. Moslem women say that they love being locked up in their homes 24/7. Roman Catholic women are hypocrites and cowards for granting to themselves total freedom to have access to contraception, but being more than willing to have their church coerce enactment of federal laws to force their 'non-Catholic' sisters to be deprived. Hindu Brahmins could care less about the destroyed lives of lower caste girls who will never be free to thrive in freedom.

The Roman Catholic Church teaches that a married Roman Catholic couple can never have sex for pleasure, but only for the purpose of producing a baby. Therefore, the 1.3 billion Roman Catholics on the globe are all morons. They have taken one of the great pleasures of being human and have labeled it dirty and deadly sinful. A couple can go to Hell for all eternity for having sex for pleasure only. Thus, we see the great importance of eliminating contraceptives. Contraceptives mean that a couple is only having sex for the immoral purpose of enriching their marital experience. But it does follow the consistent pattern of the teachings of a truly wacky, male-dominated institution. In 660 C.E. at their Council of Nantes the bishops were discussing whether females were even human. In the Third Canon they actually decided that women weren't and that they didn't have a 'soul'. They quickly rescinded that finding, however, because one of their scholars pointed out that if women didn't have a soul, then they could not be tortured in Hell for all eternity. With that decision they would have lost all control. Can you imagine what society would have been like with soulless women running around having pleasurable sex with no consequences? You might as well be Protestant.

And then, Catholic parents take their children to the building where their children will be taught that sex is dirty and evil. Sex can cost you your eternal life. Even thoughts of sex in your innermost private thoughts are deeply sinful and therefore, extremely dangerous. Don't ever think about sex unless you are within five minutes of a Confessional Booth. It is a 'mortal' sin.

Moslem children watch as their mothers and sisters are forced to never leave the house. Women are lesser beings and the evil of sex must be stopped at all costs. Even if it means that the life of every female is no better than a death-row inmate. However, this evil sex must be available 'on demand' by the male head of the household at any hour of the night or day. The male children watch and learn. God is cruel. Women are garbage. Sex is okay for men. And Allah be praised.

In history Jews, Christians and Moslems have even labeled the birth of a child as proof of sin on the part of a woman. She must have been involved in evil sex to have become pregnant. The baby is proof. And so the mother was considered 'unclean' for sixty days after the delivery.

Religionists look at the world and find a dangerous place, so they created easy answers to their fears, rather than facing and overcoming them.

Cowardly religionists see evil and obstacles everywhere.

Religionists are full of self-hatred and loathing. And with suicide an undesirable option, they often turn their hate toward 'others'.

Religionists are incapable of courageously confronting the world with new and innovative ways of bringing hope. They see AIDS in Africa and they tell the 'ignorant' there to have more babies and don't protect yourself.

Religionists have easy, simplistic answers for everything: death, misfortune, illness, deformity, and war. These easy answers excuse them from the more time-consuming acts of learning, growth and experimentation.

All religions are based on hatred of someone. Religionists will never be motivated to create Peace on Earth. Others be damned. Let their gods sort it out for them.

It could have been different, but the opportunities for humanity have been squandered by religionists for centuries. Jews, Christians, Moslems and Hindus could have recognized their common humanity and striven for greater understanding. After all, according to Mitochondrial DNA, we all have the same common female ancestor: Mitochondrial Eve. The Human Genome Project has scientifically proven that we are over 99% exactly the same! The only thing that separates us is our religious lies. Of the trillions of cells and proteins that make up who we are as individuals, we all look the same through our common ancestor of 160,000 years ago. But they all decided to play the game. All of the division and misery on earth can be traced back to these degenerate, religionist liars who squelched knowledge and learning. They created artificial realities of race, ethnicity, and nationality and started the slaughter of innocents over the centuries.

Religionists have always employed Conversion by Bullet as one of their most effective evangelistic tools through time. Whole peoples have been annihilated because they would not convert (New World, Hawaii, Indonesia, Australia, New Zealand, Peru, Mexico and others). While others converted at the point of a gun or bayonet.

Religionists speak of their religious writings as being inerrant. This means that God himself was in charge of the absolute correctness of every word in the 'holy books', which means that God really did, personally, order the killing of all those innocent people. Jews, Christians, and Moslems now stand indicted by their own protestations, that their 'books' contain the purest revelation of the God of the Universe. Someone once protested to me that his Bible was infallible, every word was eternally true, and it was exactly as God dictated. I asked if he really believed that every word in the Book of Hezekiah was true. He replied, "Absolutely, I believe that every word is true." How interesting, since there is no such book as Hezekiah. If you are going to defend 'your' god, you should at least defend 'his' book.

Religionists would never think of taking their irrational thought patterns into the work place. Work is based on FACTS. Work is based on reality. There is no private, secret zone where irrational, unscientific thinking applies. Yet, after all we have discovered in the real world, there are still adults who cling to tales no more believable than those of Santa Claus or the Tooth Fairy.

Still, there are billions who will insist that religion is the only thing that makes sense of the world and morality. The list in the next chapter reveals just how degenerate religious experience has been in our world.

Some books:

Why I am Not a Christian by Russell.
Why I am Not a Hindu by Ilaiah.
On the Gods: And Other Essays by Ingersoll.
God's War on Terror: Islam, Prophecy and the Bible by Shoebat.
Bertrand Russell: On God and Religion by Seckel.
Critiques of God by Angeles.

CHAPTER 5

If Religion Were True

- If religion were true, it wouldn't have to lie about science.
- If religion were true, it wouldn't have to lie about history.
- If religion were true, it wouldn't have to lie about medical breakthroughs.
- If religion were true, it wouldn't have to lie about evolution.
- If religion were true, it wouldn't come in Heinz 57 varieties.
- If religion were true, it would not have to be discussed in secret behind closed doors.
- If religion were true, it wouldn't have to lie about geography and nature.
- If religion were true, it wouldn't have to lie about the age of the earth.
- If religion were true, it wouldn't have to lie about human relationships of any kind.
- If religion were true, it never would have condoned the slaughter of Native Americans.
- If religion were true, it never would have permitted and *participated* in Slavery.
- If religion were true, it wouldn't have caused most of the hate, war, persecution and division, which have littered the landscape of history.
- If religion were true, it wouldn't have to keep changing its own history to fit new realities.

- If religion were true, there would be no need of orphanages. They say every child is a wanted child.
- If religion were true, all persons would get health care.
- If religion were true, it would see all humans as equal and of equal consideration.
- If religion were true, it would never discriminate, in any way, against anyone.
- If religion were true, little boys would be safe from priests and the churches which <u>hide</u> them.
- If religion were true, religionists would be able to discern the truth about political WAGS (Wild Ass GuesseS).
- If religion were true, religious gathering places would not be filled with so many mentally *unstable* and intellectually *dishonest* people.
- If religion were true, it could be learned through experiment and observations, not *only* through indoctrination.
- If religion were true, the religious charlatans, who prey on the weak and infirm, would experience the outrage of the faithful. They do not.
- If religion were true, the religious would be the ultimate caretakers of the creator's creations. "Tree huggers, anyone?"
- If religion were true, then the religious would always be on the side of the individual against the coercion of the state.
- If religion were true, most practitioners would not be storing up such massive wealth for this seemingly short sojourn on the earth.
- If religion were true, followers would more closely follow the example of the one who they claim to be following.
- If religion were true, the mix of races, nationalities, and opinions during the 'worship hour' would be far more diverse.
- If religion were true, unstable persons would not have to invent miracles to further convince their leaders.
- If religion were true, it wouldn't have been on the wrong side of every progressive breakthrough in human history: flat earth, motion of planets, discovery of bacteria and viruses, organ transplants, evolution, stem cell research, and almost every single new exciting discovery.

- If religion were true, it would have something positive to contribute to the new ways of discovering truths. Religion adds nothing but often shows up demanding to be the only voice on the ethics of the matter. If any religion has *anything* to say about ethics, it absolutely has to start with 'confession', and that alone should take centuries for any religious group to complete.
- If religion were true, the poor would have a voice. Every religion claims this. Ninety percent of humans on the earth live in poverty. "Blessed are the poor…." I guess the Sermon on the Mount was just words.
- If religion were true, it would never justify preemptive war. It would never justify the torture of prisoners. It would never justify killing innocent civilians. It would never give its consent, by standing by silently, and giving the impression of approval. Ask the Jews of the Holocaust, or the Guatemalans, or the Cherokee, what it feels like to know that the religious leaders stood by silently, or even *APPLAUDED*.
- If religion were true, why do 100% of all religionists know that the other guy's religion is false, and that its practitioners will certainly suffer damnation for all eternity? That must mean that 100% agree that all religion is false in the eyes of almost all others.
- If religion were true, why has that information only been available for less than 2,000 years, depending on your source? What about the other 4,600,000,000 years that the earth has been in existence?
- If religion were true, (or at least one version of it), then you would see a massive conversion rate from the indoctrinated 'birth-parent' religion to the 'true' religion. In fact, such conversions are less than one/one hundred thousandths of one percent of those who actually practiced another religion. "And the truth will set you free."!
- If religion were true, it could be discussed intellectually and openly. But as everyone has experienced, religious 'discussions' are nothing more, nor less, than bomb throwing contests among idiots. That's why they hide behind their closed doors, where they can safely further imprison the already deluded.
- If religion were true, it wouldn't be the coercive, dishonest, disreputable, dehumanizing thing that it has become.

If religion were true, but sadly, it isn't! Most humans will throw away most of their lives following the tragic lie called religion. They will indoctrinate their children, just as they were indoctrinated by their parents. They will do it out of loyalty, shame, or a lack of self-direction, but they will do it. As they live their lives, they will experience the reality that religion is a lie and that almost all that it teaches is harmful to personal mental health, and answers for daily living. But they will continue, in denial, mostly because all of their friends are. They will see the refuse of religious teaching, the divorced, the homosexual, the learned, the different, the foreign, and the poor. All no longer welcome or fitting in and, in denial, hope that never happens to them. Ultimately, if they ever question anything about their religion, they may just find themselves alienated and suspected by those, whose personal denial is deep, and defiant of any challenges at all.

It has always amazed me, that people believe, that the position which they take on the 'abortion' issue, puts them on a 'higher moral' plane, than the rest of society. These are the same people who lie about evolution, about religion, about scientific discoveries and medical breakthroughs. Abject lying, apparently, doesn't put a 'dent' in their moralistic armor. They are so certain about when life begins, that they are now 'protecting' the fertilized 'egg' before it even gets into the womb (no 'morning after' pills will be allowed) . Here's a *news flash* for you: we now know that the sperm, *alone*, contains all of the DNA, which is necessary, to create 'new' life. It's called 'cloning'. Watch for the new Papal statement on the masturbatory activities of priests, really amounting to the mass slaughter of 'life' in its nascent form. All that 'life' in the sheets! A good, young priest can kill over one million 'unborns' with every private session.

In the next chapter, we take a look at all of the 'attributes' attributed to god in the 'holy books'. Multiple-personalities, anyone?!

CHAPTER 6

The God Quiz

Check the Following statements that are true:

__ God is always pure love.
__ God hates.
__ God is merciful to a fault.
__ God has ordered children to be killed.
__ God never changes.
__ God changes his mind.
__ God has a mother.
__ God created all things.
__ God created evil.
__ God can forgive anything.
__ God will never forgive many sins.
__ God has done things that he will never forgive others for doing.
__ God has the highest morality in the universe.
__ God ordered that women should be raped.
__ God always tells the truth.
__ God ordered many leaders to lie and deceive.
__ God is one.
__ God talks to himself.
__ God hears all prayers.
__ God answers very few prayers.
__ God loves all children.

__ God allows children to suffer cruel, excruciating pain and offers no relief.
__ God is always for peace.
__ God is a God of war and destruction.
__ God takes sides in religious disputes.
__ God created eternal damnation and eternal suffering.
__ God demands to be worshipped and obeyed.
__ God gives his love with no strings attached.
__ God inspired perfect, inerrant books to be written about himself and his chosen people.
__ God inspired writings about himself that were filled with massive historical, chronological, geological, and anthropological errors.
__ A third of God had sex with a human woman and produced himself.
__ God promised to give immediate eternal bliss to anyone who dies while killing an unbeliever.
__ God created the entire universe just about 6,000 years ago.
__ God is a murderer.
__ God is absent from his creation.
__ God is present in every minute detail of his creation.
__ God is a male.
__ God is a female.

Now, turn in your papers, and hit the books. We've got a lot of lies to undo.

The Blind Watchmaker by Dawkins.
***The Selfish Gene* by Dawkins.**
In the Beginning: A Scientist Shows Why the Creationists Are Wrong by McGowan.
Unintelligent Design by Perakh.

As schizophrenic as all this 'history' of God is, in his own writings, in the next chapter, we get to see how it becomes even more insane in the 'lived' experiences of the myriad of lunatic fringe elements of modern 'followers'.

CHAPTER 7

Religious Outcomes from Lying Liars

I have no doubt that people have real experiences, which are difficult to square with what we know about the real world in which we live. I have no doubt that they have experiences, but it is in how they define these experiences that I have to make my challenge.

We are so steeped in superstitious religious ideas that it is easy to relate these new experiences to the fraudulent religious ideas into which we have been indoctrinated. In explaining an experience we distort it. The new experience may look a lot like what we would expect this person to say. When a Christian says that they have died and come back to life, they inevitably say that they have seen Jesus. A Muslim always sees Mohammed. A Jew always sees Moses. When faced with these obvious distortions, it becomes doubly difficult to discern just exactly what it is that they have really experienced. Religionists often sound a lot like UFO observers. If I believe it, I will see it.

Just get eye-witness descriptions of an event, notoriously defective testimony, from seven different people who were present and you will see what I mean. You may even come away thinking that they must have been at completely different events! The experience is already being filtered through a complex set of experiences and indoctrinations, which have been stored in memory and have no connection whatsoever to this new event.

One further complication is that many so-called religious events are experienced by only one person. A sample of ONLY ONE does not stand as scientific verification. You listen. You ask questions. Not too many, or they will immediately know that you are an infidel, and probably have already been eternally condemned by the spiritual star of their story.

Everyone LIES about something. Religious people already have one strike against them, in that they are already liars.

Here are the stories of a few of these liars, who told me their stories, probably in the hope that they could save my wretched soul through the sheer magnificence of what their god was doing for them personally.

Just the facts ma'am, just the facts.

A devout woman came to me with this experience. She had undergone open-heart surgery, and during the surgery had died on the operating table. She was resuscitated and the surgery was successfully completed and she fully recovered. Out of recovery, she told her doctor that she remembered dying on the surgery table. She also remembered that her soul left her body, and hovering above the surgery room, looked down on everyone in the surgery suite. She claims that she saw a white light and heard a voice telling her to get back into her body because it was not her time yet. She could fully describe everything that was in the surgery room and she remembered quite distinctly the conversations between the doctors about going golfing that afternoon and the head surgeon getting quite miffed at the surgical nurse for not being competent! She asked her surgeon if he had, in fact, been talking about going golfing that afternoon after the surgery (as if he would admit to that!). He said that he had not remembered, but later she asked a nurse who had been at the surgery if they had, and the nurse said that they had definitely talked about going golfing! She knew the color of the surgery suite. She knew all the cabinets. She knew all the peripherals, where the clock was on the wall, and a myriad of other details. She reminded me that she had been placed under anesthesia before she entered the room for her surgery.

She told me that she felt this experience had given her a whole new religious insight into the world, and it helped her to know that she was sent back to do God's work in her family and in her community. She felt that she now understood God better than most people.

She asked me if I believed. I wasn't sure whether she meant 'in her' or 'in God'.

I asked her if I could get a list of all the people who participated in her surgery and whether she would give me permission to follow-up with questions about their memories of the events. This was long before HIPPA laws, but I asked her for a release to see her medical records. At first, she refused. I reminded her that she had told me that God was now using her to reveal his truth to the world and this would certainly bring any truth to light, if possible, to support that cause.

She gave me a signed release. I can tell you that absolutely no one at the hospital was happy about this, at all. But two people agreed to talk to me.

I soon discovered that this woman was a surgical nurse at that hospital! The next fact I learned was that this woman "has a lot of problems." Her marriage was in trouble and her son had been in drug and alcohol rehab on numerous occasions. She quite often talked about needing a miracle to save her family. She also had a lot of books on out-of-body experiences and had been repeatedly warned about talking with patients about the possibility of whether or not they may have left their bodies during procedures.

I had asked her to type up a full description of what she experienced and I showed that to the two people who talked with me. One looked up the surgical records for that day and realized, to her shock, that the surgery had not been done in the surgical suite, which was described in her description. The surgery was actually performed in another, entirely different, room because the main surgical suite was under repair during that two week period.

One of the nurses laughed. "Doctors always talk about going golfing during surgery. They also talk about 'boobs' and lots of other non-surgical stuff! Anyone who has ever been a surgical nurse would know all that. A doctor berating a nurse is NOT unusual!"

When I met with this woman again, I told her about the records of where her surgery actually took place and how the descriptions didn't match. I never saw her again, but I did hear that she was still telling everyone her story with one change. Her new story contained a description of the room where she actually had her surgery. I was also told that she was collecting a lot of money for speaking to various groups.

Angels have their own language, but there are no dictionaries to look the words up.

Back in the 1970's I had just gotten out of the military and my fiancée and I were church shopping to find a church that would be a compromise for both of us. One Sunday I was asked to attend a women's prayer group. The woman who had invited me was beautiful, charismatic, a natural leader, and clearly the organizer of this group. This beautiful woman was the mother of two great kids. She had a successful husband, a beautiful home, horses, and expensive cars. She insinuated these things were blessings from God because of their faithfulness.

Everything was going along pretty much according to expectations when this woman started babbling, screeching, gyrating, and throwing herself around. I thought she might be having a seizure, but the group was only reveling in the scene! I was recording the session to play back to my fianceé who could not make it that night, but I was not expecting this at all. This craziness went on for what seemed like hours but was likely only 10-15 minutes.

Then the woman stopped. She fell to the floor. She was covered in sweat and still softly moaning. Then another woman stood up and told us that the angels were speaking through the woman who had just collapsed. The woman standing said that she had been given the gift of interpreting what the angels were saying through the other woman. She went into a long description of God's plans for his people, assembled in that group, and that we would have to redouble our efforts to support his work through this group! We were told that the interpretation was a direct translation of the words, which had been spoken in 'angel language.'

'I'm in love.' Excuse me, what is that you said about Jesus?!

I didn't go back to the group and I had forgotten that I had recorded the session. Two years later I was attending what was billed as a spiritual weekend with the author of several successful books on spirituality. She was drop-dead gorgeous and when she spoke, her voice was so beautiful that you weren't sure whether you were having a religious experience or just plain old 'country' sex. She was that good. She talked about how God had chosen her marriage partner for life, she told us how God had helped her through her first divorce, she told us how God was showing her the way to parenting Christian children, and how God was giving her strength while her children were going through drug rehab. I kid you not. No, we didn't pick up on the hypocrisy right away. I'm telling you, she was gorgeous!

In one of the sessions, she was talking about 'speaking in tongues' and how God was using her to bring the 'true' message of his will to the modern church. Then I remembered that I had my tape recorder with me and I wondered whether I still had the recording of that session which I had recorded back home in Michigan. I did.

I asked her if I could play it for the group. She thought that was a great idea. I played it and then stopped before the original 'interpretation.' She started right in to interpret this message from the angels! She was so proud that she had that gift! When she finished I told her that there was more to the tape, and I played what had been the earlier interpretation from the woman back home. She got furious and told the group that the woman back home was from Satan and was a deceiver of his people. However, the interpretations were so totally different that one of the women was absolutely a liar.

Some attendees left the conference immediately. A person, traveling home with us, said that she had seen this woman's 'manager' sneak into her room at night and not come out until the next morning. Yet she was a married woman. She didn't believe in "fornication." She told us that many times during her presentation. Apparently, she did believe in making lots of money, using fraudulent methods, and really serious LIES. Even to this day, she makes a whole lot of money and she sells a whole lot of books. Still, I doubt that any who saw her fraudulent performance that day ever bought her books again!

The sky is falling. The sky is falling. The sky is falling.

I was friends with a black, Baptist minister whom I liked a lot. He served an Inner City church and we were on the same board of ministers in this Ohio community. He was a good guy and conversations were never boring when we got together. But there was one thing which caused us the greatest consternation in our relationship. He was always, and I mean ALWAYS, talking about END TIMES. The world is coming to an end and everyone not right with the Lord is going to be left here and persecuted by the fangs of the Devil. He would get quite animated and tell me that he prayed for me every night because he didn't want to leave me behind to suffer! He really meant it.

I asked if I could pose a personal question. "Shoot brother. Hit me with your best shot." Okay.

"Do you preach to your congregation every week about the world coming to an end, sooner than they think?" "I certainly do because the Bible tells me to and because I love them."

"Do you tell them not to store up treasure for themselves here on earth and to give their worldly possessions to the Lord?" "I most certainly do."

"Have you become personally wealthier through their offerings to your church?" "I AM the work of God before this end time. We need the money to get the word out while there is still time."

This conversation took place in the fall of 1983. Everyone was talking about the book *1984* and whether God had used that to warn his people that the End would come at that time. The book really had nothing to do with the End Time prophecies, but the 'year' was a convenient tool for the fear-mongers.

I asked my friend if he knew a time 'certain' when the world would be no more. He told me that no one could know the exact time, but that God had told him that the world would cease to exist after December 31, 1983. What I did next kind of shocked my friend and clearly stressed our friendship.

I asked him if he would be willing to sign a Quit Claim Deed to all of his earthly possessions and date it January 1, 1984. He got angry and told me that would be testing the Holy Spirit. How, I don't know. But I do know that our friendship was at an end. I told him that by not signing the Quit Claim, he proved that he was a fraud, using End Times to scare his people and to coerce them into giving him money.

He lived rich, and I later heard from a mutual friend that he told his congregation that the Lord had appeared to him in a vision and said that the Devil had deceived him with that earlier date, but that God was still coming soon, maybe even tomorrow!

Please, please, please, stop hitting me. It feels so good when you stop.

One of the churches, which I attended, supposedly a young, progressive Catholic Church, was big into prayer groups and intercessory prayer. They continually solicited prayer requests for any and all needs of the members and families of the group. Occasionally, there would be a request for prayers for a really horrible, immediate need. At one time a small child was dying of leukemia and the parents begged for everyone to pray for their daughter. The priest said that he wanted to get one thousand people raising their prayers up to God on behalf of this child. I first thought why should we have to BEG God to take away this little girl's unrelenting, excruciating pain. If he has the power to do so, why doesn't he just do it? I've probably been a contrarian all my life, but when things just don't make sense to me, I ask a lot of questions. It appears that God really is just a Cosmic Bastard who has the power to take away suffering but refuses to do so without a lot of groveling. I asked the priest just how many people it would take to stop God from 'punishing' this child with pain. Is a thousand enough? Should we call the Pope and engage the Hotline? How is it that we flawed beings show more compassion toward this child than the Cosmic Bastard does with all of his eternal gifts? Is this the only child with this dire need? Shouldn't we be constantly walking down the hallways begging the Cosmic Bastard to relieve their pain as well? Or is this special perk for those of us who have been "saved"? We used to have nuns who prayed for us and when they failed, the priest was called in to put the final holy water splash on the kid!

'Judge' for yourself. This is 'class' warfare.

I have a vivid memory of the funeral of a prominent judge in my hometown. I was just a teenager at the time. The judge was really a despicable degenerate but still important to the Church. He was so important that the Bishop conducted the funeral Mass in the Bishop's Cathedral and the place was packed. One sentence in the funeral oration stands out in my memory, "Judge — will never spend one second in Purgatory because of all the prayers which will be lifted to Heaven's Gate on his behalf this day!" Now, I know that I am just Joe Schmoe, so the same benefit will not be afforded to me. Do the math: ten thousand prayers, worth about 100 years off the sentence of Purgatory for each prayer, and I will be lucky to get a couple dozen people. I'm going to be doing REAL time, not the kind you can do standing on one foot. It occurred to me that all this might just be a bunch of hooey! Similar to the burning animal carcasses on the old Jewish Altars used to appease the Cosmic Bastard of old and supposedly replaced by the kinder, gentler Jesus. The Altar is still there, and all those hundreds of burning candles are certainly reminiscent of the fires back in the LaLa Land of Israel at the Temple. It was not a comfort to me to realize that there would be a pecking order in Heaven that would certainly be no different than the one on Earth.

God, if I give you enough money will you really, really love me.

I had an acquaintance who was a Christian minister. He was the original hypocrite. His big thing was TITHING (a ten percent fee that he claimed that God was demanding from everyone out of each paycheck). He seemed to exempt himself, but he was big on it for his congregation. This guy had absolutely no talents whatsoever. He was a minister who couldn't speak well, he couldn't sing, he had a lousy bed-side manner, he wasn't well read and definitely not mentally alert, but he sure could scare people about what would happen to them after death if they didn't come through with the Tithe. One thing he could do was talk about "giving back" to Jesus with time, talents, and gifts. Sometimes he only talked about "giving gifts." Now this guy and his wife both inherited a great deal of money (inherited money does not count in the 'Tithe'). In order to support their pursuits in their church, they needed to convince their congregants—most earning minimum wage— that the Cosmic Bastard would be really ticked off if they held back on the tithe, which really belonged to him (there was a suspicion that the money never got passed on to God)! They had a ritual in their church in which they would have an Altar Call and the poor slobs would come to the front of the church, give their lives to Jesus, and the ushers would hold them upside down and shake the pennies out of their pockets. They needed to be washed by the Blood of the Lamb and coins stain the 'soul'! It was not a surprise to me to find out that both the minister and his wife were having extra-marital affairs. Lying liars are always in search of someone who is not as big a liar as they are. For religionists there is no escaping all the victims who have been created and destroyed by the constant barrage of religionist lies. In fact, I never met a priest, minister, or rabbi who was not a *THIEF.* They beg for money, do no honorable work, and pander lies to keep the 'goodies' coming. Gosh, it's great to know that there are a couple million of these liars, pedophiles, adulterers, thieves, murderers, and sadists just walking around loose!

Government approves 'snake-oil' sales by refusing to prosecute.

When I lived in Columbus, Ohio a healer came to town to hold a healing service at the State Theater. I had a very persistent pimple on my ass (actually I'm too embarrassed to tell you my real medical problem), so I thought I might just go and give it a shot. When I got there, there were already thousands of people waiting to get a seat. This guy had his own TV show and had healed thousands of different diseases right through the 'tube,' so I figured my pimple didn't have a chance. It wasn't very long before I realized that hundreds of these people in the crowd were actually undercover agents for the 'Healer.' They moved people around and seemed to direct them where they wanted them to sit in the audience. I heard them say to one man that there wasn't much room down front, but if he was willing, he could sit in one of the wheelchairs and be wheeled right down into the front row. When I got inside I saw at least two hundred of these wheelchairs with occupants who had been standing in the entryway without any assistance. They had a nice band and a beautiful choir. The lighting effects were out of this world. It felt like the premier of a Hollywood spectacular movie! And then HE came out all dressed in white! Brooks Brothers had never made a finer suit and the 'Blood of the Lamb' red hankie and tie were a very nice touch! I don't remember much about what he said in his sermon, he seemed to have an Oklahoma accent, and who can begin to understand that oil in the mouth slang? But then he got to the business of the day: The Altar Call. "Jeeeeeeessssuuss wants you to be healed, and you may never have another chance!" He ordered these poor wretches to stand up out of their wheelchairs, which they had just rented, and BE HEALED! They were in shock, because they had never been in a wheelchair before and they had certainly never been smacked on the head by an Evangelist. There they were, knocked to the ground with the Holy Spirit but obviously healed of their need for that wheelchair. "Come! Come now! God may never invite you again!" I went down. I wanted this man to put his hand on my pimple. But, on my way, I was attacked by his undercover agents who now held offering plates with long poles attached. They shouted "Make God know that you really want to be healed" and "He can't commit to you, unless you commit to him!" I never did make it down to the front.

I later learned that Billy Graham used the same undercover tactics. His Altar Calls were all well scripted shows. When the 'Call' came, all his undercover agents would get up and start making their way through the stadium to his podium. Thousands of these people worked with the Billy Graham Organization as volunteers and had been trained to interfere before all the people arrived! They had a list with the names and addresses of all the people who came forward so they could be placed on a mailing list to let them know about all the goodies they could buy from Billy to support his *SIX PERSONAL MANSIONS AND A LAVISH LIFESTYLE OF PLAYING GOLF WITH PRESIDENTS!* Billy had a personal office in Minneapolis which was larger than the largest personal CEO office, of any major corporation, in the nation. When Billy was getting older, he made a final appeal to save his organization so he could "save souls." The IRS was doing an investigation of his personal finances at the same time and found that he had *TWENTY-EIGHT MILLION DOLLARS IN HIS PRIVATE ACCOUNTS*, while telling his followers that he only took a meager salary to keep life and limb together. Billy Graham's roommate in Seminary said that Billy was the biggest liar that he had ever met in his life!

A bad penny shows up everywhere.

The Columbus' healer shows up again another time with a situation at the church we were attending in Columbus. We had a husband and wife janitor team at our church; the wife was diagnosed with blood poisoning and was on life support in ICU. The prognosis was not good. In her room was a television and there on the screen was the Healer. He said that he could see a person who had 'blood poisoning' (I kid you not) and that he could heal her, but only if she would commit her life to Jesus! To do this, she needed to send for one of his 'Prayer Hankies' and place the Hankie over the wounds. The Hankie had been blessed with the special blessing of the Healer, and had great powers. But first, she had to demonstrate her commitment to God by sending a 'thank offering' to the Healer, so that he could spread God's healing power around the world. This poor husband and wife had almost nothing, but he was willing to do anything to save his wife's life. He went to the bank, withdrew their entire life's savings, called the Healer's 800 number, and received instructions on how he could wire the money so they could expedite the healing process and save his wife's life. She died that night. He told us, that she died because he didn't have enough faith and didn't send the Healer enough money. The tales of debauchery, adultery and lies continue to be a hallmark of this Healer's family. In cases like this, you would really hope that there is a hell. But that would be just falling further into the trap of religionist's LIES.

Get ready for some great reading. Find a nice warm fireplace with a wool blanket, and that really comfy reading chair.

Deadly Blessings: Faith Healing on Trial by Bernneman.
When Wish Replaces Thought: Why So Much of What You Believe is False by Goldberg.
Miracle Mongers and Their Methods by Houdini.
Looking for a Miracle: Weeping Icons, Relics, Stigmata, Visions and Healing Cures by Nickell.
The Faith Healers by Randi.
Deadly Doctrines: Health, Illness, and Christian God Talk by Watters.
Missing Pieces: How to Investigate Ghosts, UFO's, Psychics and other Mysteries by Baker.
Flim Flam by Randi.
The Art of Deception: An Introduction to Critical Thinking by Capaldi.
Weird Water and Fuzzy Logic by Gardner.
Fifty Popular Beliefs that People Think are True by Harrison.

As gullible as 'believers' are about all kinds of nonsense, it is simply mind-boggling how much they HATE science, facts, truth, education, exploration, testing, and experimentation of the wonders that we find. So the next chapter puts it all in perspective. Hate the world, until the world overwhelms you with so much evidence, data, and truth that you can no longer be able to hide from it.

CHAPTER 8

Religious Reactions to New Scientific Discoveries throughout History

Two thousand years has given us enough time and events to see a very consistent pattern in how religions have dealt with the disclosure of their lies and atrocities.

- When the world became 'spherical' through natural observations, the religious claim of 'flat earth' was destroyed.
- When telescopes revealed the vastness of space and the true character of planets and stars, the anthropocentric and Christocentric nature of the world was displaced.
- When literary criticism exposed the forgeries of religious writers and claimants, the claims for biblical inerrancy were obliterated.
- When microscopes magnified the world of germs and viruses, the claims of divine retribution were no longer of any relevance for understanding why one person suffered while another didn't.
- When modern medicine scientifically explained the genesis of disease and cures, religion lost its footing in the claims of miracles around every event that was hard to explain.
- When students of history found documentation for hundreds of 'Jesus' like mythological characters with the same MOs, he lost his uniqueness and may have been proven to never have existed.

- When archaeology, paleoanthropology and scientific dating have been applied to the stories of the religious writers, their narratives simply are annihilated by the facts of what really happened during those times.
- When DNA was proven to be pure fact and Mitochondrial DNA pushes human existence back over one hundred thousand years, the dating of scriptures becomes simply unsustainable for any purpose, other than to continue religious lies as a way of life.
- When over ten thousand claims of supernatural 'miracle' events have been proven to be false and most often perpetrated by delusional and fraudulent characters, then science has taken away the last foolishness used by religionists to manipulate the unsophisticated.

But their pattern persists none-the-less:

1. Condemn
2. Document unbiblical nature of discovery
3. Condemn Discoverer
4. Persecute Discoverer
5. Often execute Discoverer and Followers (ostracize at a minimum)
6. After some time has passed: Take Credit for the Discovery as part of God's Marvelous and Mysterious Creation!

The following are wonderful illuminating works of scientific literature. If the truth had been important two thousand years ago, Caesar might have conducted his business on a personal computer. Lies have always destroyed progress and continue to do so today.

The First Scientist: Anaximander and His Legacy by Rovelli.
Blood Work: A Tale of Medicine and Murder in the Scientific Revolution by Tucker.
Epigenetics by Francis.
On the Origin of Species by Darwin.

The Making of the Fittest: DNA and the Ultimate Forensic Record of Evolution **by Carroll.**

The Swerve – How the World Became Modern **by Greenblatt.**

If you want to prove that every religionist is a fool, ask them the age of the earth and of the universe. They will lie, of course. Then ask them the age of the earliest human remains found on the earth. They will lie, of course. Then ask them when Adam and Eve lived (approximately). They will lie, of course. Then ask them the weight of all the cargo on Noah's Ark which held millions of species of animals, insects, flora, sea species, and so on. They will lie, of course. The next chapter is the truth, which we should be teaching to ALL of our children, but we now have charter schools, which will protect the innocents from ever being exposed to the truth.

CHAPTER 9

The Age of the Earth

Earth is approximately 4.6 Billion years old. Modern history is a miniscule portion of that timeframe. Religions would like you to think that the earth is only 6,000 years old. Their writings are focused on a timeline for history that would lead people to believe that God created one man and one woman a short time ago and then all of history happened through 'chosen' people. The problem for religionists is that the whole earth is its own natural museum with evidence of species, ages, and events which tell an entirely different story. Ninety nine percent of all species had already become extinct before their 'god' supposedly created all creatures. Religious story tellers seem to be completely oblivious concerning dinosaurs and the micro world. Today we are learning that we know almost nothing about the millions of species yet to be identified.

Compare this 4.6 billion year history and see what it would look like if it were compressed into a one year calendar. Unlike Sunday School, all times are approximate but clearly more accurate than those shoveled out by religionists.

January 1   Earth (distinct sphere from material throughout the universe) (4.6 billion years ago)

February 16   Chemical reactions begin to change Earth's environment (4 billion years ago)

March 28	Rudimentary beginnings of combinations of elements (3.5 billion years ago)
May 7	Elementary life begins forming in primordial soup (3 billion years ago)
September 3	Life forms show structures that will enable life on land (1.5 billion years Ago)
September 19	Cellular structures that will eventually be present in all humans are completing their distinctiveness (1.3 billion years ago)
October 12	Dry land still appears to be lifeless (1 billion years ago)
November 5	Sponges and jellyfish are recognizable forms (700 millions years ago)
November 21	Proliferation of life forms that will eventually evolve into all creatures on the earth (500 million years ago)
November 29	Plant life appears (400 million years ago)
December 1	Invertebrates come on land (375 million years ago)
December 2	Proliferation of life forms on land; evolution in high gear (360 million years ago)
December 3	Amphibians and reptiles populate the surface of the earth (350 million years ago)
December 9	Dinosaurs are here (270 million years ago)
December 25	Dinosaurs become extinct (65 million years ago)
December 26	Mammals appear and proliferate (63 million years ago)
December 31	9:05 PM Human-like (3,000,000 years ago)
December 31	11:48.34 PM First humans (160,000 years ago)
December 31	11:59.36 PM Hindu gods and goddesses (3400 years ago)
December 31	11:59.37 PM Moses (3300 years ago)
December 31	11:59.44 PM Buddha (2300 years ago)
December 31	11:59.46 PM Jesus (2000 years ago)
December 31	11:59.56 PM Mohamed (1400 years ago)

Don't blink or you will miss the last few seconds of history! The religionists have been misleading us for just a short time, but the massive record and history of earth are just beginning to reveal their many secrets. What a wonderful time to be alive and to discover, even with the religionists waging their last assault on reason and sanity. Science makes the lie of religion, every day, with every new discovery.

The Vastness of Time and the Fact of Evolution are now solidly proven. Only a few Cretans are still holding onto other foolish notions and billions of religionists still cling to the fraud of their religious beginnings and the unsupportable writings of their ancestors.

You're going to love these factual, scientific, proven works. And just think, I did the work of researching them for you. I know, 'what a guy!'

The Extraordinary Story of Life on Earth by Angela. (used as my inspiration for this chapter).

Wonderful Life by Gould.
Your Inner Fish: A Journey into 3.5 Billion-Year History of the Human Body* by Shubin.
99% Ape: How Evolution Adds Up* by Silvertown.
The Fact of Evolution by Smith.
How Old is the Universe? by Weintraub.
The Extraordinary Story of Human Origins by Angela.
The Voyage of the Beagle by Darwin.
The Fossil Chronicles: How Two Controversial Discoveries Changed Our View of Human Evolution by Falk.
Great Essays in Science by Gardner.

Greatest Show on Earth: the Evidence for Evolution* by Dawkins. (Please, please, please, read this one, before you go to bed tonight!)

Nevertheless, religionists have spread their 'fertilizer' over all kinds of outrageous lies, over hundreds of years (The Dark Ages – we still live there because over ninety percent of our neighbors still cling to the lies of religion, and thus, impede the natural progress of truth and light). The next chapter lists this ever-growing number of truly garbage notions. All of them can easily be proven to be total nonsense, but once indoctrinated into the mental illness of religious teachings, it is very difficult to de-program the deluded!

CHAPTER 10

Lies and Fraud derived from the greatest lie of all: RELIGION

Angels
Demons
Satan
Hell
Heaven
Ghosts
Spirits
Hexes
Curses
Sin
Superstition
Luck
Lucky numbers
Survival of death
Communication with the dead
ESP
Reincarnation
Resurrection
Miracles
Intercession
Purgatory
Limbo
Premonitions
Omens

You're probably saying to yourself, about now, that you believe in some of these things. It is clear that you have been duped or are mentally ill. Time to take stock of the garbage that has been inculcated in you by a very corrupt and sick society.

> Future Knowledge
> Eternal Damnation
> Saints
> Mysteries
> Secret knowledge
> Penance
> Holiness
> Charms
> Talismans
> Guardian angels
> Healing (extra medical)
> UFO's
> Regression memory
> Yin/Yang
> Karma
> Souls
> Out of Body
> Teletransportation
> God
> Gods
> Goddesses
> Imps
> Leprechauns
> Voodoo
> Telekinesis
> Nirvana
> Animists
> Fung Swei

Alright, I know that you really want to hang on to some of these lies because you are so accustomed to them. They can all easily be proven to be lies and the product of very low mental functioning. In the end they will not bring comfort, or confidence, or make life more easily manageable. At some point they will betray. And you will be all alone.

Remote viewing
Fortune telling
Predestination
Transubstantiation
Consubstantiation
Answered prayers
End times
Second coming
First coming
Sacred cows
Unclean foods
Gender superiority
Mind reading
Prediction
Intuition
Pre-cognition
Healing through prayer
Healing through positive thinking
Laying on of hands
Gang prayer
One true church
Rewards for good deeds
Psychics
Mentalists
Near death experiences
Biblical myths

It's time to take stock about who taught you these lies. The culture contributed. Your family certainly passed on lots of ignorance. Your religion is most certainly guilty. But now you own them and it becomes your responsibility to decide whether you will continue to pass them on to your children and to future generations.

Talking asses
Speaking in tongues
Raising the dead
Spontaneous immolation
Moral absolutes
Palm reading

Haunted houses
Demon possession
Exorcism
Dispensation
Mind control
Cults
Scientology
Numerology
(Merlin)
Wives' tales
Homeopathy
Iconography
Creationism
Flat earth
Dowsing
Big foot
Yeti/seti
Holy water

This kind of garbage is too big to take to the curb. The land-fill may not even be big enough to handle all of it. And besides, it is clearly toxic and contagious. You may have to dig deep into the scholarly works that I have proposed in order to find the best weapons for eradicating the lies and the stench.

Healing water
Apparitions
72 Virgins
Forgiveness
ET's
Good vs. Evil
Prophecy
Leviathan
Vampires
Witches
Blessings
Monsters
Spirituality
Chiropractic

Aliens
Racial superiority
Inherited intelligence
Alchemy
Royalty
Government rights
Experts
Fairies
Déjà vu
Divine rights
Divine intervention
Ghouls
Honest religionists
Medium
Clairvoyants
Acupuncture
Reiki
Hypnotherapy
Naturopathy
Horoscope
Lucky Underwear

This one is tough because I always wore my lucky underwear on every losing team that I played on.

Moral Absolutes
Past Life Regression
Life after Death
Guardian Angels
Astrology
Talismans
Emotional Intelligence
Pyramid Power
Power of Positive Thinking

Nothing of these things adds value to life. They destroy honest efforts to find true meaning. Religions tolerate most of these fallacies because anything that causes people to cling to the Lie of religion is justifiable in their eyes! Since religionists already lie about the basics of religion, it is only baby steps further to lie about anything and everything else. Every one of these lies has been used to destroy and steal the hope which comes with facts and reality. It always preys on the weak and vulnerable. You lost a loved one. No problem. We'll just talk to them and they can tell us that they're really OK. Losing your house. No problem. We'll just bury a statue of Joseph in the backyard. He will save the day. Living with danger. No problem. Everyone has a guardian angel. Except, of course, the ones who don't. God will never give anyone a ten ton load for their half ton truck. Except the billions who suffer daily. Hate your neighbor. Not a problem. God has prepared a special place of torment and suffering for them that will last for trillions of years.

Religion is such a farce!

Science: Good, Bad and Bogus by Gardner.

The Missionary Position: Mother Teresa in Theory and Practice by Hitchens.

Qigong: Chinese Medicine or Pseudoscience? By Lin Zixin.

Chiropractic: the Victim's Perspective by Magner.

Psychic Sleuths: ESP and Sensational Cases by Nickell.

Demon-haunted World: Science as a Candle in the Dark by Sagan.

Every society throughout history has been entitled to their own gods, superstitions, masochistic enforcement of the 'rules,' dread of the natural world, and loss of self in favor of the power of the state. It is not unusual to find hundreds and thousands of these 'gods' strewn across the landscape of history. Societies lose credibility, and so do their so-called gods. In the next chapter we include just a partial listing of the thousands of 'gods' who have failed to hang on!

CHAPTER 11

Gods are nothing New.

The crazy make-believe world of cosmic creatures has cursed the landscape of humanity for thousands of years. One belief in common was always held: the people who were in charge killed anyone who didn't worship their fantasy creations. Most of the following deities had much longer runs than any of our modern deities. Even though there are still over a thousand left today, followers of each still act as though they are the first and only! Here's just a short list of the mass-slaughter masters of religion through the ages. It's really quite a nice mix. Up until around 3500 BCE most of the dominant 'gods' were 'goddesses'. Females ran the world. They were the sun, the moon, the planets, and the stars. They were seasonal and fickle. They were vengeful and destructive. They were always projections of what humans wanted them to be.

And fortunate for the Jews, they made their transition from 'female' gods to 'male' gods just in time to capture their own mythologies. Well actually they didn't completely make the transition by that time, and so we find traces of Israel's god being inferior to 'female' progenitors and at war with other gods to rescue the world. It's right there in the 'holy' books of Israel. Hundreds of writers tried to erase all evidence of former mythologies in their books, but, alas, they failed.

Anu
Apsu
Damkina
Ea
Enlil
Ishtar
Marduk
Mummu
Nintu
Shamash
Sin
Tiamat
Baal
Anat
Mot
Shapsu
Yam
Yankh
Kumarbi
Hannahannas
Telepinu
Astabis
Kubaba
Re
Amun
Ptah
Khnum
Aten
Hather
Bat
Horus
Osiris
Anuket
Isis
Min

By now I'm sure you're just a little curious about some of these gods and goddesses. They were all real and can be easily searched for on Wikipedia. You might just find one that would be worthy of starting a church around. Why not, there are thousands of religions current in our world today. Everyone should have their own religion. The extra benefit is that you can get a huge charitable deduction on your income taxes for any contribution that might come your way.

Amen
Nut
Fates
Odin
Loki
Atlas
Apotamkin
Ares
Zeus
Adonis
Cronus
Heracles
Jupiter
Saturn
Venus
Mars
Diana
Hera
Neptune
Mercury
Bumba
Shango
Yemaya
Elegua
Abassi
Obatala
Eshu
Orishas
Olorun

Babalu-aye
Wandjina
Rainbow-snake
Adnoartina
Altjira
Dreamtime
Alchera
Eingawa
Baiame
Lungkata
Daramulum
Quetzalcoatl
Huitzilopochtli
Acolmiztli
Ometecuhtli
Piquete-zina
Chantico
Tezcatlipoca
Mictlantecuhtli
Tecuciztecatl
Coatlicue
Baron-samedi
Bondye
Aida-Wedo
Loa
Baron-cimettiere
Maman-brigette
Grichas
Ghede
Ogoun
Erzulie
Morrigan
Aonghus
Danu
Dagda
Cuchulainn
Arawn

Brigit
Abandinus
Cernunnus
Tuatha-de-danawn
Monkey
Guan-yu
Jade-emperor
Yen-lo-wang
Guan-yiu
Eight Immortals
Feng-du
Ao-chin
Qi-Lin
Ao-kuang
Akka
Ilmatar
Vainamoinen
Lemminkainen
Ukko
Ahti
Lenpo
Ajatar
Tapio
Mielikki
Viracocha
Cocomama
Apolatequil
Accla
Inti

Fertility cults, saviors, Mother of Creation, virgins, taboos, punishments, good-luck charms, superstitious defense against all calamities, miracle cures, suspension of any natural law as needed, future knowledge (especially helpful if you are going on a trip), invisible shields if you are going into a war zone, snake oil, wholistic medicine, herbal cures and not to be outdone the promise of immortality.

Axomamma
Ilyapa
Chasca
Catequil
Mama-quilla
Odin
Loki
Balour
Thor
Asgard
Freya
Tyr
Ragnarok
Fenrir
Dakuwanga
Tangata-manu
Abeguwo
Moai
Rongomatane
Maui
Adard
Abere
Hinenuitepo
Hiiaka
Bacchus
Lucifer
Cupid
Dievas
Chernobog
Byelobog
Bogatyri
Baba-yaga
Yarilo
Vodnik
Perkunas
Veles
Alklha
Periboriwaa

Makunaima
Sigu
El-Dorado

Jews, Christians and Moslems thought that they had it all. They are rank amateurs in the world of powerful, make-believe gods and goddesses. These lists provide gods for every purpose and most don't even ask for groveling in return. So if you are going to place a bet in the next race (your personal life) make sure you don't put your money on a dead horse.

Amana
Boraro
Bochica
Abe-mango
Aiomun-kondi
Huitica
Jin
Raksasa
Aditinggi
Agat-talai
Batara-kala
Anata-thewi
Barong
Sukreep
Bedawang
Nagpo-chenpo
Dharma-Palas
Vairocana
Adi-buddha
Samantabnadra
Begtse
Dhyanibuddhas
Palden-lhamo
Bhaisajyaguru
Tamdrin
Yahweh
Jesus
Allah

Thousands of people were killed for not worshipping these 'true' gods. Human sacrifices were burned alive to bring good luck to the nation by appeasing myriad forms of Cosmic Bastards, who were angry, and withholding their good graces from the people. When Judaism came along, it pretty much followed the same pattern of appeasing an angry Cosmic Bastard by killing their own children (ala Abraham, almost!). In the pre-Judaic cults, offspring were considered a threat to dominant males, so they just had them killed off. The transition to animals for this substitutionary purpose was common. They burned millions of animals, just so they wouldn't have to keep killing and sacrificing their own children like their crazy neighbor gods. They kept those unclean females away from the altar, the temple, and the city so that the Cosmic Bastard wouldn't get mad. It seems that the Jewish god took issue with this portion of his creative arts. Females were scum. It was Eve (symbol of a former female goddess who was in competition with Yahweh) who sinned and brought down Adam! Male gods no longer wanted females anywhere near their sacred haunts. That way they could keep them in check.

Every small detail of the Judeo-Christian Moslem faith is actually borrowed from all these other pagan religions. Jesus was man and god. Jesus was born of a virgin. Jesus was foretold by astrologers. Jesus was resurrected. And on and on. Every one of these lies was actually told about other religions'gods centuries before he was born. All his parables had been told by others, and often hundreds of years earlier. All of his supposed miracles were actually miracle stories which had been told about others centuries before. Nothing new! He never wrote anything. He never said anything new. There were dozens of so-called messiahs running around at the same time as he carried out his delusional talks. Sadly, the man was a liar, and his followers told and borrowed lies to support their own personal nefarious agendas, whatever those were!

No one worships these other deities today, not Zeus nor Apollo nor Thor nor Isis, and so on. Yet at one time whole societies were built upon the belief in these Cosmic Bastards, and they made life miserable for them too. Until they didn't. The societies died, and their deities died with them. All the eternal truths which were forced upon millions of people before our time stopped progress dead in its tracks! Now it is our turn to face the lies of our Cosmic Bastards and kill them before humanity is set back for millennia more.

In the next chapter, you get to tell the world, which branch of the LIE you belong to, and can justify, and prove (without any reservations at all) to be factually, historically true.

You'll enjoy reading: ***Mythology's Last Gods: Yahweh and Jesus*** by **Harwood**. It's a hard read, but you will never be the same after you read it. I promise.

CHAPTER 12

A Short Quiz

Place a check by the religions which are *FALSE*.

___ Presbyterianism
___ Islam
___ Christianity
___ Church of Scientology
___ Eastern Orthodox
___ Orthodox Judaism
___ Conservative Judaism
___ Reformed Judaism
___ Jainism
___ Sikhism
___ Hinduism
___ Buddhism
___ Wiccan
___ Mormon
___ Animism
___ Falang Gong
___ Spiritism
___ Unitarianism
___ Lutheranism
___ Pentecostalism
___ Adventist

__ Methodist
__ Roman Catholic
__ Evangelicals
__ Chinese Folk
__ Shamanism
__ Baha'i
__ Confuscianism
__ Zoroastrianism
__ Shinto
__ Taoism
__ Anglican
__ Episcopalian
__ Baptist
__ Quaker
__ Church of Tomorrow
__ Seventh Day Adventist
__ Greek Orthodox
__ Asceticism
__ Mater Dei
__ Voodoo
__ Shia Moslem
__ Sunni Moslem
__ Uighurs
__ Jehovah Witnesses
__ Millenialists
__ Latin Rite Catholic
__ Wahabi moslems
__ Latter Day Saints
__ Santeria
__ Native American Spirituality
__ Primitive Baptist
__ African Episcopal Methodist
__ Asatru
__ Church of God
__ Druidism
__ Goddess worship

___ Paganism
___ Witchcraft
___ Hare Krishna
___ Druze
___ World Church of the Creator
___ Gnosticism
___ Gypsies
___ IFA
___ Missouri Lutheranism
___ Sufism
___ Church of Christ
___ Echankar
___ Yazdanism

Ninety nine percent of religionists are able to identify religions as false with the exception of their own. They are able to identify them as false even though they know absolutely nothing about them. I've never met a single person in my life, who didn't believe that they had found the one true religion. Any suggestions as to why?

One thing that we know, for sure, is that at least 99% of these religions are false and utilize fabrications of the human mind. They were made up to serve a purpose other than the truth. I think we can move, even one step further, and declare that all religions are fantasy fabrications. They are made up, and they were made up by the worst kinds of liars. Now they like to call their stories myths which serve a higher purpose. Unfortunately for them, anything that starts out with lies does not become truer through the ages.

So now we can be pretty sure that you are a liar, about religion, at a minimum. The question that remains is 'what kind of a liar are you comfortable being?' The adjectives which I have used in the next chapter were all attached to religious persons whom I knew personally. They seemed perfectly comfortable with the 'zone' of their lies and had zero energy to change. What about you? Do you like being a liar? Do you think that you might be doing damage to the future, which might never be repairable, if enough 'truth' tellers are not found?

CHAPTER 13

Every Religionist is a LIAR (about religion and usually much more)

Some are listed here:
Loser liars
Filthy liars
True Wacko liars
Dependent liars
Infantile liars
Co-dependent liars
Maladjusted liars
Self-loathing liars
Pie-in-the-sky liars
Mentally challenged liars
Gullible liars
Fearful liars
Hopeful liars
Desperate liars
Lonely liars
Arrogant liars
Professional liars
Easy Answer liars
Confused liars
Mindless liars

Inattentive liars
Go-along liars
Me-too liars
Momma's boy liars
Fantasy liars
Gambler liars
Social liars
What's the harm liars
Malicious liars
Ignorant liars
Deluded liars
Manipulative liars
Innocent liars
Willfully ignorant liars
Pathetic liars
Opportunistic liars
Hateful liars
Mentally lazy liars
Intellectually dishonest liars
Purposeful liars
Obedient liars
Racist liars
Superstitious liars
Apathetic liars
Pleaser liars
Phony liars
Murderous liars
Abusive liars
Controlling liars
Rotten liars
Degenerate liars
Compulsive liars
Congenital liars
Convenience liars
Anti-social liars
Historical liars

Hysterical liars
Hidden agenda liars
Loony liars
Neurotic liars
Social climber liars
Sexually promiscuous liars
Xenophobic liars
Clanish liars
Narrow-minded liars
Politically motivated liars
Mentally ill liars
Wishful thinking liars
Coerced liars
Indoctrinated liars
Brain-washed liars
No basis liars
Unscientific liars
Stupid liars
Moronic liars
Isolationist liars
Smug liars
Conceited liars
Self-righteous liars
Foolish liars
Ego-centric liars
Blasphemous liars
Closeted liars
Spurious liars
Psychotic liars
Brilliant liars
Clever liars
PhD liars
Loving liars
Unknowing liars
Uncaring liars
Cultural liars

Group liars
Disgusting liars
Casual liars
Criminal liars
Self-serving liars
Partisan liars
Scientific liars
Academic liars
Expert liars
Childish liars
Air-headed liars
Evangelistic liars
Huckster liars
Prosperity liars
Maternalistic liars
Paternalistic liars
Power-hungry liars

Religionists will fit into one, or several, of these characterizations. When people willingly lie about what they profess to be the *most important thing in their lives*, then it becomes much easier to lie about the less significant things. Politicians will wear their religiosity on their sleeve and then proceed to rape the baby-sitter, steal from tax-payers to return favors to supporters, wrongly disparage opponents, and on and on. (In a later chapter I will expose dozens of these hypocrites, who have held elective office). Business leaders will have you watch their 'left hand' of religious diversion, while lying about their product and service. (In a later chapter I will expose several of these degenerates whom I have done business with personally). Isn't it interesting, that most car salesmen are **super-religious** in their palaver! Most medical quacks will have a heavy dose of the 'spiritual' in their formulas for why science is letting us down in terms of our health. (I will refer to Dr. Weil later. He is one of the worst). Community lies, teaching lies, geopolitical lies, all run together after the great religious lies are told, believed, and firmly indoctrinated into the minds of the feeble. Our economy is struggling and our politicians jump all over each other to prove they are more religious than the others. That just reinforces the idiocy of our leaders in my book.

Religion divides humanity into pockets of lies, which divide us into divisions of hate, war and permanent fear.

That is why religion is so **dangerous. Everything about it is destructive.**

Here's a mirror. Do you see anyone you recognize?

If you are drunk with religion, here is a book of decent, honorable people who have shown great courage through the centuries, and can 'sober' you up, if you are not too drunk!

2000 Years of Disbelief: Famous People with the Courage to Doubt by Haught.

This is an EARLY WARNING. If you are a religionist, this next chapter is 'pure science' and has nothing to do with religion, in any way! If you are at all sensitive about these matters, please do not turn the page, and for god's sake, please hide the children from any exposure to this next chapter. There, I feel a lot better. At least I warned you.

CHAPTER 14

Religion vs. Reality: No Match

The LIES of religion have contributed ABSOLUTELY NOTHING to the following fields of inquiry and knowledge growth:

>Cosmology
>Biology
>Surgery
>Cartography
>Physics
>Chemistry
>Anesthesiology
>Microbiology
>Cardiology
>Immunology
>Astronomy
>Engineering
>Botany
>Herpetology
>Oncology
>Virology
>Transplantation
>Pharmacology
>Biochemistry
>Organic chemistry

Take a break. Call your minister, priest, rabbi or imam and ask them to show you where these scientific breakthroughs are found anywhere in their 'holy' books.

Psychology
Ethology
Serology
Geopaleontology
Embryology
Morphology
Anatomy
Physiology
Systematics
Genetics
Parasitology
Geology
Astrophysics
Ichthyology
Hydrology
Computer science
Logistics
Climatology
Paleontology
Mathematics
Algebra
Trigonometry
Quantum physics
Relativity
Statistics
Phlebotomy

The world is amazing. It is so expansive. It is real. That's why these sciences could be discovered, studied and utilized for the good of mankind. People have been killed by religionists for studying and teaching every one of these sciences.

Radiology
Nuclear physics
Particle physics
Speed of light
Plutonium enrichment
Evolution
Geography
Planetary movement
Space/time continuum
Comets
Dinosaurs
Age of the earth
Age of the universe
Dermatology
Optics
Oceanography
Pleistocene age
Materials science
Hermaphrodites
Aborigines
Submarines
Airplanes
Aerospace
The periodic chart
The automobile
DNA/RNA
Genomes
Animal husbandry
Hybrid seeds
Equality
Millions of species
Ozone layer
Dialysis
Chemotherapy
Synthetic fibers
Advanced medicine

Nutrition
Nephrology
Carbon dating

If you like to do research, you can actually look up the historical accounts written by religionists about how all of these sciences were dangerous and 'unbiblical'. And today, your life is almost impossible without ALL of them in the mix.

Half life
Fission
Fusion
Particle accelerator
Solar energy
Monetism
Accounting
GAAP
Currency exchange
Mortgage loans
Annuities
Bonds
Micro organisms
Bacteria
Cloning
In vitro fertilization
Genetic engineering
Hormone therapy
Literary criticism
Textual analysis
Mechanics
Telephony
Microwaves
Broadband
Wave theory
Electronics
Ethernet

Phonology
Hybridization

Scientists whom religionists have hated: Galileo, Aristotle, Einstein, Salk, Lister, Darwin, Dawkins, Copernicus, Dr. Barnard, Mendel, Bruno, to name just a few.

Metallurgy
Logarithms
Magnetism
Planetary orbits
Axial rotation
Radio telescope
Dark matter
Dark holes
Zero gravity
Modern medicine
Disease cures
Sonar
Radar
Refrigeration
Lasers
Plastics
Volcanism
Thermodynamics
Programming
Composite materials
Electronic telescope
Light waves
Subatomic particles
Musicology
Harmonics
Sanitation
Obstetrics
Gynecology
Medicine

Zoology
Astrophysics
Genetics
DNA
RNA
Genomes
Mutations
City planning
Hygiene
Road construction
Blue-ray
Wireless broadband
Nuclear energy

Religionists are *ignorant* of the real world. Religionist writers were *ignorant* of the fact that future discoveries would expose the massive *ignorance*, which they used to influence the mentally weak and vulnerable. Today is a brand new day where anyone with the desire can discover the true facts about life and the dreadful, pathetic lies of all religionists.

Religionists try to drag society back into the Dark Ages. They aren't comfortable living there all by themselves. They want company. So the best way for them to get company is to manipulate the laws of society to take away the freedoms and progress of others. If you don't want anyone to use contraceptives, just pass laws, which make it 'illegal' for everyone. Now we're all with you. You don't want evolution taught, get on the school board and ram it down the throats of everyone! You want prayer in the school, just call everyone, who doesn't, a 'communist', or a 'socialist', or a 'fag', or an 'atheist'. That will get attention and certainly create momentum for your cause! The next chapter is your opportunity to 'shine'. Make the world know that you are SERIOUS enough about these issues, that you will lead the way to total compliance of the religious laws without any exceptions!

To summarize: Judaism is based on lies about everything. Therefore, since Christianity is totally based on Judaism, then it has also, always, been just a series of lies. Islam is a side-show of theft from these two. The

Roman Catholic and Eastern Orthodox Churches are based on the lies of Christianity, and therefore, all of their histories are just unbelievable lies, based on the nonsense perpetrated by Jesus' followers. Well, that means, that all the BS stories told by modern religionists are just pathetic lies, which follow in the direct descent from the historical liars. So, now you see, that your 'friend' who told you that 'god' had spoken to him directly, was just lying. That the televangelists, who rant on and on, about how we are being punished by 'god', because we have allowed the immorality of 'gayness'. Yup, they are just liars. Your local ministers, rabbis and priests, who tell you that they have the 'goodies' for eternal life. Yup, just a bunch of very unsophisticated liars. Everything that modern religionists tell you about religion is a lie. Even, when it is by the most sincere. They are sometimes the worst kind of liars.

CHAPTER 15

Contract on A Scarica

Since the founding of our great country, religionists have been busy bees getting all of their maniacal agenda written into Law. The process has been clearly aimed at taking away all rights and freedoms of the great Mass, who think that their fairy-tale pursuits are just that. Their dastardly laws have been passed in small hamlets, cities, most states and certainly at the Federal level.

For 'true believers' here is finally a chance to show the world that it has not been mere 'lip-service'. If they are not, in fact, the greatest hypocrites in the world they will agree to sign this Contract on A Scarica. [not to be confused with the 'Contract on a America' which was only a pathetic political 'hit' list]. Since all religionists would protest, with vehemence, that they really do believe in 'masochistic celibacy', marriage without pleasure, absence of any planning on the part of couples, death of mother over early ending of pregnancy, etc., and would prefer that we all live by them, then let's give them a chance to sign this Contract with the proviso that if they violate any provision then they are guilty of a Felony.

#1 No religionist would be allowed to have an abortion for any reason, including those only performed to save the life of the mother or an ectopic.

At present, 94% of abortions are performed on religionists. Religionists have already instituted laws that would put women away for life, for just such an act. Let's not be cruel. Priests would still be able to get abortions for their excusable pregnant diddles in the parish. No Catholic or Fundamentalist women would be allowed to use any form of contraception or be allowed to receive any form of preventative care that could be even loosely associated as pro-pleasure or anti-procreational activity. All Catholic and Fundamentalist men must go through an extremely thorough examination before being allowed to receive Viagara-like products for personal use. The questionnaire will include examination of how often the man masterbates or thinks about sexual pleasure of any kind. A physical exam will include the insertion of a three foot long steel rod into the penis to determine if this medication or procedure will enhance his procreational abilities. If not, then he will be denied. These men will also be forced to watch videos of their semen and listen to the microscopic sounds of the chemical reactions - in the semen is the fullness of life – DNA. If they refuse to watch and listen, then it will be noted on their permanent medical records.

#2 No religionist would be allowed to get a divorce for any reason.

At present, over 80% of divorces involve religionists. Religionists have so destroyed the fabric of society by infecting the domestic courts of America with draconian rules and expensive procedures. Religionists will be saved all that because they won't even be allowed in the process. If religionists are not allowed to use the courts for divorce, other legal matters decided in court will speed up tremendously!

#3 No religionist will be allowed to receive medical treatments for any disease, which has 'evolved'. Religionists don't believe that anything has evolved.

Evolution is going to be a real killer here. The evidence for evolving diseases and microbes is overwhelming and vastly documented. Medical science has advanced on the basis of being able to study these evolved realities and creating treatments to cure them. The religionist, to be consistent with what they want to be taught in our schools, will have to demand that modern medical science refuse to treat them or their children if they have to use 'evolved' knowledge to do so.

#4 No religionist will be allowed to have access to any medical breakthroughs which have come through embryonic stem cell research.

Fair is fair, you shoved your ASS in the face of America and told us, that over your dead bodies would you ever allow this research to take place. Sign at the bottom, so that we can know you are as serious about denying these breakthroughs to yourself, as you are about denying them to us!

#5 No religionist will be allowed to violate the laws of their own religion, including but not limited to adultery, fornication, envy, greed, sloth, gluttony, and avarice. They will not be allowed to pick and choose the ones to keep or not keep—leave that to the Catholics.

#6 Religionists will only be taught what is included in their holy books and nothing else. They can be excused from class and wait in the hallway until the teacher has finished teaching science, math, conceptual and free thinking, great works of literature, music through the ages, evolution, and nutrition. Since religionists demand that all sciences should allow for opposing opinions to be taught in their place, then let's have the Bible give counter-arguments for biology, chemistry, physics, quantum theory…not just evolution.

#7 Religionists agree not to marry outside of their religion, race, gender or species.

Imagine all the laws that have been written throughout the ages by these mutants to interfere with the freedoms, rights, and libido of the rest of us. They like to say that times were different then, but their smarmy ancestors were the same degenerate leaders who people the churches and synagogues today. As we uncover more and more of how those fraudsters really lived, and who they really slept with, we realize that they wrote their laws for everyone but themselves.

#8 Religionists will not be allowed to participate in premarital sex of any kind.

It is against the laws of the Roman Catholic Church that any human being should ever have sex for pleasure. It must always be for pro-creational purposes only. That makes for a pretty awful post-menopausal time of life. It would make Stephen Hawkings existence even more draconian than it already is. It is a level of foolishness that boggles the mind, but religionists have pledged to follow the 'commands' of their church, fully aware that the church has given a binding sentence of eternal damnation for those who violate this law.

#9 Religionists can never express DOUBT, ever. They must talk about their faith in absolutes always. They must defame anyone who disparages any aspect of their religion. They must never show much concern when their country is involved in war or killing innocent civilians who just happen to belong to one of the FALSE religions.

#10 Religionists must give ten percent of everything they have to their religion. They must agree to be audited for this purpose. They must agree NOT to take a tax deduction for these voluntary losses because their LORD told them to give to Caesar what is Caesar's, and to God what is God's.

Sign on the bottom line so we know that you are serious about all of this, and not just another run of the mill hypocrite.

"These are my absolute intents, my beliefs, my life and I ask that I be given the full punishment for violating these eternal principles handed down to me by my inerrant church."

Signed:

WARNING LABEL: All other societies which have followed these strictures exactly are now extinct.

Now that we have agreement on these central issues, let's take a look in the next chapter at what your brothers and sisters have been busy doing in this society, which claims to be 98% religious!

CHAPTER 16

Liars Who Have Impacted My Life and Community

Many of these are so obvious, that we will just note them in a cursory way. Bear with me in this accounting of the lies that have invaded every corner of our lives. It is important to realize that lies are never innocent. They destroy. They create winners and losers. They victimize, even when they are presented as 'victim-less'.

Government and Politics

Democrats

This is the Party of the Little Guy. When is the last time that you saw a Little Guy at one of their $1,000 a plate dinners? It's almost a cliché that you only see politicians during a campaign for your vote. After elections they go to work for the group that paid for the plates.

Republicans

This is the Party of the Big Guy. Enough said. It is a little unseemly that they let those Wall Street types reach into their pants and fiddle, while Tea Partying us that they are for Small Government. Excuse me Senator, is that spilled tea on your pants. No, that's urine. I got so excited when Rubin,

Lies Have Ruined the World

Fuld, Blankfein, Cox, Shapiro, Bernanke and the boys gave me millions to defeat my clueless opponent.

Presidential Cabinet Members

Let's just say Robert McNamara and leave it at that. Our wonderful Secretary of Defense under President Lyndon Baines Johnson. Who after the slaughter of 60,000 of the finest Americans ever in Vietnam, tells us in his book that he knew that it was all a lie, but extremely hard to stop once you get started.

Supreme Court Decisions

Plessy v. Ferguson, Dred Scott, Williams v. Mississippi... It is still a crap shoot, even after 200 years, for unpopular causes –women's, gay's, minorities' et al, which should have been receiving the guarantees that the Constitution provided at the beginning. The Court is not interested in, nor concerned about the TRUTH; they exist only to microscopically examine the fine points of legalese. Lifetime tenure anyone? Alzheimer's, senility and the Dancing Ito's. O.J. is innocent, Casey Anthony is innocent and the public is screwed, but at least we know, because even courts on the local level can see very clearly what the Supreme Court is all about.

Government Agency

When I was in graduate school I had a summer job doing industrial roofing. The work we did took place on airport hangars three stories high where the government stored medical supplies for troops around the world. The composition of the roofing was the old style six-layer roofing with gravel and tar. First we had to tear off the old roofing (a job created by the most sadistic s.o.b.'s in the world), replace rotted wood beams and layer on gavel, topping off with tar heated to 500 degrees. We would apply the hot tar with 'hod' buckets that we manually pulled across the roof at a 45 degree slant towards the ground. This was extremely difficult work and was usually done with a roof temperature exceeding 150 degrees. One day a guy whom we didn't know came onto the roof. This was a high security area and so we immediately confronted him for why he was there. He flashed some kind of ID and told us to get the f— out of his way. Then he started tearing up a section of the newly laid roof, which we had completed hours earlier. He got out a camera and started taking pictures of the roofing which he had just destroyed and then left. We called the super's office to complain about this mystery man and to find out what was happening. We were told not to worry about it and to repair the roof. Later at the bar he told us that the guy was a government inspector. He really could care less about the quality of the job, but he did want a new sailboat. The super told us that the company received a one million dollar bonus for every hangar that was completed before the deadline. The inspector knew this and wanted to let them know that if he didn't get his sailboat (and other 'bennies') that that one million would be in danger. The inspector had told our super that there were thousands of political appointees, just like him, and that was one of the benefits of being related to a politician! There were seventeen huge hangars that we reroofed that summer, so you can do the math.

I've heard that the 'Oil' inspectors who work for the government in the Gulf States area live like royalty, travel extensively, and have never, ever disappointed anyone in the Oil Companies! After the Oil Disaster in the Gulf, none of them were fired, none of them were demoted, and none of them could care about what happened to millions of American taxpayers!

As we continue to get more and more reportings of Salmonella and E Coli, after-the-fact, when people have already died, we now know that not a single government inspector or political appointee has ever been fired, demoted or even inconvenienced.

Presidential Press Secretaries

If you want to master the art of lying, you will have to attend the press conferences at the White House. Although one would have to say that Fleischer, Gibbs and Carney have taken these skills to a whole new level of 'sewerage'!

The President of the United States

Thank you for Vietnam! It saved me from a lot of long weekends partying with my friends, who never came home. And thank you for admitting that it was all a mistake. And a special thanks to all the other presidents for a series of unconstitutional 'undeclared' wars. The widows, orphans and untreated veterans at the few remaining VA hospitals are especially thankful.

FBI Lab Workers

How could governmental scientists, working at the main labs for the FBI, have submitted falsified evidence in trials across America for over TWO DECADES and not have anyone know or report it to their managers? Ordinary citizens have to know and be confident that the massive machinery of their government will not be used in a massive assault against their freedoms. The 'whistle blower' laws have proven to be an absolute failure in protecting safety and private citizens' rights.

A Police Officer

A policeman of the Stow, Ohio police department threatened a 16 year old witness to an accident that he would be brought up on a trumped-up drug possession charge, if he didn't change his statement about an accident that involved a relative of the police officer. The young man's mother told the police officer that her son was going to tell the truth. The police showed up at his house with a search warrant, signed by a local judge, on suspicion of possession of illegal narcotics. He never testified!

Military Officer

Every soldier who has ever had to put their life in the hands of a military officer can tell you the sheer terror when it is discovered that the officer is lying and incompetent. No one wants to come home dead. During Vietnam it was not difficult to discover that a whole lot of people in our government and military were lying about everything.

The Fields of Healing and Dying

Chiropractor

Charged every patient for every procedure that their insurance would reimburse. Most patients had GM insurance - this was a GM town - and since there were no co-pays at the time, the patients would never see the bills. The companies really had no way of knowing what services were provided or not. This person, a leader in our small community, went one step further, he never actually performed the procedures. A friend of mine had taken a job to do billing for him. When she saw his charade, she called me in tears. I told her that she had to report it. Apparently that was what the previous billing clerk had done and had received threats to keep her mouth shut. My friend just quit. But this filthy back-cracker made another kind of mistake that would bring him down. A lawyer friend of his would send him patients after accidents with instructions to treat to the greatest extent. Some patients went for subluxation every day for three years (supposedly). But Doctor Greedy didn't stop there. He billed for accident patients, who never actually came to his office to the tune of over six million dollars for accidents and workman's compensation cases in ONE YEAR! He was number one in Ohio and soon had the authorities on his back. He pled guilty to the fraud. His sentence: he had to promise to never do it again. He must have invented the 800 hour day because that is how many hours he would have needed to see all the patients for which he charged.

Health Insurance Salesman

I had a health insurance policy for over fifteen years and never used it very much because I had a healthy family and we didn't need to go to the doctor often. My daughter needed to have serious surgery, so we followed all the procedures and had a second opinion which verified the need for surgery. Our insurance company gave us the go-ahead. After the surgery the bills started arriving. The hospital told us that the insurance company had declined paying for the surgery. The doctor's office sent notice that the bill was our responsibility because the insurance company had declined payment. I called the insurance rep who told me he was surprised that his company was denying payment. He told me that they had determined my daughter's condition to be 'pre-existing'. $23,000 in bills. I asked how the condition was 'pre-existing', since she had never been diagnosed with the condition before. He told me that seven years earlier my daughter had complained of pain in her abdomen, at a routine office visit, and that the doctor had made that notation. I got a lawyer (I know, scum). He did give me good advice, however. He told me that, in Ohio, if you sue an insurance company and win, you can still only recover the medical costs and not any legal fees or court costs. He had no doubt that the insurance company would simply stall the process and drive up my legal fees until they would exceed any judgment that would be rendered in my favor for medical costs. He told me that if it were any consolation to me, I was clearly in the right and that the insurance company and rep had lied to me. I felt pretty sure that I was the only person to have ever had this happen to them. Time to move on.

Funeral Director

After the families would leave to get into their cars to go to the cemetery, the funeral director would close the casket for the final time. Well, not quite. He would remove all the jewelry and valuables first. To give to the family, right? Well, not quite. He would box them up and ship them to an associate in the Bahamas. This went rather well for several years, until one day, a relative got a court order to have their family member exhumed on the basis of a 'tip' from an anonymous phone caller. The jewelry was actually not the most startling part. He had removed all the gold from the man's teeth during embalming as well! After experiencing all this firsthand, I have decided to never die. I had officiated at some of these funerals and never had the stomach to tell the families what I had found out. It would have just opened up the grieving process all over again.

Nursing Home

A visiting doctor would lean his head into each room and say hi! He would make just about 90 visits in less than twenty minutes. The nursing home was just fine with this atrocious behavior until a family saw this exhibition from the lobby and asked the doctor how their mother was doing. He told them she would be fine. Their response: that's interesting, since she died three hours ago! I was there with the family and the doctor was a friend of mine. I never discussed it with him, because I have a violent temper when confronted with injustice. I guess that makes me a coward.

Pharmaceutical Companies

Thalidomide, LSD, Vioxx, Trovan...but in the main, we are really fortunate to have the wonderful scientists continually working on medications that will make all of our lives better. Just don't lie to us anymore. Do you really want me to start listing the millions of victims of your products by name?

Doctor

Can anyone say UNNECESSARY tests that have nothing to do with good diagnosis, but a lot to do with CYA for the doc! But how do you know? I never got to ask him directly. This is what we would hear in his waiting room: "The doctor's nurse's assistant will see you now." Oh yeah! Every time!

HMO

When your doctor gets paid more if he doesn't treat you, then someone is lying. That's not capitation, that's decapitation or is it castration?

Media

Fox News

Life just isn't that one-sided, regardless of what side of an issue that you are closest to. Writing a story should come after the observation of an event. If the story is already written and just looking for an event to 'glue' to it then who needs shamans to shrink our heads any further? Try this for your own sanity: When a talking head is about to say something, set the *record* button on and turn the sound off. Then write down what you think that talking head is about to say about the subject. If you are always right about what they will say about every topic, then you don't need them anymore! That way, you don't have to waste your time listening to the greatest liars in the history of the world: Rush Limbaugh, Bill O'Reilly, Sean Hannity, Rachel Maddow, Laura Ingram, Karl Rove, Glen Beck, Ed Schultz, (anyone on CNN or MSNBC)....in fact, there is not a single talking head in the media today who is not a congenital liar, who understands their audience, and where the pay point comes for their opinions!

Turn your TV off. Quickly read *Media MythMakers* by Radford. You will never turn your TV back on, or if you do, you will never watch with the same old gullibility.

NPR

This public media has really found a rapid path to the bottom of journalism. My favorite time of the week used to be early Sunday morning. I could listen to NPR programs and read my NY Times. But now, Krista Tippett on Sunday mornings starts off the week with the most disreputable gibberish of religious inanity known to mankind. She is an apologist for the most unsupportable, anti-intellectual religious garbage that can be found anywhere. Her statements make you wonder if she has trouble getting in touch with reality. In some quarters that might be an indication of mental instability. On Saturday mornings the "People's Pharmacy" fills the airwaves with fear-mongering and fallacious lies in their discussions about alternative and holistic medicine, touch therapies and a never-ending gathering of unsubstantiated, unscientific fools. When many of their guests quote Dr. Andrew Weil, they come as close to absolute 'subhuman' garbage that is possible. This man has stolen millions of dollars from unsophisticated fools in the public. But, to be fair, you can't cheat an honest man, right?

Stop now and quickly read: *Denialism: How Irrational Thinking Hinders Scientific Progress, Harms the Planet, and Threatens Our Lives* by Spector.

You will never allow Weil, or his ilk, anywhere near your life again. He is a thief and a degenerate!

Also read: *The Vitamin Pushers: How the "Health Food" Industry is Selling America a Bill of Goods* by Barrett.

Then we get to listen to the nonsense of Diane Rehm. She is tough on subjects and speakers, whom she doesn't agree with, and who don't support her Liberal agenda. She wants you to know that 60 Minutes has nothing over her! Then a religious speaker comes on her show and her brain goes to 'mush'. She oohs, and aahs, and purrs, she regains her ability to speak, she is, after all, a defender for her Catholic faith, and wants us to know that she is very tolerant of all kinds of religious nonsense. And then there are other times while listening to NPR that I have to check the dial, because it sounds an awful lot like I'm listening to *Radio Free Israel*. The Israelis can do no wrong, and the Palestinians are always subhuman vermin. To be fair, a large number of the reporters and producers (very competent in most subjects) are Jewish and you certainly wouldn't expect them to betray their true loyalties, now would you?! NPR government subsidies have been cut, so they had to make drastic cuts to stay on the air. They have decided to cut out the FACTS, which used to be the cornerstone of justification for their existence. And just to prove that they are 'in touch' with their audience, they play seventy year old 'jazz' pieces, all day long. It does give me an opportunity to find out what is being said on other stations. Thank you. Their recent ad fund-raising campaign claims that 170,000,000 Americans listen to NPR, so now they've added an obvious 'lie' to their repertoire.

A challenge to my former friends at NPR: do an investigative report on the hiring practices of NPR, CNN, Fox, ABC and ESPN. How is it possible that over 60% of the positions of executive management and production are held by persons who come from a group that is less than 2% of the American public? With over-representation there will always come bias and prejudice in so many ways. The lies become so subtle because everyone seems to be in sync with their handlers. When we only saw 'white' faces delivering the news in years gone by it was very easy to see every story only from a 'white' perspective. That made it easier to lie and to be mystified that 'blacks' seemed to be so offended that their points of view were never presented. Openness in hiring is the only way to expose the build-up of lies that accumulate in a pre-determined mind-set. But I suppose that we will continue to be bombarded with 'Stale Air' and 'All things Jewish' until the lies are finally challenged.

Journalists

They only write what they are told to write, or what they are allowed to write. Give me the name of any journalist, tell me the subject that they are writing about and I will tell you, almost verbatim, what they will say.

Slants, bias and pre-determined script are always the final product of lies and delusions.

Michael Moore

He gets his own special section, because he is just such a huge presence in our society! When he goes after the 'lies' in our country, he is a 'vicious' attacker! He takes no prisoners and he shows no social graces for his victims. He is, after all, the greatest seeker of wisdom and truth for us all. Except.... when you ask him about his Roman Catholic religion. Then, it is off limits. He reserves the right to have his own pocket of lies and foolishness. He certainly doesn't approve of your invasion of *his* private space.

Documentary Film Maker

Global Warming is a very important topic. Our world needs to face the facts and make intelligent, adult decisions concerning the impacts on the future. It does not need a liar like Al Gore to distort or sensationalize. Lies about science only confuse the public and give grist to the anti-scientific, moronic denizens of the 'far' right. As brilliant as Nora Ephron is, she should have known better.

Advertisers

Everyone knows that there is so much lying and deception in advertising, not to mention manipulation! The field is totally unregulated. What can you do if an advertiser uses outright fraud, call BBB or the local prosecutor? In court they will say that they can only help you recover your losses. That is meaningless to ANY company. Go ahead and sue.

Here's a better solution. Never buy anything that is advertised. The cost of advertising is significantly included in any product that you buy.

Here's a better idea. Force all advertisers to create a Standard for Advertisers that will appear on every advertisement. If the advertiser violates any of these standards for any company, they will not be allowed to use this Seal of Approval on their ads until they correct their ways!

When I was growing up, going out to eat at a restaurant was a special event which was only done on special occasions. The restaurant, Republic Hotel, thirty miles away in Bay City Michigan, had white linen table cloths with matching white linen napkins. The dishes were china. There was real silverware and nice glassware. The waiter had a linen towel draped over his arm and always had a pitcher of ice water ready for our needs. There was always a very nice fresh floral centerpiece. The waiter took our orders, one at a time, with very special attention and recommendations. The music playing was often live or at least high quality elevator music. The chairs had arms and were always thickly padded. The waiter would clear each course of the meal as we finished and he had a little petite broom that he used to make sure that the table was completely clean for our next course. At the end of the meal, all was cleaned and the dessert was served. When McDonald's came to our town, for the first time, it was a very special happening. You went to the kitchen to order your own food. They served it on plastic trays, which were paper, plastic or cardboard, with plastic utensils. You found your own seat and sometimes cleaned the table of the previous person's mess yourself. When you finished your meal, you cleaned up your own garbage. What was McDonald's slogan for the new dining experience: "We do it all for you!" Now there's advertising! But it was obvious to us that the standards had been wiped out.

I used to travel a lot, so the only time I could do my banking was on Saturday. One Saturday I went to the branch that I always used and found this message taped to the inside of the door: 'Closed on Saturdays for your Convenience.' It was a couple of weeks before I was back in town on a week day. I went to my bank and closed all my accounts. They asked me why. I told them that it was for their convenience!

Commentator

Food for thought. Not anymore. It used to be with commentators like Edward R. Morrow and others that you would always come away with lots to think about very important subjects. Now you just get screech from annoying hyenas who are not persons of substance themselves. I used to enjoy PBS because of the research and thoughtful programming on lots of subjects. But just recently I have noticed that the 'sponsors' for these programs – supposed foundations – have leaned heavily to get the slant that they want from these programs. Stories on the 'truth' of the Bible should not be sponsored by the Jewish Foundation or the Templeton Fund. You don't make a program on truth by getting your money from liars.

Home Shopping Network

There are only two left! Call now! Operators are standing by! These are one of a kind! It is really important to assume that the great majority of Americans are really stupid and gullible. That's how this works.

eBay

I put a very expensive item on eBay. It was my first time. The seller suggested that we have a 'reserve' limit to guarantee a higher price. What did I know? He told me that no bids met the 'reserve', but that a buyer in Japan was very interested and would pay me $2,500. I thought the item was worth four times that. He told me that this was the way the system worked. So I agreed to sell. A friend who recognized my item called me to tell me that my item was on eBay at $8,500. You guessed it. The seller was the guy who talked me into selling to the mystery buyer in Japan.

Retail Businesses

Auto Repair Shop

My daughter was in college, and I was just coming back from a business trip, when I got a call from her. She was distraught. She had taken her car in for an oil change and the independent garage told her that she would need to have her brakes replaced (pads, rotors, etc.). She was told that her car was absolutely unsafe to drive. The cost of repair would be $450. Being a student, she didn't have the money. I told her not to do anything. I will go to the repair shop when I get off the plane. My daughter didn't know that I had just had the brakes replaced before I left on my business trip. The repair shop was owned by a Lebanese Christian and I had been there before. When I went in, I saw Christian symbols all over the walls, and I remembered that the owner had told me that his little business was putting his son through medical school and his daughters through college. He told me that the brakes were in terrible shape and needed to be replaced immediately. I asked him if I could take a look in the bay. When he put her car back on the rack and took off the first wheel, it was obvious that the brakes were brand new and, in fact, had been replaced, at his shop, just recently. He told me that his mechanic must have looked at the wrong car. Now I got serious. I told him that the last thing that he would want, in his new home in America, would be to have his reputation destroyed. So I made him a deal. He would replace all of the fluids in her car with premium fluids, flush the air conditioning system. and recharge, all while I watched. He would do it for free. If not I would take both his estimate of repairs and the documentation of the previous brake replacement to the BBB and to the local prosecutor. He was a thief and I should have just turned him in. Some people think that taking advantage of students and females is some kind of sport. I was not amused.

Retail Store

Every single 'sale' item would ring up at the normal price when I would go through check-out. Every time I went to their store! I would complain to the manager and quickly recognized that he had a 'could-care-less' attitude. This was before Wal-Mart existed. It was K-Mart and they finally filed for bankruptcy, surprise, surprise! It is still in existence. I had not shopped at one of their stores in over 20 years, but recently saw a coupon in the paper for a children's toy that I was interested in for my granddaughter. I went back to the shelf, saw the sale 'tag' on the shelf and took the toy to check-out. It rang up with the regular (non-sale) price! I told the clerk that I would see them in twenty years, if they were still around. But that day I did not do business with them.

Electronics Store

I bought a desktop computer outfit for each of my daughters. The sale claimed "Buy one and get the next one half off." Good deal. That was my first time going to Radio Shack, but they had a recognizable name and had been around for a long time. The deal was that you took a copy of the sales receipt and sent it in to a company that would process the REFUND. Six months later, still no refund. I went back to the store, where I purchased the computers, and asked what was going on. He told me that the company that did the refunds was not connected to Radio Shack in any way. This company 'bought' the 'refunds' and then waited, and hoped that people would forget to apply for their refund. I finally tracked down a branch of this company in Minnesota and tried to talk to a woman who had a very strong Chinese accent. She told me, "we already pay you!" I called the Attorney General's Office and explained the situation. The company was well known, but not for a good reason. Somehow the Attorney General convinced Radio Shack that they would padlock their doors, in the area, if these situations were not resolved immediately. Six weeks later, I got my refund. But even my bank warned me that they would not 'clear' the check for 20 days, because of problems with this bank in San Francisco. I shouldn't have used Radio Shack's name, they are not responsible for the promises that they make.

Car Salesman

I actually had a good friend who happened to be a new car salesman. He knew that I had done consulting for a major auto manufacturer and was fully aware of most of the 'ins' and 'outs' of the industry. In fact, I served on a Board of Directors with the owner of his dealership. I told him that I was interested in buying a new car and that I had done a large amount of research on the Internet while also calling contacts that I had with his Auto Nameplate. I told him that I wanted his best deal and that I would not accept any 'lies' from him. We looked at the car, looked at the price and I told him to give his best offer and we would make a deal. Even knowing all of this, HE STILL LIED TO ME about the price. When I confronted him with what I knew, he got very defensive. I knew that there was a factory rebate on this vehicle for another $1,000 discount that was supposed to be passed on to the customer. He told me that his dealer liked to keep that rebate, since it was never advertised to the public. I gave him one more chance to reduce our agreed upon price by another $1,000 dollars. The dealer wouldn't budge. This dealer was one of the dealerships that were closed when the manufacturer filed for bankruptcy.

Car Dealership Owner

I could skip this part completely and everyone could fill in the blanks about these degenerate liars, but I want to relate this one experience. This Dealer was going to hold a 'Back to School, Teacher Appreciation Sale'. Any teacher who brings in their ID will receive $1,000 off the price of any car on the lot. We have to support our teachers! I asked the manager of sales how this was even possible. He told me that they would raise the price of every car on the lot $1,000 two weeks before the 'Sale' was announced. He also said that the discount was contingent upon using dealer financing (which is actually a greater source of profits). Many of the cars were recently purchased at auto auctions and only carried a one month extremely limited warranty! And, of course, they didn't raise the price of the real 'dogs' that they wanted to get off of the lot anyway. The Dealer was a deeply religious, anti-abortion, self-righteous jerk. So I asked him how he could justify this fraudulent sale. He told me that it was up to the customer to determine the truth or falsity of any statement. That he was not responsible for what others did! He might have said 'caveat emptor', but he was too stupid to know what that meant. He inherited all of his wealth from family, so I didn't expect him to respect the hard earned money that people brought to his dealership. I ran into his 'buyer' at a pub one night and told him about how horrible I thought the dealers ethics were. He told me that that was not the worst part. Many of his used cars were 'swimmers'. They had been totaled out in flooded areas around the country and purchased by this dealer for pennies on the dollar! Of course, he never told the buyers that these cars will eventually have all kinds of electrical problems. The frosting on the cake came when he told me that the dealer would send him to auctions in other states, so that he could buy cars, which had been totaled out in accidents, bring them back to Ohio, re-title them, and never mention that they were in any accidents. "One owner car" it would read on the windshield on the Dealer's Lot.

Business and Industry

Corporate Directors

We are revising our published quarterly statements for the last five years. The revised profit/loss figures have a confidence rating of 20%. You can take that to the bank. We already have! And so millions upon millions of investors have lost millions and millions of dollars because they trusted that leaders of multi-billion dollar businesses would not lie to them. They also trusted that their government was performing an oversight function to give them a level playing field. The loss of trust and confidence has proven to be even more devastating than the loss of money.

Manufacturer

I owned a Corvair - unsafe, a Vega – five engines, an Oldsmobile 88 – axle fell off, a Ford Escort – spontaneously caught on fire from 'unwrapped' electrical wires running through the back seat, and a Corolla – my first car that rusted out throughout. I was greatly saddened to find out that these manufacturers knew about the defects in these vehicles years before I was informed. I guess I was the test case for finding out just how much a customer could take.

Union Leaders

How can unions justify the salaries of Committeemen who make $50,000 with overtime while working on the floor and, after being elected, are making over $200,000 and coming to work in a Limo? One of the ways to make this happen was to have someone clock in for overtime on behalf of the elected official for every shift, even when he was not there. On the Eleven O'clock News I got to see one of the thieves getting arrested by the FBI in his pajamas, at home, while clocked in at work. You really want to know why GM went bankrupt? Have you got a couple months to hear all the stories? And lies!

An Agribusiness Company

Got one of my companies, ShaneAgra, to build a prototype processing plant (cost $1M), at our expense, to prove that we could take the effluent flow off of their processing of fruits in Oregon (this company is one of the largest food companies in the world). The effluent 'wash' is rich in sugars that can be captured and turned into edible foodstuffs. At the time it was only gooey waste that had to be disposed of, at great expense. We built the plant. It performed as we had stated and we had a contract to build a much larger plant. The company reneged. My last conversation was with a Vice-President of the company in Pittsburgh. "So, sue us, we've got 700 in-house lawyers just waiting for 'the little people' like you." Do you throw good money after bad, or do you just accept that they were too big and we were too small? We were also told that the courts did not take too kindly to lawsuits that might threaten their corporate 'sponsors' in the Pittsburgh area.

Tobacco Company

CEOs from the largest tobacco companies testify before Congress that they didn't believe smoking was harmful to a person's health and subsidies to tobacco farmers in the US were the only way to save jobs in small communities throughout the South. One of the CEOs, was named Mr. Bible! My losses have been multiplied millions of times by friends dying because of the lies of these executives, who for decades presented their product as safe to an unsuspecting public.

Telecom Corporate Exec

I was asked to consider a consulting project with a telecommunications company. The CEO invited me to join him for lunch. He picked me up at my office and we proceeded to the restaurant. When we arrived he pulled into a handicap parking spot, pulled out a handicap sticker, and put it on his rearview mirror.

"Are you handicapped?" I asked.

"No, but my mother is and we got the sticker for her."

"But she isn't with us."

"No problem, I do it all the time."

Shocked at his behavior, I asked that he take me back to my office and explained that "I would never do business with anyone who would be so dishonest over such a trivial matter." He called me for the next three months. I never returned his calls. Business ethics are far too important to sell or buy for a few lousy bucks.

Business Partner

Is it possible that someone could be born a low-down no-good lying thief and that you are only able to discover this over time? Fortunately, for us, it turned out that he was only lying when his lips were moving. I wish that I could print his name right here, because I know that I would get over a thousand confirming phone calls within an hour.

Home Builder

Wrong cabinets, no insulation, wrong brick, patched carpet, wrong flooring, wrong doors, and everything that was installed was of cheaper quality than specified in the plans. I had to call in three state inspectors to verify claim for possible lawsuit. Six month delay left us in a rented apartment, having sold our house earlier. I forced the builder to write out a check for $27,000 before we would sign off on final draw for the loan. Home design was unique and we had a clause that prevented the builder from ever building that design again. At last count, before we moved out of the area, he was up to over twenty exact duplicates!

Airline Pilot/Business Acquaintance

This particular taxi driver in the sky with less education and no second language ability called to tell me about a genius in the computer and telecommunications field who would like to meet me and talk about a possible investment. I asked the pilot if he had vetted this guy. He told me that he had and that he had personally invested large sums with this genius—all of which proved to be false, as I later found out. To my amazement this guy was in Boston but wanted to catch the earliest flight to Cleveland to meet with me (I know, RED FLAG stupid, no multi-millionaire drops everything to meet you in a coffee shop in the airport in another city). We met three hours later. He showed me documentation that he had a PhD from Northwestern and a master's degree from Berkeley. He also stated that he would have competed in the Olympics, but Carter cancelled American participation. He told me that he had worked as a consultant to NASA and had been one of the designers of Linux. He showed me profit statements from his five companies that had a revenue stream of over $100 million. He gave me the names of five prominent persons in the financial field with contact numbers. I called them in New Zealand, London, Scotland, Costa Rica, and Australia unaware that they were part of the scam. Everything that he ever said was a lie. He never went to college. NASA didn't know who the heck we were talking about, but that others had made similar inquiries. Linux lists everyone who has ever worked on their project and his name never appears. I learned all this about ONE MILLION DOLLARS too late! Another businessman who had been swindled out of millions of dollars himself hired a detective and found out all of this damning evidence. When I called the pilot to confront his lies, I found out that he was mad at me because he had finally invested about $50,000 and wanted his money back. This was the twenty-eighth company that this loser, the swindler, had supposedly started and LOST all of the investors' money. There never were ANY companies. Oh by the way, the feckless pilot, who got me into it, did get his money back. He's from Youngstown and convinced this low-life fraudster, that if he didn't get his money back and soon, that he would be beaten to death with a baseball bat by a member of the MOB. He showed me the bat! I called the FBI, the IRS, I wrote to Charlie Crist, who was the Attorney General of Florida at the time. I presented documents that PROVED the fraud with all the offshore account information (Nevis, Vanuatu, Barbados, Grenada) and nothing happened. You see this little thief's cousin was a personal advisor to President George Bush and met with the President every day! Confidentially, an FBI agent told me, that anyone who pursues this case will have their career shortened! The order came all the way from the top! It was case closed. There will be no FOIA, because no documents are

IN EXISTENCE (as I was told by the agent)! Over the years nearly 300 people—including an accountant, a lawyer, a real estate mogul, a financial advisor, an insurance company owner, a minister, a retiree, a politician, a TV personality, a dentist, a colonel, government execs from Costa Rica and New Zealand, a member of the Financial House of Noble—have contacted me to tell me that this low-life had taken their money. All of us should have known better, but we didn't. I passed the messages on to his parents, who live in Malibu CA (his father was a writer for Star Trek and wrote musical pieces for several artists), but apparently they are the ones who taught him to do all this!

Potential Employee/Client

I had a person interview for a position in one of my companies in Costa Rica. We advised lots of clients on many diverse business issues. Our advice had to be thoroughly researched and very timely.

"Do you know what we do in our business?"

"Yes, you do research, gather data, analyze the data and make recommendations to Company owners."

"Correct. What do you think a company would do if they saw us acting counter to the preponderance of data that we had uncovered?"

"I'm sure it would cause them to doubt the integrity of your work."

"Correct, and that's why I'm not going to hire you. When you arrived, I saw you smoking a cigarette out front. Do you believe that there is a preponderance of data that conclusively proves that smoking is dangerous to your health?"

"Yes, of course."

"It scares me to think what you might have done with OUR data."

Lies come in many forms. There are straight up deceptions. There are lies of omission. There are lies of ignorance. There are lies that seem insignificant. But in our business lies are deadly. We were often called in to help companies overcome the effects of lies that had brought them down.

One evening I met a client for dinner. When his food arrived, he began to put large amounts of salt on it before he had even tasted it. I realized that this was a person who had no time for research, data or alternatives. He was a person of impulse who had been lucky in his career, until he wasn't lucky anymore. I knew that his company was in serious danger with him at the helm, and I told him so. He was not pleased but his business was in peril of collapsing, so he listened to what I had to say. I told him that he needed to hand over strategic planning to others in the company, who could sharpen the pencil and analyze their 'real' options. We got the job done, and he was promoted to Chairman of the Board. He did ask me to suggest a Board of Advisors who could keep him abreast of the issues that created the greatest risks to the future viability of the company. Out of that process, I suggested that they seek out a friendly buyer for the corporation. They did, and the companies were sold for a very handsome profit, and all the execs received enough compensation to retire comfortably. If this executive had continued on the course that he was going in the beginning, thousands of people would have lost their livelihood. I could sadly tell you about several others that were destroyed by a head exec, just like this one.

Service Sector

Movers

When my wife and I had a major move, big enough for a moving van, we were all excited about moving to our new home. An hour after we got on the road, we got a call from a friend back in the community from which we were moving. "You should know that your moving van ran over the curb going through town and we could hear all your stuff tumbling around in the van!" When we got to our new home about six hours away, the van pulled up, and we asked them if there had been any problems. They said NO! When the movers opened the side door of the van, we could see smashed furniture, lamps, and broken boxes. Their next move was well choreographed! "You're going to have to sign a release on any potential damage, or we'll have to come back next week with your stuff." My wife was nine months pregnant and we were exhausted. We signed. This actually nullified any claim of insurance that might have been due to us. Our daughter was born two days later, so we sort of forgot all about it. Let's just say that the moving company is still not a name that should be brought up in our house.

Plumber

I suppose I should be thankful that these people are always able to find ten other emergency needs that should be taken care of immediately. Well, that is, of course, after they go back to the shop to get the necessary part and tool. And, oh by the way, each trip back requires and extra $75 service charge on top of the repair.

Tax Planner

If you have earned lots of money offshore, you only have to report it. You don't pay taxes on it until you re-patriate it. If you hire a 'hick' tax planner, you get a 'hick' tax planner.

Loan Officer

Why are there always hidden fees? You would think that after a loan officer had been doing the job for twenty years he would know what fees will be charged. Truth in lending. Sounds familiar, but I'm not sure where I picked that one up.

Banker

He used to live in my neighborhood. But now I'm sure that he doesn't even live in yours. With Federal Reserve rates at zero these birds can spread their own investment portfolio far and wide with very little risk at all. I'm getting .0025% on my passbook account, how about you?

Broker

What the heck are viaticals and REITs anyway?! Whatever they are, my money just disappeared and so did the securities broker who sold them.

Financial Advisor

Everyone who has ever lost money through the advice of a financial advisor please send a copy of this book to a friend. NY Times top ten list here I come.

Education

Parochial School

The governor of the State of Ohio asked me to be a consultant to work on turning around a major public school system in the State. Our research and data indicated that this school system had strengths which were not taken advantage of or widely known. We instituted a fiscal plan that saved the schools over $15 Million in the first year. My company, along with the school board, created a public awareness campaign that we titled "….. Schools #1 and Getting Better!" The schools had recently had two students who earned perfect scores on the SAT. They sent more students to the best colleges in the US, than any other schools in the State. They had the only certified nursing program on the high school level in the US. They had a complete driver training course on campus. That year they won the state championship in football. The achievements and accolades continue. The local major corporations and unions that had been inspired by the campaign called to see how they might contribute to taking the schools even further. The contributions to success, from hundreds of entities, were an inspiration to all involved. Unfortunately, not everyone in the community was happy about all the attention that was given to the public schools. The local parochial school system was livid, to say the least. They got most of their tuition-paying students by claiming that the public schools were corrupt, deficient, and dangerous. They started a BILLBOARD campaign that stated "Come to — where we teach REAL values and a quality education is the STANDARD for all of our students." Their billboards displayed pictures of families attending college graduations of their former students and sitting around the fireplace enjoying the benefits of a better education. Most important, they had billboards featuring a "winning'" football team. Since I have been a doubter all of my life, I asked to have an appointment with the head nun who ran their school system. When we met, it brought back old memories of the arrogance of a church, which had lost its meaning centuries before, but no one had told them. She was a haughty, overbearing relic from the past. She didn't like our public school campaign at all. Her enrollment was down and she wasn't going to take it lying down. She claimed that the community knew the parochial school had "superior values and better families." After she finished her rant, I asked my questions.

Do you accept mentally retarded students? NO.

Do you accept ADD students? NO.

Do you accept any student who has a juvenile record? NO.

Do you offer seven foreign languages? NO.

Do you offer a certified nursing program? NO.

Do you teach evolution? NO.

The community is 52% black; what is the percentage of black students in your school? Less than 2% and all athletes.

Are you allowed to recruit athletes from anywhere in the world for your program? Yes. The public schools were limited by geographic boundaries (Usually a portion of the county).

Can you name over 300 graduates of your school who have gone on to prominence in the United States? The public school can and the names would blow most people away!

Did you know that your average scores on the SAT are lower than the scores of the public school? NO.

Do you know that your school has consistently scored lower on math and science than the public school students for the last 15 years? NO.

Did you know that more graduates of the public schools eventually go on to graduate school, than your students do? NO.

Did you know that your teachers, on average, earn 60% less than their counterparts in the public schools and your teachers have fewer benefits? YES.

Did you know that the public schools have instructors with master's degrees in every subject and your school has none? YES.

I informed the nun that I had written three letters to the Editor detailing what we discussed. I had already contacted the Editor—who helped design the public campaign and is very supportive of the public schools—and asked him to hold copies of these letters until I give him the go ahead. I want the billboards to come down tomorrow or the letters would be published.

I never give up and I was educated in public schools! When I was growing up it was strongly insinuated that Catholic schools won athletic competitions because they had superior family values and morals. It may have had something to do with unlimited recruiting territory, when others were limited. When Notre Dame had winning seasons, this was always the insinuation. When they had losing seasons, they just fired the coach—in fact, many coaches. Perhaps 'forgiveness' is not one of their core values. God also had a little help here in undergirding this claim by having ND play over half their schedule against Girls' Schools for the Blind.

When you take the cream of the crop and produce 'average' that is really nothing to brag about.

Please read: *The Case Against School Vouchers* by Doerr.

Autobiographers/historians

There seem to be many reasons for writing an autobiography/biography. And truth does not seem to be one of them. Autobiographers often want to make sure that their side of the story gets told. Or they want to even some scores. Or they might want to 'titillate' the public. Or, or, or. Biographies (Lincoln has over 200, most filled with so many lies that they aren't worth the paper that they are printed on). Historians always want to emphasize their slant on history. I'm sorry, their version of the truth. If you like this kind of distortion, go ahead and read biographies on Bush, Cheney, or Reagan. There are better things to be reading.

Community Sector

Civil Rights Leader

I have been involved with Urban League and NAACP and other Civil Rights organizations over the years. One thing that I could always count on was that someone in the organization had their finger in the till. Society was never too keen on punishing these offenders. It was a sensitivity issue, but it sure cut deep into the credibility problem.

UN Leader

Have we ever figured out who stole the billions of dollars that the USA gave for relief efforts in the Middle East? It just disappeared. It apparently was all in one hundred dollar bills too. Kind of easy to spot in Iraq, if someone were really looking. Rumor was that the son of a UN leader was the last one to see the shipment before it went missing.

Environmentalist

Not everything is bad. Not every bit of progress will destroy the world. Get off your soap-boxes and join the discussion in the real world where extremely difficult decisions need to be made every day. There are people starving today in Third World countries because environmentalists have stopped progress dead in its tracks to save a newt at the expense of millions of starving children.

Lawyers

Get out the phone book, cover your eyes, and just randomly point at any name.

Priest

I have personally known dozens of families which have been destroyed by the actions of these immoral priests. They were further devastated by the actions of a Church which claims to have the highest morality of any church on earth. Their cover-ups left families shattered. There is no recovery. There is only a tragic level of acceptance that the world is an unsafe place and the ones chosen to make it safer have turned out to be the worst kind of criminals that the world has ever produced.

Prosecutor

Prosecutors make deals. That's just part of the job. Judges want to avoid trials at all costs. So the message is clear. If the criminals want to plead to a lesser charge, the judge will approve. But not all deals are of equal value. Pick up your local newspaper and see the outcomes for several crimes that have happened in your community in the recent past. Now look at the final disposition of the case. 'Murder One, dropped to probation.' What? Local official has drug charges dropped, because evidence is missing from the evidence locker. Teacher, and son of prominent local politician, has sex charges with a minor dropped. And so, the local prosecutor becomes 'the law' or lack thereof.

While teaching business classes on the Graduate level I ask a very simple question, 'Have you ever been lied to or cheated by a business?' The floodgates are then OPEN. I always thought that I must have been extremely unlucky to have experienced all these things until others shared literally thousands of stories of lies, deception and outright theft on the part of companies with stellar reputations!

SO WHO DO YOU TRUST? You have to trust someone, or you will never be able to function in the real world. I truly believe that most people are gracious and wonderful. I also know that all of them lie. You must determine for yourself the truth or falsity of everything that is ever said. It only becomes a problem, when the lies steal your freedom and tear away the fabric of life, which should be a never-ending search for the truth. This is a list of businesses and persons who have done great damage to me, my family, and my hopes. Wisdom shouldn't have to come at the end of life to work for people in a free society. We have to expose the lies and the liars, and further, we have to do something about it, or our children will drift further into the Dark Ages, where solutions will become more and more difficult to acquire.

I invite you to join this never-ending search for truth, regardless of whether that means you will have to expose your parents, your elected officials, your priests/rabbis/ministers, your friends, yourself. It won't be easy, but it will certainly be gratifying in the end.

The next chapter will show us that lies are never innocent. They cause damage to the pursuit of a better future and hope, so that they become a permanent fixture in the slavery of the world.

CHAPTER 17

A Lie Begins the Loss of Freedom

Many lies seem harmless, but they always deprive the audience of choice. Without choice there can be no truth and without truth there can be no freedom. Tragically, the victims of lies unwittingly go along with the lie because they have been so indoctrinated and brain-washed that they really believe they have chosen their way of life.

A few of the Freedoms destroyed by Lies and when not present a state of slavery exists:

- ➢ The freedom to say what you want to say.
- ➢ The freedom to express your own opinions.
- ➢ The freedom to disagree with popular *truths*.
- ➢ The freedom to dress as one chooses, rather than submit to what others have predetermined is appropriate.
- ➢ The freedom to write whatever a person has devised as a part of their own personal discovery.
- ➢ The freedom to believe or disbelieve whatever a person has concluded, on their own without indoctrination or coercion.
- ➢ The freedom from governments and rulers making endless laws, not based on freedom, public safety or sound judgment, but the whims of 'self-serving politicians'.
- ➢ The freedom of one's person not to be harmed, molested, detained or abused by anyone.

- The freedom to pursue whatever field of interest a person desires without the approval of the culture, society or government.
- The freedom not to be labeled for any reason—not for convenience, the Census, or accounting. The freedom to be a human being without any discounts to their humanity by compulsives, who simply want a tidy, meaningless world.
- The freedom not to be imprisoned for *moralistic* offenses. Moralists would just-as-soon put everyone who disagrees with them in jail. And just remember that the person who yells the loudest about moral offenses is probably the one who should be investigated.
- The freedom to expose the lies of religion and the hypocrisy of most of religions' public stances. Don't expect to ever hear an intelligent discussion on this topic in the public media.
- The freedom from unwarranted search and seizure of property, communications, movement, business transactions, et al.
- The freedom of a citizen to live wherever they choose, and to travel wherever a person's dreams may take them, without government creating a permanent nanny state to second guess the freedoms and thoughts of its citizens.
- The freedom not to make up the deficiency in taxes created by granting total tax exemption to religious groups. Religions have over Seven Trillion Dollars in property in the US, tax free. The rest of us have to make up the tax shortfall. And then constantly listen to how their religious freedoms have been torn away from their communities.
- The freedom not to have to compete against Large Corporations, which receive subsidies from the government, while small businesses pay from penny one without any honorable breaks. The poorest individuals in the US pay a higher percentage of their income to IRS taxes, than do corporations (income, sales, property, personal property, etc.). A state of slavery already exists, and the foundation for the theft of property from slaves has existed for a long time.
- The freedom to be whatever it is that a person yearns to be. In their personhood, in their activities, in their private lives. Without

> this freedom a state of slavery exists, and is perniciously enforced by the 'norms' of a sick society.
> The freedom to choose how a person deals with their own body, their own pain and their own death. The government has decided that 'former' sins are now ok. Such as alcohol, gambling and tobacco. So leave the rest of the drugs and pain relievers to the discretion of the individual. To do otherwise is to create a state of slavery, in fact.

Our elected officials foolishly think that they gave these freedoms *to* us. The founding of our nation was supposed to be recognition that those freedoms were always *ours*.

A liberal professor once recorded an interview with a former slave in 1923. The professor was quite proud of his openness to equality for all people. In the interview he insinuates that he supported the rights and freedoms which had recently been given to former slaves. The former slave woman, in her gravelly voice, stated, "You still got the disease. My freedoms and rights have always been mine, you didn't give me nothin." The professor was obviously put off by this display of hubris on her part. Just like our elected officials who perpetuate governmental lies and have the arrogance to believe that our freedoms are gifts to us and that we should show a little more gratitude for the wonderful work that they have done on our behalf.

The next chapter discusses why our elected officials have become such disreputable liars and thieves of what should have always been ours.

CHAPTER 18

Elected Officials have all been influenced by MONEY

EVERY elected official has been bought, and heavily influenced, by 'money' interests! We have too great of a track record in our history to even venture that that is not a *proven fact* – a list of a few of the criminals will follow later.

This great LIE has disenfranchised Americans for over two centuries now. It is time to propose a solution to stop the rape of our great society.

- **First**, elections of presidents, senators, congresspersons, and governors should be publicly funded (to start, other offices later). No member of the candidate's family, or extended family, should receive any compensation or expense reimbursement from these, or any other funds. No corporation, union, or any other entity would be allowed to volunteer campaign workers for use in a campaign while they are on the payrolls of these entities. No advertising or media companies would be allowed to *gift* services to any campaign. Incumbents would receive only three-fourths of the amount of funds that a challenger for the office would receive.
- **Second**, senators and congresspersons and their staffs are NOT considered Federal employees. They are employed by the states and districts from which they are elected. All compensation,

benefits and reimbursements become the sole responsibility of these local entities. The medical benefits for a senator should not exceed the average benefits of his/her constituents. Representatives must apply for *all* reimbursements for activities of their office from their local districts. As a result greater scrutiny will be applied, especially when massive cuts are being taken by everyone else in their district or state.

- **Third**, NO political campaigning may commence more than six months before the date of election. Americans are sick and tired of constant campaigning! NO candidate may expend any money for any campaign activities, whatsoever, previous to this time. No candidate may expend any *personal* money, at any time, while running for office.
- **Fourth**, to become a candidate, a person must gather signatures from five percent of the number of people who voted in the last general election. No one can become a candidate until these signatures are verified. All persons gathering signatures must be volunteers. No candidate may have their name on the ballot in any state for a primary or caucus without having gathered these *certified* signatures in that state.
- **Fifth**, for a person to be elected president, senator, congressperson, or governor from a state, they must receive in excess of FIFTY PERCENT of the vote. If no candidate receives in excess of fifty percent of the vote, then a run-off election must be held within SEVEN days between the top two candidates. One of the choices for each office must be the option of voting NO. In a run-off election 'NO' must still be an option. Then, if no candidate receives over fifty percent, the candidates are disqualified, and a special election must be held with new candidates. Everyone is so tired of getting stuck with the 'other guy' in these extremely important positions!
- **Sixth**, no elected official may hire any family member to be compensated on his staff or any offices that he/she may have influence over. If any family member is hired by any corporation, union or other entity, then the elected official must recuse himself/herself, when dealing with any issue remotely affecting those

entities. No elected official may propose or influence the action of others to benefit entities from which his family may benefit.

- **Seventh**, no elected official may receive any benefit of any kind from anyone while in public office. That means NO meals, transportation, or benefits to any family member. NO free meal while giving a speech. NO transportation costs covered to meet with or address any groups. No junkets of any kind may be paid by anyone other than the elected official, and the junket cost must be approved in advance by the entity which elected them. Any violation should be considered a breach of oath of office and should be taxed at 100% of benefit received to be paid out of the personal funds of the office holder.
- **Eighth**, politicians have been very fond of loyalty oaths. So fond that they have forced children to pledge loyalty to abstract concepts of religion and commitment of life, liberty and personal possessions. Even adults quite often do not have a clue as to the meaning of these oaths. Since we have required our children to Pledge Allegiance to the Flag, it is only appropriate that we create a Pledge of Allegiance for our elected officials to take *before* being seated in the chambers of power. Of course, we all pledge our fealty to support, protect and defend the Constitution of the United States. Elected officials should go one step further and promise to never lie to nor deceive the public in any form, whatsoever. The Pledge could go something like this:

"I pledge to you that what I am about to say is the truth, the whole truth and is not intended to be deceptive or lacking in information as to deceive the listener. If I am not telling the truth or if my words are lacking in sufficient information, such that the outcome will be the deception of the listener, then I ask that I be charged with the offense of violating my oath of fealty to my constitutional duties and that I be removed from office." It will be understood that upon taking public office, this pledge applies to every written or oral communication made by the elected official until he/she leaves office.

Now there's a pledge with teeth!

Further Requirements:

- All senators and congresspersons are required to be in their respective elective districts for three two week periods each year to attend open forum meetings and answer questions from local voters.
- All senators and congresspersons must communicate with their constituents on every vote that they cast. If the representative voted for the legislation, he/she must list the five main reasons why they voted in the affirmative. They must also list five reasons why they would have voted against the bill.
- No elected official will *EVER* be allowed to vote for their own wages or benefits.
- Every contact between a lobbyist and an elected official (or his/her staff) must be recorded and reported publicly online. Every written document from any source must be recorded as received and made available to the public. No proposed laws can be written by anyone other than congressional staff. Absolutely NO laws, in any form, may be submitted by outside sources.
- An elected official who misses 5% of the votes taken will be reprimanded, and they will be expelled if the voting record does not improve.
- A separate Ethics Committee outside of the purview of the elected bodies - NO elected officials can ever serve on this Committee - will hear ALL ethics charges and make referrals to the appropriate criminal and civil authorities. Just the foolishness, that has already been made public, has made the Congress of the United States a laughingstock to the rest of the world.
- The President of the United States will serve a four year term. At the end of thirty-eight months of the presidency a national vote will be taken. The voting public will determine whether or not the sitting President will be allowed to run for a second term in office. If the vote is less than 50% in the affirmative, then the President is ineligible to run for re-election.

- All Senators at the end of five years in office will face a vote in their home state that will determine whether or not the senator will be allowed to run for another term in office. The senator will need a final vote of at least 50% in the affirmative or he/she will be ineligible to run again.
- NO CAMPAIGNING WILL BE ALLOWED PRIOR TO THESE VOTES.
- No seniority will be allowed in the Senate or House of Representatives. Seniority diminishes the power of representation of constituents in other states. All Senators and Representatives enter each Term on an *equal* footing.
- All elected officials must declare, under oath, that they do not have any money offshore. If it is discovered that they do, they will serve a two year prison sentence in a Federal Penitentiary. Financial disclosures will be required of all elected representatives and no amending will be allowed after being sworn in.

Provisos for Elections:

- Funding for election campaigns will be determined by the number of citizens who voted in the last general election in each jurisdiction. For example, if ten thousand people voted for representative from their district in the last election, then the total amount for the next election will be a dollar amount per vote cast.
- No ads or funding will be allowed by any entity residing outside of the state/district of the election.
- No elected official may campaign in a jurisdiction other than their own.
- Free and equal airway time for each candidate will be mandated by the Federal Election Commission.
- Any ads which are clearly *factual lies* used to coerce the electorate will be punishable by law.
- No food, music, or entertainment will be allowed at any campaign meeting.
- No endorsements, on behalf of any candidate, by any elected official will be allowed.

- All elected officials must maintain a website where the public can easily follow all of the officials' actions. The site will also contain an accurate listing of all expenses and expenditures which must be kept up to date.
- Any support staff must be compensated from the home district funds. This includes benefits, travel, health care, and other expenditures.
- All laws passed by Congress—including discriminatory, liability, and disability acts—must be applied to those serving in Congress as well with NO exceptions.
- The minimum air and water standards, which are legislated for the EPA, must be maintained by the air ducts and water pipes in the Congressional Offices at all times. If a certain amount of lead, mercury, arsenic, or other effluents are acceptable to be in the air or water in a mining town in West Virginia, then that level of air quality must be maintained in the air systems of government buildings. The water quality will be checked in a border town in Texas, and then, those levels with be maintained in the water system in all government offices.
- No separate medical or retirement plans will be permitted other than the plans that the general public has available to them.
- Any excess monies from a campaign must be returned to the FEC immediately after the election has finished. Any debts, beyond the legal limits of the campaign, may cause the candidate to be disqualified.
- Former elected officials cannot work for any company which is registered as a lobbyist organization for a minimum period of ten years after leaving office. The former elected official cannot work for any company which does work with or receives compensation from lobbying firms. If the former elected official's wife or immediate family member works for any of these entities after the official leaves office, then the former official must forfeit pension, benefits, and prerequisites.
- No former elected Official may use *Emeritus* status in the halls of government. When the person leaves office, they can no longer eat in the dining hall or meet with officials for business of any kind.

- o An Elected Official may NEVER take the Fifth Amendment for any purpose while serving in office.
- o No benefits will be given to family members of elected officials, whatsoever. This includes tuition payments or breaks, travel on government airlines without compensation, appointment (or special hiring) to any government jobs for friends or relatives, or 'perks' which they have not earned through their own efforts and merit.
- o All Elected Officials—including the President, Vice-President, Senators, and Congressional Representatives—upon leaving office must be subject to an extensive exit interview. They will be asked penetrating questions about their actions, statements and positions. The interviews will be conducted by 100 of the most respected historians in the United States. All records will be sealed for 15 years. If, when unsealed, it becomes obvious that the elected officials were lying about substantive issues, then remedies and repercussions may be implemented. A violation of constitutional authority will be considered on the level of violation of National Security.

Some might say that all this looks like we don't trust our elected officials.

We shouldn't trust our elected officials, and we have been given substantial reason through the years to have come to that conclusion.

The following is a partial list of elected officials in our most recent history who have disgraced their families, themselves, and the United States. These former officials have been censured, convicted of crimes, or resigned in disgrace:

- **John Edwards**
- **Ted Stevens**
- **John McCain**
- **Bob Torricelli**
- **Richard Nixon**
- **Spiro Agnew**

Dennis Richard Proux

- John Ensign
- Larry Craig
- Duke Cunningham
- Anthony Weiner
- Joe Walsh
- Joseph Kennedy
- Jim Wright
- Jim Traficant
- Charles Rangel
- Bob Livingston
- David VitterT
- om Delay
- Jon Corzine
- Barney Frank
- Newt Gingrich
- John Glenn
- Don Young
- Laura Richardson
- Pete Visclosky
- Dennis DeConcini
- Bob Ney
- Jerry Lewis
- Mark Souder
- Dennis Hastert
- Walter Fauntroy
- Mary Rose Oakar
- Walter R. Tucker III
- John Doolittle
- Vern Buchanan
- David Wu
- Dan Rostenkowski
- Ken Calvert
- Alan Mollohan
- Nathan Deal
- Rick Renzi
- William Jefferson

- Buzz Lukens
- Carl C. Perkins
- Carroll Hubbard
- Nicholas Mavroules
- Austin Murphy
- Wes Cooley
- Barbara-Rose Collins
- Joe Kolter
- David Durenberger
- Lawrence J. Smith
- Joshua Eilberg
- Mario Biaggi
- Dan Flood
- Pat Swindall
- Frank Thompson
- Anthony Lee Coelho
- John Jenrette
- John M. Murphy
- Albert Bustamante
- Richard Kelly
- Michael Myers
- Jesse Helms
- Harrison A. Williams
- Bill Clinton
- Martin B. McKneally
- Cornelius Gallagher
- Alan Cranston
- Donald W. Riegle, Jr.
- Richard T. Hanna
- Charles H. Wilson
- Herman Tallmadge
- Fred Richmond
- Charles Diggs
- Helen Chenoweth
- Henry Hyde
- Gary Condit

- Jon Hinson
- Robert Bauman
- Fred Richmond
- Daniel Inouye
- Allan Howe
- Robert Leggett
- Wayne Hays
- Thomas Evans
- Charles Robb
- Wilbur Mills
- Ted Kennedy
- Arthur Brown
- Dan Crane
- Robert Packwood
- Gerry Studds
- Jim Bates
- Brock Adams
- Gus Savage
- Arlan Strangeland
- Ken Calvert
- Mel Reynolds
- Dan Burton
- Raymond Lederer
- Maxine Waters
- John Connally
- Otto E. Passman
- John T. McFall.

This is only a partial list, which only includes the ones who got caught. While their shenanigans were going on, they were creating budgets and rewarding themselves and buddies with taxpayer money. It really is a nice assortment of Republicans and Democrats. No moral highground here.

The major obstacle for getting reform accomplished:

OUR GOVERNMENT IS A LIE

The writings of the early founders of America laid out a convincing case for freedom: government should only be established through the CONSENT of the governed. The earliest form of the US Government was clearly limited so that FREE people could determine their own destinies without the continual interference of any tyrannical governmental leaders and actions. The signings of the Declaration of Independence and the United States Constitution were seen, as much as a protection *from* government, as they were a formation of a new government.

The United States has failed to live up to its own sacred agreements, which were made with the citizens of the United States.

The 'Consent of the Governed' means the consent of *ALL* the governed. Women were denied the right to vote for the first 144 years of the existence of the United States. Then, with an amendment, which never should have been necessary, made female voting possible. It was still discouraged through overwhelming cultural ignorance promulgated by male domination, which might as well have been written in stone by the Founders. As a result, over 50% of the governed were abused, denied property rights, and lacked standing in the courts of law for almost 150 years and counting. This tragic abuse continues in many ways, but especially in the pathetic tokenism which is dragged out every time a woman is nominated for any position of authority, or jurisdiction. Only women are asked what they will do about their children, if they are given a demanding position. Only women are described by the clothing they are wearing, whether or not they wear make-up, or the possibility that they will become emotional at certain times of the month.

The United States has never operated based on the 'consent' of the governed. This great system, which we pretend to be exporting to the rest of the world, has never happened here. It is a grand lie that has destroyed many lives.

"All men are created equal." The founding fathers all signed their names to that statement. They then proceeded to establish a government which denied the vote to women, blacks, slaves, Indians and non-landowners. Blacks could not vote for nearly 200 years. The United States was supposed to be a great human experiment where total freedom was finally possible for ALL people. It didn't happen. We did overcome royal rule, slavery, sexism, and xenophobia, but not because the Founders wanted it that way or because the government took action to do something. Change was forced upon government leaders, and it was always seen as them giving up perks –the great white male bias - that belonged only to them. Discrimination and denial of rights is still rampant in the land because some know that politicians can be bought.

The words were right and the desire for freedom was universal, but the actions were those of political leaders who abhorred the thought of being considered equal with the riff-raff that made up the United States of America. Not only was the GREAT LIE that they wanted freedom for everyone, but it was a heinous denial of basic human and legal rights.

After the boys signed their wonderful documents of Freedom, Jefferson and Washington went home and raped their defenseless slaves. It's hard to justify that kind of behavior, under any circumstances, but to call it consensual behavior on the part of a twelve-year-old black slave with her ankles and arms in iron shackles is to further victimize the victims. We are so proud of all the progressive liberal ideas—incorporated into the documents of our beginnings as a nation—brought about by Jefferson. But he had the time to do so because he had free slave labor creating and sustaining his wealth. Two hundred thirty slaves working for free is a benefit to which many modern corporations aspire!

The Founders' disgusting and depraved attitude toward women gave them the opportunity to have sexual affairs with hundreds of women who had NO power over their own lives. Many women, in the first two hundred years of this farce of a democracy, knew that they could only have anything *through* men. They couldn't own property. They had no parental rights in a divorce. They had limited educational opportunities. They could even be brutally beaten and considered the 'instigator' of the beating. Too many laws—many still on the books today—plus too many cultural norms prove

Lies Have Ruined the World

that the government still doesn't have the *"consent of the governed."* When Tiger Woods refused to play at any golf club which did not admit blacks, he guaranteed his own place in the sun. Yet when he continues to play the Masters at a club which does not admit women, he proves that there is no freedom in our society, which is free from the bigoted mentality of our Founding Fathers.

Have you seen black injustice which takes place daily? Have you seen the many blacks and Hispanics who have been released by the 'Innocence Project'? The Consent of the Governed has never involved blacks! Token appointments and token laws are not the same as black participation in the process of governing on an equal footing.

The Founding Fathers believed that only the rich should have a say in governing. This has never changed. The promise of the United States has been a lie.

Today the RICH choose who will run. The RICH pay for campaigns. The RICH lobby. The RICH pay lawyers to write the laws the way they want them. The RICH decide the winners and losers. The RICH buy the judges but not justice.

Washington would have been so proud that Thomas Paine never got his way in seeing every person as equal and free in America! (*The Rights of Man, The Age of Reason* and *Common Sense* by Paine). In fact, Paine wrote, printed and distributed *Common Sense*, totally at his own expense! It was the most widely distributed pamphlet in the Colonies. Some even said that it was the most important tool in winning the Revolution. How did we thank him? Washington, Adams, Jefferson, and others made sure that Paine was shunned because of his ideas on equality, and the religious leaders of America made sure that he was shunned because he was an atheist. He died despised, abandoned, and alone, in a make-shift borrowed space on a farm in New York. Truth-tellers and true visionaries, like Paine, are always trampled by the leading liars of the day. Having discovered truth in so many venues, I can tell you that the liars are just boiling with hatred and vengeance toward stopping anyone from hearing it.

The American public keeps hoping that a candidate will step forward who will really listen to and care about the common person, but instead we get a barrage of candidates who pander only to the wealthiest one percent and a collection of 'village idiots'.

When Adlai Stevenson ran for the presidency in 1952, he gave one of the most moving orations ever by a candidate. After the speech, a woman approached him and told him: "That was the greatest speech that I have ever heard. Every thinking person in America will vote for you." "That's not enough ma'am, I've got to get at least 50% of the vote!"

The only hope for America, and indeed Freedom, is that we get back to the principle of the "Consent of the Governed" by forcing our representatives to be accountable to us. They must be forced to be answerable to the citizens who elect them.

Are our elected representatives swayed by money? Drag a dollar bill through the halls of Congress on a string, but make it a 'long' string, or you might just get trampled to death! Since our elected officials have been well known to be quite fond of whoring for dollars, I propose the following:

- o If the unemployment rate in the US exceeds 5%, then the wages of all elected and appointed officials will be **cut by 10%.**
- o If the unemployment rate in the US exceeds 7%, then the wages of all elected and appointed officials will be **cut by 20%.**
- o If the unemployment rate in the US exceeds 8.5%, then the wages of all elected and appointed officials will be **cut by 30%.** We would soon find that our clever elected representatives will figure out a *different way* to calculate the unemployment rate. The only way that a person would be considered 'unemployed' is if they agree to a drug test and *deep cavity search*. Sadly, most will accommodate this ridiculous law because they have already suffered the unbelievable degradation of not feeling useful.

My advice: attach money to whatever it is that you want Congress to do and that will be your greatest chance for success.

Some good reading:

Architects of Ruin: How Big Government Liberals Wrecked the Economy and How They Will Do It Again if No One Stops Them **by Schweizer.** You will cry!

The Fruits of Graft by Jett.
Reckless Endangerment by Morgenson.
Griftopia by Taibbi.
Politically Incorrect: a Guide to the Constitution by Gutzman.
Great American Hypocrites by Greenwald.

One aside, which I believe is important. Our government has been very active in creating 'states' outside of our own, without the consent of the governed in those territories. We have discussed how that has had an effect upon the 'rightness' of our own governance. Now I would simply want to mention the damaging effects upon others. Why is it that we don't have a State of Cherokee, or State of Pharaoh, or State of Prussia, or State of Gaul, or a State of Inca? We have a State of Israel. Its justification for existence is that 'god' gave that land to them! And since we know that their 'god' does not exist, it makes the argument specious at best. These other groups also claimed that their 'god' gave them their land, and these other groups actually occupied their lands for a longer period of time. Not to mention, that the present State of Israel is far larger than the land mass which their ancestors ever occupied. The citizens of Israel have certainly been victims in a very cruel and unjust world. But that never should have been the justification for taking the land away from others, and giving it to them. The lie of Israel has been, and will continue to be, a massive, impossible problem for the world to solve. If something starts with a lie, it doesn't get any better with 'blinders'.

So now we have discovered that there are no 'experts' in religion. There are no 'experts' in government. In fact, there are an inordinate number of liars. The next chapter reminds us that, in fact, there are no experts in any subject matter area, whatsoever. There are only liars, who use their position to manipulate and deceive the public for personal advantage. So let's prove it.

Government is Responsible for:

Disaster Relief	Grade: C-
Border Security	Grade: D+
War Powers (Justified wars only)	Grade: F
Regulation of Wall Street	Grade: F
Regulation of Banks	Grade: F
Oversight of Federal Reserve	Grade: F
Food and Drug Safety	Grade: C+
Mine Safety	Grade: F
Oil Drilling Inspection	Grade: F
Immigration	Grade: F
Equality of Taxation	Grade: F
Balanced Budget	Grade: F
Fair International Trade	Grade: F
Child Labor Laws	Grade: F
Control of Firearms	Grade: F
Highway and Bridge Safety	Grade: F
Recovering Medicare Fraud	Grade: F
Mortgage Lending	Grade: F
Corporate Fraud	Grade: F
Social Security Funds (Lock/Box)	Grade: F

According to this 'report card' the government is a failed enterprise. It should therefore have its funds confiscated by a 'charter' government which can prove to be a better use of our taxes. It does explain the government's program of 'No Child's Behind Left', however.

CHAPTER 19

If you see an 'EXPERT', you have been fooled.

There is no such thing as an expert!

While many claim to be experts in various subjects, it is impossible to be an expert in anything. The word "expert" means to have *perfect* knowledge of a subject such that his/her opinion on the subject would go unchallenged. The world is far too complex and single subjects far too narrow to be validated by the claim of inerrancy. Some individuals have a great deal of knowledge and years of practice in a given field, but that doesn't come even close to having perfect knowledge. Religionists were the first to bring us this irrational notion of inerrancy. They wanted absolute power over people and punished those who asked questions or challenged their authority. Their irrational stances, even in the age of modern science, are still shouted in the marketplace as though people are incapable of individual thought. Perhaps they are too often right about that assumption.

We see this when a pope speaks and demands that everyone believe that 'god' is really moving his lips. We see this when we hear government officials speak with such arrogance about subjects that they have never researched even on a very superficial level. We are exposed to this from medical practitioners who want us to just accept any 'pabulum' that they put forward because they went to medical school. A person says 'I am a scientist' and they expect that everyone will just bow down to the ground –face in the dirt – and become robots to whatever they say. Persons sit on the witness stand in court and declare that they are experts in a particular field and then some years later an 'innocent' person is released from jail because the 'expert' was a liar and a fraud, while at the same time carrying 'tenure' at a prestigious university. The FBI Labs send out 'experts' in numerous fields which have proven to be bogus at best. I could list every single field of endeavor and there will always be so-called 'experts' in every one of them.

And they would all be liars and deluded fools. And after they smugly go home with stipend in hand, the truth dies and innocents lose life, limb and hope.

The further tragedy of this misuse of the word "expert" is that many who call themselves experts simply cannot restrain themselves from having opinions on lots of other subjects, of which they have superficial exposure at best. They present themselves to be experts in morality, child parenting, politics, criminology, on and on ad infinitum!

The data-base to draw from to show that there is no such thing as an expert in any field is massive and readily available in every single human endeavor, for instance:

- Cemeteries are full of people who received care from an expert surgeon.
- Prisons are full of innocent people convicted on the testimony of experts in various fields.
- Bankruptcy courts have thousands of documents filed on behalf of clients who received expert advice from their financial advisors.
- Medical science has been impeded for centuries because of the expert opinions of leaders in the field.
- Expert literary critics have been universally wrong about some of the greatest classics ever written.
- Expert economists have led the vulnerable economy of the United States through one major recession after another.

- One of the greatest criminals in human history, Alan Greenspan, has stolen more money from more people and destroyed more lives than any other group of amoral, vicious tyrants combined.
- The experts at Credit Rating agencies gave us Enron, the mortgage debacle, and so much more.
- Of the many experts in the field of parenting, Dr. Spook (not his real name) was personally responsible for the infant-crib deaths of over 60,000 babies for demanding that parents teach their babies how to sleep on their bellies. The other clowns in this field are far too numerous to mention, but let us simply say that over the most recent decades they have managed to turn most normal mothers into paranoid wrecks by convincing them that they are terrible parents for just about everything they do.
- The experts in military operations have caused the deaths of innocents on the other side and thousands of members of their own troops. They don't even know war! Let alone the realities on the ground, that they have consistently messed up now for seventy years or more. The British said that the Americans didn't fight fair. "They hide behind trees, like the Indians." The Americans won. American military say that the Taliban don't fight fair, yet they are still in power.
- I must say that Donald Rumsfeld is personally responsible for me poking sticks in my eyes and pouring acid down my pants, because every time he opened his ignorant mouth, I lost it! Mr. 'Expert' on everything "Who knew?"! "You go to war with the army you got!" Is it illegal to say that we would all have been better off, if this 'two bricks short of a full shit house' had never been born?! Thank God we had George Bush and Karl Rove to keep us on the right track (now there's expertise). Oh my God, the acid on my private parts has gone to my brain! Beam me up Obama!
- The experts at NASA convinced us that manned missions were the only way to accomplish the sophisticated work that needed to be done in space. In fact, that was never true and cost taxpayers of the US over one trillion dollars more than was needed because unmanned missions would have accomplished as much, or more, and at far less risk to life.

- Many experts convinced us of the "war on drugs." They claimed that if we didn't spend nearly one trillion dollars to intervene in this dastardly activity, there would be illegal drugs everywhere in our society. They would be easier to obtain than cotton candy by our children. However, drugs continue to be easily obtained and we still wasted the trillion dollars on enforcement, interdiction, broken foreign relations, and incarceration for drug-related offenses that massively outnumbers anywhere else in the world.

There are NO experts! Even the ones who shamelessly carry the title for themselves will have to surrender that title within a decade of the modern era.

It is amazing that when someone openly presents a problem over the Internet and asks for individuals to submit possible solutions that more often than not, a wonderful solution is suggested by someone who is not even in the field. 'Experts' will always eventually take credit or ownership, but it doesn't diminish the fact that breathtaking insights are often a random occurrence throughout humanity.

Accidents bring breakthroughs as often as intention. Experts with their blinders on will more often deny, ignore, or demean the new insights!

We need people to be diligent about in-depth learning in many fields, but when they attach the label "expert" to their name, we need to look them in the eye and clearly say, "Look, Mr. Arrogant, we've got a dialogue going on here with life. Join the discussion or get out of our way. We have serious problems to work on here."

For some interesting reading, just go to the library, and pick up a biography, of anyone, who was considered to be an 'expert' on any subject in the 1930's. Then proceed to the 40's and don't stop there, just because you are now laughing out loud. When you get to the nineties and you come across the name Greenspan, and you see that when proven wrong, continuously, he doesn't stop blaming everyone else. "The lousy world is wrong and it messed up all of my work. If only it had listened to me." It did listen to you. Now, crawl back into that deep hole, in the murky swamp, which you crawled out of. You can find Mr. Greenspan's advice regularly featured on MSNBC. Now there's a repository of 'expertise' and 'swill', that you just can't get anywhere else!

I know that you have finished all of the other books, which I have recommended, so here are a couple of real good ones for tonight!

Greenspan's Bubbles by Fleckenstein.

Fooled by Randomness: The Hidden Role of Chance in Life and in the Markets by Taleb.

So now we've killed all the priests, government 'official' liars, and experts. It's time to kill all the lawyers! Their lies have stolen trillions of dollars from the public. In the next chapter we recommend very strong actions to stop this thievery and restore our freedoms, which have been lost for so many generations.

CHAPTER 20

All Lawyers are SCUM

Writing that "lawyers are scum" may seem to state the obvious to many people, but there are deeper LIES in the legal (so-called Justice System) of the United States which have caused the loss of rights, freedoms, and wealth for millions of Americans.

The legal system in America is broken. Lawyers are the ones who broke this system, yet they refuse to fix it.

Lawyers seek to make fortunes and they do so by maneuvering through the maze of foolishness that is the court system. The Courts are filled too often with corrupt, incompetent, and lazy people.

To start, the entire legal system in America is closed to the average citizen. Everyone in the system is a lawyer. The judges, the clerks, the advocates exist to protect the financial interests of the lawyers.

The courts are not established to **determine fact and truth.** They exist as a purely adversarial system that is more impressed by pretty boy lawyers than they are by diligent thought. Too often the courts look more like gladiatorial forums for dancing, wrestling, and performing circus bears.

The community has been hoodwinked into believing that they can choose their judges through open elections.

This is a joke! Not one person in ten thousand even knows the names of the candidates who run for judicial office. In addition, the judge is chosen before the election even takes place. Prominent law firms hand-pick the persons whom they want to sit in the judges' seats. Other potential candidates quickly find out that they can't go up against law firms that can and will destroy them. These law firms make sure that they pick judges who will run their courts in the best financial interests of the lawyer community. Delays occur when the lawyers want to run up massive bills for a client, rulings are made that prejudice the proceedings, and off-the-record conversations take place that shape the outcomes.

Judges are often appointed based on their preconceived opinions on abortion, unions, employment, science, and religion. In medicine they call it a 'pre-existing' condition. In the courts they call it a 'pre-existing' opinion. There is no such thing as an impartial judge in this system of political favors and backroom deals. The judges' beliefs must align with those of the law firms and politicians who appoint them. Biased decisions—clearly in line with the judges' prejudices —come down every day, regardless of any factual data that is presented! The average citizen with no legal background can tell you how the Supreme Court Justices will rule before the case is even presented. This is a travesty! A lawyer once told me that if you don't know how a judge will rule before the case begins then you shouldn't be practicing law! The most important part of the case is getting the right judge—the one who holds the lawyer's same prejudices. These judges work very hard to stay on the bench because most of them are not intelligent or industrious enough to make a living practicing law, and that is exactly where the lawyers have them in their pocket. Judges know that if the most powerful law firms don't want them on the bench anymore, then they are out.

Every judge becomes an unbearable moralist on the bench. They know better than anyone else how the world should work and how citizens should behave, even if their views are extra-legal and inappropriate. It is eerie to see how much a courtroom resembles a church or synagogue. The judge wears a priestly frock and sits behind an elevated altar while spectators sit in pews. The national, religious symbols—often the Ten Commandments—adorn the walls. Oaths are taken in god's name while a Bible is used as justification for truth in testimony. Punishment is decided in terms of sin and repentance, whether or not the defendant is guilty. Some court sessions even open with prayer. It is no wonder so many judgments are completely irrational.

The United States incarcerates more people than the ten next largest free nations in the world combined. Judges take out their vengeance on the poor souls who are unfortunate enough to enter their courtrooms. Televised trials have convinced Americans that the courts are thorough and meticulous. When the cameras are turned off, the railroading begins. The courts are fully aware that there is almost no chance they will be brought under scrutiny for running the hate mills they call courts. The chance of having a case even heard by an appeals court is almost zero. Remember that these judges are also lawyers. They don't want to make their colleagues look bad. They know that they serve at the behest of the LAWYER community and can be removed at any time. The biggest reason that few cases are ever heard on appeal is that judges are monumentally lazy. The only way a case can be heard is if a point of law is challenged meaning it is totally subjective as to whether a case will ever be heard by an appellate court. These judges went to the same schools, belonged to the same fraternities and sororities, and married into the same families as the judges whose cases they are deciding to review. Justice is impossible when you put all these elements together.

The courts must be separated from lawyers and law firms.

No lawyer should sit in the judge's seat ever again. Judges should be trained in a separate educational system that no lawyer should be allowed to enter. Most judges are incompetent. They are generalists who have no expertise in any facet of the law. They fumble around, violating the rights of citizens, and try to cover their inept performance. In the future all judges should go through an extensive training program, become certified to sit on the bench before they are ever allowed to decide in cases that affect the Constitutional rights of citizens.

How many innocent citizens are rotting in jail today because of an ignorant judge with moralistic hubris? Adding salt to the wound, the greatest majority of decisions that are handed down are not even written by judges. They are written by their clerks! These clerks are too lazy or incompetent to make a living practicing law as a professional, so they attach themselves to judges who are too clueless to know whether their clerks are writing proper decisions.

Lawyers steal from their clients every day.

They overbill. They steal from estates. They charge for work that they already charged another client. They charge for research that they obtain with one click on a pre-written database available on their computers. They charge high fees for work done by their secretaries. They charge for the work of multiple associates when only one lower associate actually did the work. They write unnecessary briefs with the collusion of the courts. They create unnecessary delays, so they can charge for their services over and over during that time period. They work with lawyers on the other side of the case to create the illusion that they need to answer the huge pile of paper that the other side "just sent." They charge for lifestyle expenses that have nothing to do with the case, such as expensive meals while they supposedly talk to a witness, expensive trips to take a deposition, or even an oil change on the Mercedes!

When the billable hours of the thirteen largest law firms in the nation that do work for the Federal Government were totaled for one year, the number of hours exceeded the total number of hours in a whole year by a factor of three times. Everyone at the law firm would have worked around the clock, every day, every week, and every month, with no bathroom breaks for any of them. The total number of lawyers, legal aides, paralegals, secretaries, and runners were used to divide into the number of billable hours and there was still no justification for these charges. When the government was informed, no audit was ordered. The panel that made the decision not to audit was comprised entirely of lawyers.

When injustice hits home.

A few years ago a friend at work got the sad news that his uncle in Alabama had died. His uncle lived alone and his wife had died some years earlier. My friend was the only living relative. He went to the funeral from his home in Michigan. After the funeral he went to his uncle's house to make an inventory of his uncle's possessions and to determine what needed to be done to finalize his estate. He contacted a local attorney for advice. The attorney informed him that in that small community the judge usually appointed someone to look over the interests of the estate. With that, he went home to Michigan and waited to hear from the court. Nothing happened, so he contacted the court to find out what was going on. He didn't like what he heard from the court administrator, so he made a special trip to Alabama. When he got there everything of his uncle's estate was gone including the real estate. He talked to the attorney, to whom he had talked before, and got all the bad news. The judge had appointed his own nephew as executor of the estate. His nephew was the minister at a large local church. The minister then appointed his own son to appraise the value of the estate. They each got huge salaries for taking on this unpleasant task. An auction was held and all the possessions were disposed of, including the real estate. The real estate had been condemned as unlivable by a local official who was also an acquaintance of the judge. When my friend went to the church of the minister, who was the executor, to ask questions about the estate, he was shocked to find his uncle's furniture, television, and stereo in the lobby of the church. The land was quite valuable because a strip mall builder had wanted to buy it for years and had now purchased it from a local minister. The lawyer he consulted told him to just lick his wounds and move on. "Besides, two of the appeals judges are relations of the judge!" My friend figures that he lost about $200,000 but considered himself lucky that he didn't end up in jail. The judge's court sent him a bill for unpaid expenses that were still owed on the court's processing of the estate. I can't print what he had to say about that.

This type of thievery goes on in probate courts all across the nation every single week of the year. **Billions of dollars of citizens' wealth are regularly stolen**, and there is absolutely nothing that can be done about it, except to change the system. We need certified judges who have never been lawyers and are not appointed by corrupt politicians and degenerate law firms.

Domestic Court. It sounds so sweet. Like "Haven of Rest." Yet, domestic court judges are the most moralistic, unfiltered bags of excrement that the world has ever known. They claim to want to save the nuclear family, yet they do so by dragging families through torturous proceedings that have absolutely no value and ultimately tear families apart. Lawyers complain about divorce cases, but these are the greatest source of legal ATM money for these scumbags.

Whatever it costs for a marriage license—approximately $50 to $100—it costs thousands for the cheapest divorce. Lawyers have figured out how to milk their clients out of every last penny. Divorce is actually quite simple: The fact that the marriage is over, the estate, the children. Even couples with no children are persecuted in these courts in order "to protect the sanctity of marriage." When I went through my divorce, I found it ironic that all the judges, lawyers, and clerks were divorced. Our judge had been a nurse and after she went through her divorce, she decided to become a lawyer then a judge, so that she could get even with men. Both lawyers agreed that she was a 'man-hater' and that no father had ever gotten custody of his children in her court. So much for impartial justice. The lawyers wanted to drag this case out for years and they did. One of the bailiffs invited me downstairs at the courthouse to buy me a cup of coffee. He told me that he had been doing his job for over thirty years and he was retiring that week.

The facts, just the facts.

"One thing you need to know. Everyone up there is getting paid: the judge, the lawyers, the clerks, the aides, the bailiffs, the janitors, the social workers, all of them. Everyone except YOU. And YOU are paying the bill!

Most of these cases could be decided in a month, but the system needs to drag on for the benefit of the courts, not the families, who tragically have to come here. I've heard the conversations of lawyers and judges about their clients, and they're not very complimentary. I've even heard the judge agree to punish 'that no-good S.O.B.' and have both attorneys agree. Lawyers only make money if they work together against their clients. I know that sounds ridiculous, but these guys will go golfing together after court using the money that they will coerce out of their clients who get caught up in this unjust quagmire."

Fair play? Hardly. Better read: *A Family Divided* by Mendelson.

The next time you hear about the terrible back-log in the number of divorce cases that are pending, please look that person in the eye and tell them 'A pox on you and *your* family!' The greatest amount of damage to the American family is done by domestic courts across the nation, and the greatest theft of wealth (from which most families never recover) is stolen by these degenerate judges and lawyers.

The Ironclad Contract.

Another lawyer once told me that there is not a single contract that cannot be broken. I asked him to tell me more. He told me the reality is that most contracts are so poorly written that you could drive a truck through them. He told me that one of the great ironies about laws, passed through Congress, is that they are purposely written to produce work for lawyers. Wiggle words, poorly defined words, obscure sentences are all fodder for millions of dollars of legal work. Lawyers love it when Congress passes new laws because it means decades of job security for millions of otherwise useless, unemployable lawyers.

Let's say that you have an ironclad legal contract and someone wants to break that contract. First they will hire an attorney who will fire the first shot to let you know that you are about to incur massive legal fees to defend what you think will be protected by the courts. This will be your first mistake: the self-righteous position of knowing that you are right, and therefore, have nothing to fear. Then your opponent will file a suit followed by the request for documents, order for depositions, filing of briefs—all to protect an *ironclad* contract. Now it's getting expensive and your attorney makes it clear that you will be asking for attorney fees and costs as part of the penalty for having to defend this litigation. Your lawyer tells you not to worry; it's ironclad! The courts assign a judge—unfortunately one who has made negative rulings against your company in the past. Your opponent's lawyer asks for delays and more depositions. The costs are clearly in the hundreds of thousands of dollars and the whole darn contract is only worth half a million. Then they provide witnesses who have nothing to do with the contract but are listed as challengers to the validity of the whole contract process. The judge holds a meeting in her chambers with just the lawyers and berates the defendants' attorneys for wasting time on her court docket. She wants a compromise and a settlement before this whole mess goes to court. She insinuates that the defendants need to compromise, settle, and pay legal fees, or she will come down hard if it goes to court.

Another ironclad contract crushed by a corrupt court, a lazy ignorant judge, and a clever set of lawyers who count on the court system having nothing to do with truth, impartiality and integrity. Unfortunately, this event really happened and the lawyer told me the story with all the pride that he could muster. He told me he makes the big bucks because "they ain't no rules in a knife fight, and they ain't no judge that can't be bought!" The settlement was over $350,000 and he took 60%. Fees were not on contingency and his client got money that he really didn't deserve. The decision could never be appealed because it was settled and sealed. Let the games continue.

Some reading this chapter may be tempted to claim these are merely stories of 'bad apples' in the legal profession and these people are being sanctioned and removed. However, the people who make those decisions are all lawyers who sit on Supreme Court review boards in every state. Even lawyers, who have stolen millions of dollars from clients' estates, have only received a slap on the wrist. The system is corrupt to the core. The lawyers in this country have stolen more money than all the organized crime syndicates put together. It must be changed, or the promise of freedom in our Constitution will remain just a Fairy Tale for suckers.

A judge in Akron, Ohio used the money collected for court fees to buy a new car for himself and one for his son. When it was discovered that he had done this, a complaint was filed. After a short investigation, the prosecutor stated that there was no violation of law because there were no stated limitations for what the court fees could be used. He did say that it didn't look good, but that was just a personal, and not a legal, opinion.

I will admit that it's the ninety-eight percent bad lawyers that give the other two percent a bad name.

The legal system in America is broken and cannot be repaired. It must be destroyed and rebuilt brick by brick, or the grave injustice meted out every day in America will never be set right.

The problem lies with lawyers. There has **never been a lawyer** in the United States of America **who has not cheated a client** out of money and there are thousands of ways to do it. From fraudulent billable hours to stealing from estates to incompetent work to unnecessary filings to unconscionable and unjustified delays to coercion to secret agreements with other attorneys to outrageous lies and scenarios to manipulation of trusts to unnecessary lawsuit filings, lawyers find the means to deceive and steal.

Hundreds of law firms involved in work with our governments charge for more billable hours than there are hours in a year. It is standard practice, but highly illegal, immoral and unconscionable.

They control the judicial system from A to Z. The courts have become nothing more than a giant ATM for easy withdrawals by lawyers.

Since judges are lawyers, therefore the scum that rises. Judges aren't really elected; they are preselected by powerful lawyers who have a lock on the system. Lawyers want judges who understand that the courts are money machines for lawyers. They want partisan judges as long as their views align with the lawyers. They want judges who clearly understand that they will only stay on the bench if they stay in the good graces of the power brokers who put them there.

These judges couldn't make a living practicing law, and they choose clerks who usually graduated at the bottom 5% of their class. Judges always seem to have strong political, religious, and generally biased views in sync with the brokers who got them there.

Ninety nine percent of what average people will ever know and experience about the court system in America happens on the local level. This is where the lawyers wring the last few pennies out of their clients. A major cause of poverty in America is a result of what the local courts steal from average citizens, day in and day out: divorce proceedings, speeding tickets, estates, trusts, parking tickets, employment violations, petty disputes, theft of property, and the list continues. What the lawyers don't steal, the courts will take.

The system is broken and corrupt. Please read: *Presumed Guilty: Why Innocent People are Wrongly Convicted* by Yant.

If a person doesn't like a judge's ruling then they can just appeal it, right? They can hire a new lawyer (more scum), be assigned a new judge (more scum), and submit new filings and briefs to new clerks (more scum). All this just to wait through delays while charges add up and the appeal is eventually rejected by more lawyers—appropriately dressed in black to signify the death of justice in America. These are, for the most part, cronies and political hacks who understand that certain issues will never be heard because they would hinder the agenda of the ruling party. Abortion, labor, employment, environment and other issues like these will never see the light of day. These political hacks will see to that. **The courts have never been in a search for the truth.** In fact, they all have a standing army of over 10,000 that will rise up at even a hint of truth trying to enter the sacred halls of justice.

Appellate judges—even though they have never had an original idea in their heads—can faithfully recite the political, religious, and bigoted party lines that got them there.

How do you know how a particular judge on the Supreme Court will rule, even before any evidence is presented? NON-PARTISAN judges don't exist. Through the appointment hearings in the Senate, it became easy to figure out why these people had been nominated and exactly where they stood on all the major issues of the day. When I volunteered for a political campaign, I met a powerful lawyer from a prestigious law firm involved in the process. I know because he told us that he was "a powerful lawyer" from "a prestigious law firm." He made statements about how our candidate was going to do this and that after being elected to office. I told him that I was a little uncomfortable about over-promising and not being able to deliver after the election. A lot of these issues had to be decided by the courts and, therefore, was not a slam dunk. He retorted, "Not a problem." We don't *rent* judges, we *own* them! I told him that I had a hard time accepting a level of corruption that would rival anything even the Mob was doing. He mentioned five issues before the Ohio Supreme Court. He told me what the decisions would be and who they had in their pockets on each issue. He told me that certain judges were up for re-election and therefore vulnerable and compliant. He was bragging. Unfortunately, he was absolutely correct. I will never work on a political campaign again. But it did make me realize that if we don't change the system, it will destroy us!

Just a little bit of this tragic history of our 'Supreme' Court: *Inherently Unequal – The Betrayal of Equal Rights By the Supreme Court 1865-1903* **by Goldstone.**

Justice used to be a right. Then it became a privilege. Then it became a privilege for the few who could afford it. Now it only belongs to the elite. Please read *With Liberty and Justice for Some – How the Law is Used to Destroy Equality and Protect the Powerful* by Greenwald. And then, never turn back to your personal enslavement.

With absolute corruption at the top, what are the chances that the judges' underwear is any cleaner at the bottom, on the local level? Not a chance.

Judges make rulings based on nearly everything but fact. Republican, Democrat, Catholic, Protestant, white, black, ties to a tobacco or an auto manufacturing state. Whatever their demographics, the law and case before them is totally irrelevant. They will decide on the basis of personal history, bias, and prejudice. Thousands of cases presented before the Supreme Court of the United States have been decided on bases that have nothing to do with justice! These deluded fools claim to be unbiased supporters of the Constitution during the confirmation process. Yet, we have suffered these fools for over 200 years.

A SOLUTION

- ✓ Separate the profession of lawyers from the Justice system of America. Create a chasm that there will be absolutely no avenues to cross over.
- ✓ Never again should a lawyer be allowed to serve as a judge in the United States of America.
- ✓ Since most of the judges today are incompetent, lazy and partisan hacks. When elected they go through three days of orientation, in most states, and then, OJT the heck out of the public. This must be replaced with rigorous certification.
- ✓ Establish a special college for the training of judges in which no lawyer, law professor, or politician would be allowed to attend. The thoroughness of the training would be enforced through internships, residencies, clerkships, research grants and observational assignments.
- ✓ The New Judicial System would be intensively educational. Only graduates with the highest qualifications will ever sit on the bench. Judges will be evaluated quarterly, and every case will be scrutinized for juris prudence. Every judge will be required to attend three months of intensive postgraduate education every three years.
- ✓ Any judge who leaves this Judicial System will be banned from studying law as a career for ten years and will also be banned from working for any law firm, directly or indirectly, for a minimum of five years.
- ✓ No lawyer would be allowed to serve in any function in any part of the Justice system. All courts—municipal, night, district, domestic, appellate, probate, supreme—would be required to have a certified judge.

- ✓ Since 99% of the general public's exposure to the legal system is at the very local level, they will receive the finest and most just system in the world. A system that will be subject to continual improvement every single day of the year.
- ✓ All lawyers would remain officers of the court and would be under a strict code of ethics enforced through the justice system. Additionally, all bills of service must be submitted to the courts by way of registered U.S. mail for approval before being submitted to any client. A violation of billable hours would be subject to loss of license and incarceration.
- ✓ The United States would be divided into ten judicial districts. Each district would have a board of twenty certified judges, each serving on the bench at the same time. Each judge would serve a term of only five years and cannot serve on a district board again until a five year period has elapsed. Discipline, for all judges in the district, will be handled by this Board. No political appointees will ever be allowed to serve in the Justice System of the United States.
- ✓ No judge can remain in the same Judicial District for more than fifteen years.
- ✓ This Board will oversee the thorough and extensive training of all judges. The end result will be a competent judge sitting on every bench in America.
- ✓ No judge will ever be allowed to sit on the bench of any court for more than ten years. No judge will ever be allowed to be a judge in his home community.
- ✓ No judge may belong to any political party, religious organization (other than attending services), social club, country club, social movement, or boards of directors.
- ✓ Judges will run their courts with an iron fist. Dates will be set and kept. Filings will be timely and follow legal guidelines. Lawyers will be fined heavily for abuse of standardized procedures. Divorces will be heard and settled within six weeks. Civil cases of less than $10,000 will be heard and settled in less than eight weeks. Liability cases will be thoroughly documented, heard, and settled within ten weeks. Night courts will be established which will clear all petty matters within a week of presentation and the

night courts will remain open—up to 16 hours a day—to clear the entire docket.
- ✓ A special committee will be established to review all laws on the books in every community in America. All archaic, clearly unconstitutional, or foolish laws will be stripped from the law code. It is estimated that over 90% of the present laws will be easily targeted for this cleansing.
- ✓ There will be no more manipulation of the justice system by lawyers ever again. Every lawyer must be certified to practice law in each area of specialty (wills, divorce, corporate, liability, labor, employment, etc.). There will be no general practice lawyers. Getting a law degree and passing the Bar will no longer suffice. A person must actually practice the law to be a lawyer. If someone becomes a politician, corporate legal advisor, or any other job, that person will no longer be allowed to practice law in the New Justice System. The courts will assume that their skills have diminished, and they will no longer be able to credibly do work for their client. Each lawyer must submit the amount of billable work that they performed during the previous year. If there were none, then the lawyer must go through the process of becoming re-certified.
- ✓ Every lawyer must be available for jury duty. Every member of the lawyer's law firm must be available for jury duty. Every lawyer must contribute 5% of their previous year's billable hours for pro-bono assignments from the court.
- ✓ When there is a vacancy on the Supreme Court, the Ten Districts will each elect one delegate from their District who will meet with the other delegates. These ten judges will examine the vita of judges considered to be the best in the profession. They will then choose ten candidates whose names they will submit to the President of the United States. The President will then choose five candidates from the list to be submitted to the Senate and a final choice will be made by the Senate. The division of power will be preserved.
- ✓ The Term of Office for the chosen Supreme Court Judge will be ten years. No candidate for this honored position can have any conflicts of interest, whatsoever, in their personal life. No member

of their family can be politically active or belong to any of the groups to which the judge could not belong. A judge can only serve on the Supreme Court for one term of ten years and then can never serve on the Supreme Court again.

- ✓ No judge can own any stocks. No person who has ever attended law school or worked for a law firm can ever participate in the new selection of judges or become one.
- ✓ No judge can have their name attached to any building or school. If they want to understand real honor, they should go to the CIA headquarters and observe the wall, which honors all the great heroes who gave their lives for their country and will remain anonymous forever.
- ✓ After each trial, the judge will complete evaluation forms for each defense attorney and prosecutor and evaluate the jury's verdict. The competency of counsel, the proficiency of the state's representatives, and the judgment of the truth, fairness and justice of the verdict will then be sealed and can only be opened by a supervisory panel, which will hear any appeal of the verdict. This process of evaluation will enable the system to better determine whether the system has fulfilled its purpose to bring justice to citizens and fairness to process.
- ✓ Cameras will not be permitted in the courtroom so the focus remains on the trial itself.
- ✓ Lawyers, judges, and jury members will not be allowed to speak with the media. A violation of this rule will be met with harsh penalties.
- ✓ Each community will have a standing pool of 300 vetted jurors who will be ready to hear the next case. There will be no more use for jury consultants. The pool will always maintain the 300 level throughout the current court session. At the time of trial, a court officer will pick 24 names at random from the pool. These names and their vetted information will be forwarded to both sides in the trial. Each side may remove four names. Of the remaining 16, the judge will select at random the 10-12 that will comprise the sitting jury and the remaining persons will serve as alternates. A

"jury of one's peers" will, again, return to the notion of average citizens sitting in judgment of truth and justice.

A book: *We the Jury…the Impact on Our Basic Freedoms* by Lehman. Please read this book and see what we could have had, but have lost to history.

- ✓ The Grand Jury System will be instituted in every community. No lawyer may ever enter this hallowed space for any reason.
- ✓ Every judge in America will be drug tested monthly. No one will sit in judgment who does not surrender to enforcement of all of the laws. Every judge in America will be audited by the IRS every year and 'ignorance of the law' will be no excuse.

Let's make a decision to hold all lawyers accountable. Let them practice real law, a great centerpiece for the freedoms which we all cherish. Let's do it right and do it now.

Let's help our lawyer friends to regain some sense of dignity and decency in America.

One last issue: There is a constant drumbeat for tort reform. We have to protect citizens from the occasional abuses, which they suffer in our society. To do that we will need to say something about the worthless bureaucrats who make up our governmental agencies. There are supposed to be so many protections for citizens all along the way with new laws, enforcement and fairness that there should never be any doubt as to the safety of citizens. The **FDA (Food and Drug Administration)** is supposed to protect us from being poisoned by drugs or foods that we have legally brought into our homes. When a drug company continues to advertise and sell a drug which they know causes heart attacks, they are only partly responsible for this happening. The executives in the FDA were supposed to perform oversight and enforcement. The FDA claims they do no testing because they are understaffed yet hundreds of doctors wrote to the FDA about the problems with Vioxx and the FDA chose not to act. The work created for external lawyers should have been totally unnecessary. If the

FDA had been doing their jobs, this would have been caught years before plaintiffs' lawyers started drooling over multi-billion dollar settlements. The agency could have put a stop to the manufacture and sale of this killer drug. The FDA could have stopped production, determined level of liability, and compensated victims. That's what a government agency is tasked with doing.

And to the heads of the FDA for not performing their duties to protect the citizens of the United States, the top ten officials will be fired immediately! The next ten officials will have their wages reduced by 40%, immediately. Hello, is anybody listening! Somebody died. No more! Never again! If someone dies in the public, then someone in government is going to pay with their career.

It would be easy to reform tort through every agency of the U.S. Government. **Energy Department.** Where the heck were you when BP got their plans approved for their deep water drilling project? Not a single degenerate bureaucrat in the energy department lost his/her job, or was reprimanded, or even demoted! The cost to the citizens of America was in the billions, and much of it will never be recovered in a lifetime.

The top ten officials at the energy department should have been fired, immediately! The top ten government inspectors in the energy department with responsibility for the oil fields should have been fired!

Hello, is anybody listening?! All claims for damages should have been filed through the Energy Department with a simple two page form and no lawyers. The Energy Department should have sent out notice, to all companies even remotely connected to this disaster that they would need to set up reserve accounts amounting to $500 billion in total.

There is not a single person in the **SEC (Securities and Exchange Commission)** who is not a person whose interests are not in conflict with the citizens of the United States! Madoff was just the tip of the iceberg. Insider trading is so common, that it is on the menu in over 100 restaurants in NYC alone! The SEC is supposed to do oversight. They should be required to register every single complaint that comes into their office, and file a copy with the Justice Department. The top twenty-five officers of the SEC should be forced to resign for every complaint that was not followed up on, that resulted in an investor loss of one million dollars or more. No one should serve on the SEC Board for more than four years. And absolutely no one should ever be allowed to move from the SEC Board to another governmental post in a period of less than eight years. All complaints of illegal activities should be submitted to the SEC, where damages will be assessed, and paid from their fines of financial entities! (Again, no lawyers please, we don't really need you!) Did anyone ever hear about the fraudulent rating of swaps and mortgage values? Apparently the SEC remained clueless until just yesterday, when a bellboy asked the Chairwoman if she had ever heard about the swaps and she replied, "It sure was news to me!" She may have been distracted, however, because Greenspan was standing next to her, with his hand on her posterior, and mumbling something about how it fooled everyone! There are enough laws and standard practices on the books, they just need to be enforced.

The Alcohol Tobacco and Firearms agency is within the **Department of Justice.** Don't get me wrong, they have stopped the importation of grenade launchers in 'groups of a thousand', dead in their tracks. There are millions of illegal small arms in every city in America and they just can't seem to get a handle on the problem. So, let's make them responsible for getting these small arms under control. Anyone who owns a gun which is used in a crime goes to jail, no exception. And every gun owner must be fully insured, up to one million dollars, to cover the liability of injured persons and property, because of the misuse of said gun. The ATF can collect the insurance money, and compensate victims. See, no need of lawyers here, either. An unregistered gun, in the hands of anyone, is an act of terrorism with a punishment up to, and including death. This agency should have a goal of taking 'one million' illegal guns off of the street by next January. If not, the top five execs will lose their jobs, next February!

The USDA. There is not a reason in the world why salmonella or E. coli should ever make it to market. Companies have to be self-responsible and our government has to punish them when they fail to do so. If someone dies, the top ten officials at USDA will lose their jobs immediately. Any claims of damages will be filed with the USDA and paid from their fines.

Mine Safety. Talk about a joke. I've got a good one for you. Anyone dies in a mine in the US and the manager of the mine, and the CEO of the parent company, will be charged with manslaughter. Is anyone, at all, in this agency looking out for the welfare of these miners. Each, of the last ten presidents, has sent condolences to the families of dead miners. Enough is enough. Some of these useless bureaucratic place-holders must follow through on their regulatory jobs.

There will be no need for lawyers because the agencies will be charged with collecting the claims and paying out from the fines of the companies, which have violated the law.

If we get every agency to do their job and follow-up when damages occur, then we will have eliminated the need for tort and our courts will be free to practice justice again.

Patent Law. In America it is every man for himself and the little guy gets crushed in the system.

This is a government agency, which should exercise oversight and protection for American citizens, but doesn't. I could list thousands of inventors in American history, who have never gotten a dime from their creative inventiveness, but had the proceeds, instead, stolen by clever lawyers and entrepreneurial thieves.

The British system is much better. All patents belong to the Queen and Queens don't take kindly to theft. So if anyone tries to steal your idea from you and your new partner (the Queen), they are going to be in royal trouble. We could do that here in America. We could partner with the US Government. No lawyers needed. The Patent Bureau will take care of all that for you, because they are your new partner. Anywhere in the world, when anyone tries to steal your idea and make money from it, you will have the protection of your partner, Uncle Sam. In fact, the term "royalty" comes from the payment for use of patent rights.

Some tragic patent stories:

Story of Goodyear: An Inventor's Obsession and the Struggles for a Rubber Monopoly by Korman.
The Telephone Patent Conspiracy of 1876. The Elisha Gray – Alexander Graham Bell Controversy and Its Many Players by Evenson.
The Story of Television: The Life of Philo T. Farnsworth by Evenson.

Even Bill Gates has admitted stealing from Steve Jobs, but that's OK, because Steve learned well enough to steal from Samsung and others. Karma? Nah! Not really. Just stealing and hundreds of lawyers have gotten long-term employment just fighting over very simple ownership concerns.

We have all these bureaucratic agencies in the US government, and now it's time for them to step up and do their jobs, with the side benefit of practically eliminating the need for tort. **Now that's tort reform!**

In the next chapter we talk about the fabric of our society. With so much lying going on in church, in congress, and in the courts, you would think that there couldn't be much other damaging stuff going on. But you would be wrong. The divisions that we will disclose next, in many ways, are by-products of the lies of all of these institutions. Underneath the ugliness of lies is the hatred that has been endemic since the religionists first killed their neighbors back home!

CHAPTER 21

The LIE of Race, Gender, Ethnicity, and Nationality

The Lie of Race and Gender

There is no such thing as "race." This label is a tragic contrivance, a human fabrication that attempts to categorize the world into recognizable and usable data—usually for malicious purposes.

When persons use a label like this, they believe that it gives them a quicker and easier understanding of the world. Quite the opposite is true; it leads to erroneous assumptions and, devastatingly, to high levels of hate and discrimination.

Imagine a black person. What do you picture? Chances are, your mind has already jumped to hundreds of erroneous conclusions because the image you concocted is likely based only on stereotypes.

This person is an aboriginal. Your mind quickly advances to further conclusions, which are equally erroneous, but nevertheless, you feel fairly comfortable that your mind is feeding you accurate and useful information about this person. You may even have a clearer picture in your mind, which narrows quite significantly the possibilities of who this person might be, and at a minimum look like. You know you are getting really close to a definitive idea about who I am talking about.

This person has a graduate degree and serves on Company Boards in Australia. This person speaks six languages and is married with two children. Has your image changed at all since you first realized that this person is 'black'? Probably not much. Our prejudices around the LIE, which is RACE, are deep, and so indelible, that the bias against this person was already activated when the term 'black' was first applied. But there is no such thing as race. It is nothing more than a destructive lie. It builds walls between human beings that are not rational and destroy any real hope of peace on earth.

This person is a woman. This makes it even worse. Prejudice and bias against blacks and women have placed over half the human race at a decided disadvantage. And we all pay the price from lost opportunities, productivity and the creative energy of billions of our fellow human beings.

You probably want me to start over with another example and give you a chance to prove that race and gender labels are not all that pre-determining or as destructive as it seems. Can't do that. We have too much history of this kind of pre-judging and hate to not know what has really taken place. Maybe a new generation will reject all this race nonsense, before it destroys the world.

I have gone into more detail in other parts of the book about the Lie of Gender. It is not that gender does not exist, it is just that gender has always been used to discriminate and destroy. A woman in America has thousands of disadvantages —many of which are hidden. A woman in the Middle East has thousands of disadvantages that are glaring and cruel. The boxes 'male' or 'female' have no place on any form being filled out in the civilized world!

The Lie of Ethnicity

Imagine a Serb. What do you know about this person? Chances are you don't know anything about this person at all, yet your mind already jumped to a number of conclusions. These conclusions would be tragically wrong and would only serve to build a wall between you and this person, depending on your own background.

This person is extremely religious. Oh, oh. We got problems here. We know about 'very religious' people who are Serbian.

This person is a weapons expert—qualified at the highest levels of marksmanship.

You still know very little but when assumptions are tied to ethnicity, problems multiply. We want to quickly make sense of the world, even when it gives us a totally erroneous sense of the world.

There is no such thing as ethnicity. It is a meaningless concept. At the microscopic DNA level, it may have some value in understanding disease or disease susceptibility, but at the macro, social level it is totally worthless, baseless, and has led to destructive biases and prejudices.

This person lives in America. Yeah, but where are the true loyalties? We have to ask that. We have to consider these questions because our prejudice cannot be complete without more biased information, which can complete the suspicion that has already been set off by our preconceived ideation. An extremely religious Serbian, who is a weapons expert, living in America. What religion is it? It really matters. Does it?

Do you know anything about this person at all? You formed opinions based on a biased knowledge of ethnicity and you are wrong.

This person has always been an American. In fact, he only found out that he had Serbian heritage through a genealogy site just last month. He served in Iraq and received two Purple Hearts for his heroic service. He is a devoted follower of the Assembly of God church—not that it matters but you likely made an incorrect assumption. He is missing one leg from the war. He has adopted two special needs children to honor a pledge he made to God when he saw the terrified children in that village in Iraq. But his so-called ethnicity would have subjected him to unwarranted prejudice, discrimination, and hate.

The labels go on forever. We think the labels give us understanding, but they leave us deeper in our own ignorance. Irish, Polish, Venezuelan,

Palestinian, Puerto Rican, Mexican, Chinese. These labels are vapid and meaningless. They tell us absolutely nothing. The U.S. Government must stop labeling people in their census and in the myriad bills written by Congress. We are all human. That should be enough.

When people are introduced with the artificial labels, walls are built and we stop prospering from each other's lives. Labels are misleading and ignorant and the users of labels are lazy, shallow persons, who need to be avoided at all costs, for the sake of sanity, if nothing else.

Ethnicity and Nationality are sometimes seen as being closely related, but there are subtle differences that divide and destroy while the power-elites of the world insist that borders are necessary for the safety of the world.

The Lie of Nationality

Nationality comes from the arbitrary drawing of lines on a map. That's it! Over time, those lines are redrawn, time and time again. The people within those lines are told their nationality and that they better obey the government which drew those lines. If you lived in Texas, before it was stolen from Mexico by the United States, you were a Mexican, then a Texan, but the next day you were an American. Puerto Ricans are Americans because Puerto Rico is a protectorate of the United States. This gets confusing because they don't look American! In America we do a magic trick. We take people of different nationalities from all over the world and we turn them into Americans through a process called citizenship. They, however, have to give up their previous citizenship. Once you step inside these drawn lines, 'presto change-o', you have a new nationality.

This can only mean that nationality is an arbitrary designation, which means anything that world leaders want it to mean. Why are there hundreds of wars going on right now because of border disputes? Because you can't really hate someone until you know their nationality. Let's get the borders straight so we can more carefully align our hatred toward them. Just imagine how complex this is going to get when Israel moves their borders back to what they were in 1967. Who's 'in' and who's 'out'? And when can we start killing again?

Hatred based on nationality is getting so complex that it is turning ordinary citizens into psychopathic stress-bags. We all hate Iraqis, right? But wait; thousands of them came to the United States and did the magic citizenship thing, so now they're American. But they don't look like "us." They look, and act, like "them." Is it okay to continue hating them? What is *nationality* good for if it doesn't sort out the hated from the haters?

Nationality is a worthless designation. It is meaningless and tells us nothing. It teaches us that what we thought was the purity of our Nationality (White, Anglo-Saxon, Protestant) was always a myth, a LIE, a fabrication of some narrow, degenerate minds.

However, with education and openness, truth will eventually have a chance to bring about world peace.

I have stated that Jews, Christians, and Moslems—included not as *labels* but self-designations—have been proficient haters and killers throughout history, but if you want to find a group which has become really good at it, you've got to read the following book:

Why I Am Not a Hindu by Ilaiah.

They don't even have to kill the body, they just get really good at demoralizing, discriminating and denying every natural right of humans!

The next chapter speaks to the issue of overcoming tyranny, and the many false starts, which have only led to more disappointment. Morally courageous leadership might have changed all this in history, but leaders were few, and the task was often insurmountable.

CHAPTER 22

Truth is Truth A Lie is A Lie Hypocrisy is Hypocrisy Debauchery is Debauchery

Words have meaning. We are too easily led astray by the misuse of words and quite often that misuse is quite intentional on the part of the speaker. How often have we heard someone say 'well, I was taken out of context?' If you don't call a thing what it is, then you have not identified it. If you allow religionists to always use excuses for their misbehavior ('well, we're all just sinners anyway') while condemning others for the same behavior, then madness and insanity have become the norm. If we allow politicians to use one obfuscation after another not to answer very simple, straightforward questions, then we almost deserve the outcomes that we suffer under. If we act like gullible sheep, then we have to accept the fact that we will someday be dinner.

Martin Luther King, Jr. was the leader of an important movement, one that was essential to the progress of a truly free society.

However, he was NOT a great man. He lied through school. He lied to his wife and family. He cheated on his wife. He degraded others for his physical pleasures. He was famous among his followers for holding sex orgies and using prostitutes.

Although his private life was inconsequential to his work with civil rights, he presented himself as a LIE to his followers. King gave eloquent speeches about how citizens were forced into demeaning, low-wage work by the forces of discrimination. He decried how those in power took advantage of the poor in our society. Yet he justified hiring prostitutes who were forced into demeaning work because of their circumstances. He refused to acknowledge that he was the power broker and they were the disadvantaged victims of poverty. On the day he died, he talked of the terrible injustice that was being done to the garbage collectors in Memphis, who were at a great disadvantage because of these same kinds of discrimination. Rumors suggest that he was returning from a sexual tryst shortly before he was shot.

Of course, King would never have allowed that life for his own daughters. He spoke of truth and yet lied to his wife on whom he repeatedly cheated. King was, and always will be, one of the great hypocrites of history.

Unfortunately, a devoted follower of King who continued his public and private legacy is Jesse Jackson. He used his power to destroy the lives of his sexual victims. Jackson even used tax exempt 501(c) 3 contributions to pay for his illegitimate child, bought a home for his prostitute, and sent her generous sums to keep her mouth shut. Now, for the rest of us, that would be a felony and we would be in jail. We would not be able to manipulate the authorities with the threat of racial unrest if we were jailed.

Falling into the same deceptive path is Al Sharpton, a man who would yell "fire" in a theater just to get attention. Tawana Brawley was his creation, pure and simple. He lies for a living. He stirs up his less intelligent followers to become enraged at every made-up and imaginary slight. He is not always wrong, but it is more on the scale of the 'even a blind squirrel can find an acorn in the forest on occasion.' Sharpton dines with the elite and wears thousand dollar suits, but he makes his living manipulating and 'playing' the role of friend of the poor.

Liars are liars, hypocrites are hypocrites, debauched persons are debauched persons. They will always attach themselves to just causes and charities, because that becomes the best place for them to hide! Three of these individuals claim to be 'ordained' Christian ministers. Maybe we are wrong in expecting something better from them.

Unfortunately, thousands of honorable individuals fought for these same causes and you will never know their names, sacrifices, or the good that they have accomplished for us all. Liars make better MEDIA coverage and blood sells.

In order to achieve progress in a free society, citizens must commit to stop watching NBC, ABC, CBS, CNN, FOX, and MSNBC. These media outlets will always pander to the unsophisticated listeners in the public and attach importance to non-events on slow news days. They will forever interview Jesse Jackson, Al Sharpton, Bill Clinton, and other people who should not be granted access to a microphone or an audience. One has to remember that the national media audience, out of laziness, is just looking for sound-byte quotes to justify their illiterate thoughts.

According to most media outlets, Bill Clinton became an expert on everything after he left office. When he was President he couldn't talk his way out of a sex scandal, yet now he gives speeches about the wonders of democracy and justice—for exorbitant fees—to free societies like Qatar, Kazakhstan, and so on. It is now a proven fact that Bill Clinton and Robert Rubin, in consort with Alan Greenspan, did more to damage the world economy than any other persons in history! Just read *Reckless Endangerment* by Morgenson and then give me a call.

Please read: *Unequal Justice: Wayne Dumond, Bill Clinton, and the Politics of Rape in Arkansas* by Reel. But only if you would like to have a truer picture of our former president.

Why do we allow these losers to run our country? We have institutionalized our presidents as LIAR IN CHIEF, and we may never get away from that pathetic standard.

We glorified our civil rights leaders, but their flaws almost guaranteed that they would undercut the movement from truly being successful. In so many ways minorities in America are in a worse situation now than they have ever been. A few bright spots will never negate the sufferings of millions. Someone with honor and integrity must step forward and bring us back to reason and purpose. Only when our glorious Constitution moves us to fulfill its clearly unfinished business will we be "free at last."

Please read: ***My Bondage and My Freedom* by Douglass.** Frederick Douglass was one of the greatest Americans of all time! He was single-handedly responsible for 'shaming' Abraham Lincoln into, finally, writing the Emancipation Proclamation. If Douglass had been around in the 1960's, our nation would have made much greater progress. MLK was unworthy to even carry this man's dirty underwear.

Discrimination goes beyond societal lunacy. In the next chapter we will explore the inequality of the tax system, which enslaves and destroys the hopes of most Americans. The Tax System is a perfect formula for rewarding the rich and punishing everyone else. Read on and let the lies of taxation harken back to the days of the original tea-party bandits.

CHAPTER 23

The United States Personal Income Tax System isn't FAIR

The tax system in the United States is not fair, equal, or even rational. So what do we do?

First we have to acknowledge our own part in this mess because we elected those degenerate, depraved people to represent us ever since the first Income Tax law was passed almost 100 years ago. Our representatives took advantage of the law, doing favors for friends, political contributors, and lobbyists to win favors and contributions. As long as we allow these degenerates to handle money, they will steal from us by making laws to benefit their own bank accounts. These sickos are still there because they crave the *filthy lucre* which they can get by betraying their constituents, and the great mass of American citizens.

To stop the insanity we must first start by having all elections funded by the public and the rules strictly enforced by the elections commission and courts. We'll talk more about this later.

Tax Law can be greatly simplified by removing political influence from the equation. Each congressperson, senator, and president has influenced changes to the tax law to help their friends and contributors. All that must end.

No more deductions for any purpose whatsoever.

There used to be a deduction for sales tax on the purchase of a motor vehicle. Guess who got that into law? There is a special deduction for farmers – sometimes to NOT plant crops – guess who got that put into the law? There is a deduction for interest payments on a home mortgage. Guess who got that into the Code? The stronger the lobby, the greater benefit. Most of these are recognizable, but I could have quoted thousands of totally unknown deductions that would be shocking to most any sane person.

You would absolutely be shocked at what deductions corporations get for giving out the goodies to their executives….tickets to major sporting events, trips to luxurious resorts to talk about business over the phone, while romping with their families on the beach, personal grooming…. and on and on.

In order for our government to run, politicians must set a fixed amount of money each year to be collected from all of us through taxes. When one person or group gets a deduction, the amount owed by all is not lessened, but shifts to all the others. If large numbers of people or groups get massive deductions, then the tax burden becomes onerous for those who did not. While feckless representatives tell their constituents they are making the world a better place by writing tax write-offs for their friends, they are, in fact, creating an unintelligible 600,000 page tax code that only works to hide the mischief they created to benefit their friends.

We must correct all this criminal activity on the part of our elected representatives. We must take the tax code away from them forever.

No more deductions will be offered for anyone, for any purpose. The government sets the budget for the year and taxes are assessed to meet that budget.

The Tax Code will be simple and straight-forward:

- Income $00.00 to $20,000: No personal income taxes whatsoever for any purpose.

  Try living in America making less than $20,000 a year. It is a great myth in America that anyone can rise above poverty with hard work. The fact is that less than one percent of all persons born into poverty ever rise to the level of financial security. The government is especially efficient at taking 'dollars' from everyone and then giving back 'crumbs'. Yet eighty percent of the wealth created on Wall Street will go to less than one percent of the population – not at the bottom.

- Income $20,001 to $30,000: Tax rate of 10% on the amount over $20,001 only.

This is an effective tax rate of only 3% at maximum.

- Income $30,001 to $50,000: Tax of 10% on the amount $20,001 to $30,000 plus Tax of 20% on the amount $30,001 to $50,000.

This is an effective tax rate of only 10% and covers 83% of American Families.

- Income $50,001 to $100,000: Tax of 10% on the amount $20,001 to $30,000 plus Tax of 20% on the amount $30,001 to $50,000 plus Tax of 30% on amount $50,001 to $100,000.

This is an effective tax rate of only 20% at maximum. Upper middle class families keep 80% of their earnings and probably save thousands of dollars in accounting fees. For example: a family making $80,000 would pay an effective tax rate of only 17.5% or $14,000.

- Income above $100,000:   Tax of 24% on total income.
- Income above $300,000:   Tax of 27% on total income.
- Income above $600,000:   Tax of 31% on total income.
- Income above $1,000,000:   Tax of 34% on total income.

- Income above $5,000,000: Tax of 37% on total income.
- Income above $10,000,000: Tax of 39% on total income.

Social Security, Medicare, and other government-funded programs will be taken out of Gross Receipts (we need transparency back into the system – are we paying our way or not) received and will not be limited by an income ceiling. For far too long the government has been playing 'smoke and mirrors' with borrowing from Trust Funds and the illegitimate printing of money.

Businesses will not pay withholding taxes. However, they will collect taxes, on a pro rata basis, on behalf of the government. They will also be responsible for delineating all perquisites, which are received by employees and are thus taxable. Businesses will collect taxes on behalf of the government, at a pro rata plus 3% basis so that everyone will have to file a return in order to get their money refunded.

- Every citizen must file a return whether or not they have income.
- Since there are no deductions of any kind, the whole process is made much simpler and should be a huge savings of time and money to all citizens. There will be no joint returns because there is an advantage for couples to file separately anyway, since they will each be in a lower tax bracket and taxable amounts are not assessed until after the first $20,000.
- Since there are no deductions for anything, it makes it easier for individuals to make decisions about what is most important in their own lives without the government piling tax burdens on the little guy. Contributing to organizations is a personal decision and others, who do not support your organizations, should not be responsible for picking up the lost taxes. If you want to buy a house, then that will again be a very personal decision that your neighbor will have no added tax burden for you to enjoy.
- The IRS will make an allowance that all filers—who file before the April 15 deadline, pay taxes owed, and have the correct personal information—will be eligible for a drawing to be conducted by PriceWaterhouseCoopers. This lottery will allow 1000 people to

win $100,000 each, 5000 to win $50,000 each, and 10,000 to win $10,000 each. Rewarding individuals for the correct and timely submission of their return will be far less than the cost of agents investigating average citizens. The cost of $450,000,000 for an almost 100% totally compliant tax system will prove to be one of the greatest savings in our history. What does the IRS cost us now? What is the compliance rate, now? What are the enforcement rates? They are clearly not in a range that gives us a fair system of taxation, nor one that encourages compliance.

The best part of this new approach is that it leaves absolutely no room for elected officials to award give-away money to their friends and cronies. Everyone pays and everyone pays according to the same rules. I am not so foolish to believe that the criminals in Congress won't get to work on a way around this, but maybe we might just catch them sooner.

- Every citizen who makes over $50,000,000 will be audited every year.
- The value of any benefit which comes to an employee or executive will be taxed as ordinary income, including health care, use of vehicles, club memberships, tickets to sporting events, etc.
- All bonuses will be taxed at the 50% level. If a corporation does not pay the minimum 20% of gross receipts tax, bonuses will be taxed at the 100% level for all employees receiving bonuses in that year.

It is criminal that one of the five largest corporations in the world (General Electric) paid their top executive a bonus of $13.8 million while the corporation itself paid less in their total taxes the same year. Also note the huge campaign contributions they gave to Obama.

- Deductions will no longer be given for charitable or 501(c) 3 organizations. If these people truly believed in these causes then they will continue to contribute. The largest recipient of religious tax exemptions in the United States is the Roman Catholic Church. On average their constituents give about 1% of their annual income to support their church. This is the largest 'religious' organization receiving the largest amount of 'free' taxpayer funds for their church and then they have the 'nerve' to say that they don't want to have to 'obey' federal laws in the use of these funds. That is the very definition of hypocrisy.

- Consider that Bill and Melinda Gates and Warren Buffett are involved in charitable work in Africa which you, the taxpayer, pay for. They set policy for American taxpayers by supporting various projects in Africa (although these works may, or may not, be laudable) they are conducted without the permission and lawful consent of the persons whose money is used. They do this by not paying taxes on the income that is deducted for "charitable use." Literally billions of dollars are expended by using money which we lost through the present tax system. With all the worthy causes in the United States, they have decided to take their billions offshore. In fact, most of their expenditures have found their way out of the country. Further, they have taken their good fortune in producing wealth in the US and have now become so-called experts in education – with no background in education, whatsoever. They are now using taxpayers' money to affect educational systems around the country and force their scheme for education on our children. Gates, Buffett, and Walton can spend their own money on any project they want, but they can't spend *my* money on anything without my permission. The rich have perfected 'taxation without representation' to an art form.

- Re-institute the Inheritance Tax. All estates are taxed at 50% upon death for estates valued at $1 million or more. Estates valued at less than $1 million are taxed as ordinary income to receiving party. Any citizen may give away a portion of his/her estate while living at any time. All transfers from one person to another will be taxed as ordinary income to the receiving party in the year in which they received it. One exception is that a person may transfer up to 1% of his/her estate to a son or daughter each year with no tax consequences. Anything over the 1% is taxed as ordinary income.

- Any money that is received by an individual—from any source—is considered ordinary income, and that income is taxable at the rate of the person's total income for that year.
- Life insurance proceeds are taxed at the ordinary income level of the recipient. Any life insurance proceeds under the $200,000 level are not taxable.

This has been one of the favorite tax dodges for corporate executives for decades. Corporations buy their executives an expensive life insurance policy, and then offer the proceeds tax free to the beneficiaries. Nice scam, if you can get it. Let's stop the baloney. Pull your own weight. Pay your own way. Stop shifting the tax burden to the everyday citizen. Tax the benefit when it is received by the executive and tax the proceeds when they are received by the recipient.

- No retirement plans will be tax exempt. Money placed into a retirement account, or 401k, is first taxed as ordinary income in the year in which it is received.
- All investments are taxed as ordinary income in the year in which proceeds are received.
- There will be no write-offs for losses on investments. Each investor must use prudence in making his/her own personal decisions.
- Any charity that receives gifts will be taxed at 1% of total. Every charity must file a tax return. If no tax return is filed, then the organization will be taxed at the level of individual personal income based on total receipts.
- No more foundations will be set up in the name of or run by a relative of a congress person—I'm looking at you, Barney Frank.

Politicians use this tactic so that the money they receive is not considered a campaign contribution or bribe—I'm looking at you, James Johnson. Fannie Mae provided this service to so many congressmen that the final total amounted to over $200,000,000 in just one year—just in time for the hearings on privatizing their organization.

- Every corporation will be taxed at 20% of gross revenues. There will be no deductions for any purpose. The government will not be in the business of saving insolvent or poorly managed businesses. These same businesses should cut costs and deliver value to customers, rather than have the government play patty-cake with their executives. No more postponing profits to a later year to avoid taxes. Some corporations have postponed paying taxes for as long as fifty years.
- Corporations cannot move their headquarters to Bermuda to avoid taxes. Any corporation that has shifted headquarters during the last twenty years must still be considered American for tax purposes. Any business which does business in the United States must pay a minimum of 20% of gross receipts for all their operations internationally. If they pay 5% to Japan, then they owe 15% to the US. If they pay 0% to Bermuda, then they must pay 20% to the USA. An international agreement will be established to AUDIT any company records, of any company, which operates under the free trade agreements.
- Any corporation which keeps any funds in a numbered account offshore will forfeit the funds, and the corporation will be dissolved by the courts of jurisdiction in the US. Any bank that keeps numbered accounts for any citizen or corporation in the United States will be barred from doing business in the United States forever. Its subsidiaries and future owners, if they should be sold, will experience the same permanent ban.

Most companies give nothing to charity. The average annual gifts are less than 1% of net profits. At the same time they spend billions telling us how important they are to our communities. Build us roads for free. Give us total tax write-offs for decades. Build larger schools to accommodate the increase in students. Excuse us from paying property taxes. Build treatment plants to discard our toxic effluent. Give us a one week heads-up for any safety inspections of our facilities. Don't bother our executives with traffic violations or any other petty local issues. I lived in a community where an automotive manufacturer was the dominant presence and had almost all of these advantages. The son of the top exec was going 100 miles per hour on a 35 mph street and hit and killed a pedestrian! The police called the exec and encouraged him to get his son out of the country, ASAP, before he could be charged. The exec simply told the police chief to 'fix it now'. "Remember, that we could move our operations out of this flea-bag town, at any time!"

- Personal and business decisions will no longer be based on the tax code and its consequences. Smarter decisions will be made and wiser distinctions can be a part of how we determine value and manage our own affairs without government games.
- When we ask a bank for a loan to buy a house, the banker can no longer rob us by telling us that the huge interest payments are tax deductible. He is forced to give us value for our money by lowering interest rates and fees, both closing and documentation.
- Builders will begin to build more appropriately-sized homes, thus driving a less costly, needs driven market, instead of the 'I've got twenty-three bathrooms, how many do you have?! market.
- A businessman can no longer afford to be sloppy about his decisions. There will be consequences for dumb.
- A broker can no longer deceive you about making up for your losses on the winners, which he is recommending to you now. A loss will mean that you will hurt your family, not the neighbors, who will have to pick up the taxes, which you got out of paying!
- If families want more kids then it is within their rights to have them. However, parents will not be given deductions for each child. Fairness in the new tax system will reward wise choices for those who make decisions based on current resources.
- The insanity will stop immediately. The inmates will no longer control the country.

I believe in paying taxes. I believe in my country. I believe in our government doing what only it can do best. I do not believe in politicians. They are all the worst kind of liars because they have created this mess and refuse to correct it. I have never met an elected official who didn't believe that he or she had not become royalty the first second after being elected.

In one district where I lived, we elected a local barber to Congress. He was not elected to a second term but came to our Rotary meeting and bragged about coming home a millionaire from Washington after only one term. That may have been the only time he ever told us the truth. He went further to say that anyone who is elected to Congress and doesn't become rich is a dimwit. "There are so many buyers for what a congressman has to sell!" I would just like to stop the shopping list of what they have to sell.

We must change these tax laws now. We all know that they are unfair, and we have seen examples of the graft and collusion which drive the system. An acquaintance of mine brags that he hasn't paid taxes in fifteen years. He lives in a house appraised at over $1,000,000. I turned him over to the IRS by writing a formal complaint. I was told—on the basis that it would be denied—that it was true this person did not pay taxes but was strongly protected by political interests because of large contributions to major political candidates.

When the income tax law passed in 1917 only the top 1% of the richest Americans paid any tax at all. Then wars came and the nation needed funds badly to pay for all that lunacy. A complete schmuck, Milton Friedman, got in Roosevelt's ear and they came up with a plan to withhold pay from soldiers serving in the war. His reasoning was that we take the money out first-through payroll deductions - so then we have it. 'Most of these guys may be killed in battle anyway, so they will never ask to get it back, or will only get it back after we have used up the 'time' value of money. It worked so well that they have continued doing it to this very day.

Our government should create a food stamp card for all Americans living under the poverty line. This card would only be issued to families who file an income tax return, whether or not they have income. Their address must be correct, and all the information on dependents must be correct and verifiable. This service would provide recognition that every citizen is entitled to a certain level of nourishment to survive. We are no longer going to give subsidies to farmers of any kind.

Foods grown or manufactured, exclusively, in the United States are eligible to be purchased by this card and no other foods would have the validated barcode to be purchased. Over $200,000,000,000 worth of foods *grown in America* will be purchased through this program, and it would be the most dramatically targeted, direct distribution of benefits in U.S. history. Hot meals in school districts would also be targeted for use by this program. Every penny would go directly back into the economy, and farmers would have a guaranteed return on their efforts.

The present tax system is a lie created by the most depraved kind of liars. It will take courage and the determined pressure of taxpayers to stop the insanity.

As a consultant, I would analyze the 'non-value added' jobs in a client's business. A 'non-value-added' job is any job that does not contribute to the products, services, or profits of a company. Over time, a company will accumulate "feather-bedded" jobs which add nothing to the business's mission and goals. Whole departments—which no longer contribute to the company's future—exist within a company. Sometimes it was advantageous to eliminate those jobs, while at other times, they could more easily be outsourced at a huge savings to the company.

The Tax System of the United States is the greatest producer of non-value-add jobs that the world has ever seen. My proposal will eliminate the need for tax accountants, tax lawyers, tax consultants, tax negotiators, IRS agents, tax courts, and imprisonment institutions for tax violators. It's just going to be a whole lot less taxing on all of us!

The government is far too clever to stop at taxing as a means of getting the last dime out of your pants pocket. They have other schemes: fees—clear or hidden, gambling games, fines, licenses, tolls, pass-through invisible taxes to the target, tariffs, and on and on. Where is the best place to get most of this money? The State, of course. In the next chapter we are confronted with the reality that most states have 'lost their minds'. They are clever about lying to their citizens, about where the money comes from, and where it really goes. They have to lie because the truth would shake citizens to their core. States are bankrupt and have been for decades. State politicians are thieves and liars. Their hands have been in the till so long that it almost seems like it belongs there. They have no intention of balancing budgets or running the government, strictly for the good of the 'people'. They pander to the public with foolish religious palaver or made up controversies, but they never talk about what they are really doing. We only get to read about what they have done years later, or just by reading the next chapter. A word to the wise.

CHAPTER 24

Lies Told by Your State

When I was growing up in the 40's and 50's, all forms of gambling were illegal and even condemned as deeply immoral. The Mafia, in addition to their many crimes, was accused of corrupting society by running illegal gambling games. Gambling did nothing but steal from the elderly and poor as well as corrupt innocent human activities, such as baseball. We put people in jail, sometimes for life, because they were caught gambling. Even private poker games were illegal, and the participants were stigmatized as the worst of the worst in our society.

When my parents were growing up in the 'teens and 20's, alcohol was illegal, and the same criminal elements were at the center of this illicit activity. Can anyone say 'Kennedys'?

Alcohol, gambling, and tobacco, once illegal habits, are today - thanks to the mismanagement of State budgets by incompetent, inept elected officials - essential sources of revenue . Don't misunderstand, they are still villainized, but no state could even hope to gain enough revenue without the taxes and proceeds from these activities.

Motorists driving under the influence have cursed our highways. Cancer from cigarettes has killed millions of Americans and added billions of dollars to medical care costs. Betting is nothing more than a devastating tax on the backs of the poor and the unsophisticated.

In gambling, our states have given two new labels to their citizens: sucker and loser. Think of it as forever walking down the midway of a county fair and placing dollar bets to win a fifty cent toy. Only that return is many times greater than anything the state offers.

99.99% of all people who place their *first* dollar bet will lose more money than they will win over their entire lifetime! This is simple statistics and the state knows this fact. The gamble of choice does not matter—slot machines, casino games, football pools, fantasy sports, lotteries, or bingo. Gamblers do not own the game. That's why they are called gamblers! It is estimated that over twenty-six trillion losing bets have been placed in the last century alone.

Michael Jordan, Charles Barkley, Alex Rodriquez, and others gamble, not because they are rich, but because they are stupid. They could care less that the lesson they are teaching to the unsophisticated will actually destroy lives.

The ones who own or, in some cases, rig the game are another story. They are called elected officials.

Consider the lottery, which is sold in over eighteen states. The odds against buying the winning ticket are listed at over 195,000,000 to 1. This is statistically equivalent to every household in the United States paying their utility bill twice a week, every week of the year, and only having ten homes (on average) annually getting electricity to turn their lights on. **The rest will live in darkness.**

If you played the lottery game every week it would take over two million years—at a minimum—for all of the possible combinations to come up. Can you see what the state is doing to you? They know that you are hurting. They know about high unemployment. They know that your daughter is sick, and that the medical bills are tearing your family apart. So, instead of getting off their feckless rear ends and fixing the economic problems, which they created, they devised this scam to take away your final ten cents. Their solution: Create more lottery games, cut unemployment benefits, raise taxes and then, attend your daughter's funeral. Every state official is personally responsible for this horrible mess, and they will never stop cheating us until we throw them all out.

We need a new law dictating that every elected or appointed official in the state would be required to purchase $50.00 worth of PowerBall Lottery tickets every week. It can be a simple payroll deduction. That would add millions to the state revenues. As we know, "you can't win, if you don't play!" Their chances of winning would be close to zilch, but if one of them does win, the citizens of the State would win doubly since the official would likely resign their position. That is, unless the position already gives them access to millions of unearned dollars already!

'Lotto' is a little better. It only takes about 250,000 years for all the combinations of winning numbers to come up. Some computer programs suggest that it is more likely to take about 16,000,000 years for all the combinations to actually be drawn, but this is not a time for quibbling. Sadly, a lot of people play their kids' birthday numbers and end up blaming their poor kids for being born on the wrong day.

For all the Pick Four fans, the odds are 10,000 to 1! If the state game picks four numbers twice a day, 365 days a years, that's 730 numbers picked out of 10,000 in any given year (not even counting the same numbers being picked more than once) and it would take a minimum of over 13 years to cover all of the combinations. Still, the winner only wins $5,000 if the proper straight bet is placed.

No one ever comes out on top in this scam perpetrated by the state except the state!

Of course, no one who gambles would ever stop after winning just $5,000. That's not enough to be rich, and that certainly would not replace all the money which had been wasted on this game leading up to the win.

The State loves the suckers who play scratch-off games. The stated odds of winning the big prize are just an illusion. Assume that the state produces one million scratch-off cards. Only five percent of these cards are distributed for sale at any given time. The largest winning amount may not even be available to the public because it was not in the cards for sale. The State recognizes that it may make the most money on the game by retiring it before all of the purported large prizes are won. Multiply the odds against winning in this game by a factor of about twenty and it would be closer to your chances. The State never loses. The sucker never wins. It is a tax on the gullible. Fortunately, the state produces these suckers by providing such a poor public education so that mathematically-challenged bettors will tax themselves to death. Of course, these are the same people who scream whenever that state raises sales tax by one penny to actually create public improvements. Don't be fooled by advertisements that declare these funds will go to better education in the state. The gambling money was not an add-on to education; it just replaced the education money in the budget, long, long ago!

Benefits we receive from how our modern state governments are run:

- 325,000 people die every year from the use of alcohol (legal)
- 300,000 people die every year from the use of tobacco (legal)
- 150,000 people die every year form medical malpractice (legal)
- 75,000 people die every year from taking the wrong prescription drug (legal)
- 60,000 people die every year in automobile accidents (legal)
- 10,000 people die every year from use of cocaine (illegal)
- 5,000 people die every year from food poisoning (legal)
- 5,000 people die every year at the hands of a family member (???)
- 1,600 people die every year using marijuana (illegal)

One of these areas receives over $50,000,000,000 per year to control. Which one would you guess that it is? And are our citizens any better off from all this governmental protection? All these funds are used to control a problem that has gotten even worse since the time that the state got involved. Weed and cocaine are everywhere. Rights to privacy have been violated. Violence is present everywhere and the state is bankrupt with few funds left to run a progressive, modern state.

85% of the cocaine and marijuana in the United States is consumed in upper middle class to rich neighborhoods. Arrests for illegal drug possession in these wealthier neighborhoods amount to less than .00001% of all drug arrests in the United States. Representatives, Senators, Sheriffs would never be so stupid as to invade the neighborhoods of their 'true' constituents. And so the poor have the 'jack' boot of the law at their doorstep and the ghost of poverty to contend with to survive. And all the money spent by the state is lost to their great potential futures.

Sad thing is that I could go to Congress today and buy these illegal drugs. They have passed laws that protect them from being searched while 'busy' doing the country's business! But they are there.

LEGAL guns. The state wants everyone to own one and to carry them everywhere. It is extremely rare that a *legal* gun is ever used to protect oneself against the actions of a stranger. And the domestic violence cited above, most of these family members were killed by a 'legal' gun held at the residence.

So the state provides the 'fool' with a losing lottery ticket and a weapon of violence more likely to be used by a member of his own family against a member of his own family.

All this comes right back to the State and the utter neglect which they have shown to the educational system which is one of their primary responsibilities. But as terribly neglected as the schools have been, the fault lies equally with the imbeciles who raise many of our children.

"Daddy, why do you smoke?" "Mommy and daddy smoke, sonny, because we never finished Third Grade. We don't believe all that 'guberment' crap and science stuff about cigarettes. It's a conspiracy to take away the last little pleasure we have left. Why, look at that 96 year old woman, who lived about 14 miles down the road. She smoked a pack a day, every day of her life, and without those sissy filters!"

The next day junior shows up for school. "OK, students, today we're going to look at the impact which DNA has on our immune systems." NOT a snowball's chance in Hades!

Not one single person who smokes can ever be listed as being above average in intelligence.

A special book, just for smokers: *Cigarettes: What the Warning Label Doesn't Tell You* by Meister. Also, *Beyond the War on Drugs* by Wisotsky.

And for all the gamblers, smokers and gun-toters: *The Darwin Awards: Countdown to Extinction* by Northcutt.

Read: *The Numbers Game: The Commonsense Guide to Understanding Numbers in the News, In Politics, and in Life* by Blastland.

There are solutions, but the state would have to shoot itself in the foot to accomplish them. They want us to think that they are already working so hard and these problems are so intractable. Truth is that these problems are never really addressed, they bring too much power to the power elite already in place.

First of all, every child from age seven and up should be taught about the foolishness of gambling, smoking and irrational hatred. They should receive visual demonstrations that clarify the total nonsense of such activities and why people become vulnerable to such schemes. They should be taught that politicians have failed their citizens by incompetently running the affairs of state.

One of the major flaws of our present day society is the lack of consequences for personal behavior. Much of that has been legislated away. There was a time when a student who failed a grade had to repeat that grade again, but this requirement is no more. Now that student is simply passed along to the next teacher. How often have you seen a student graduate who couldn't even read his own diploma?

How many DUIs are needed before the courts get these murderers off the road? It is the repeat offenders who are the 'killers' on the road. These are not 'happy' drunks. They are your neighbors. Whether doctor, laborer, secretary or what not, they will kill you just as dead. The state makes millions off of the sale of booze to them. So why do we read every single day of someone dying in a crash involving an alcoholic who had been arrested multiple times before and NEVER sent to jail. The state got their money, where is our safety?

I had a professor in Graduate School, who told me that I should hope, every day, that I never get lucky, at anything. "The first time that you don't earn what you get or pay the consequences for your behaviors, from that day on, you will always hope to get lucky again." The drive to succeed through personal efforts, and force of will, will be diminished. If you don't study, then failure is the consequence. If you smoke, then you will lose seventeen years off of your life expectancy, on average. If you use illegal drugs, then hundreds of unexpected consequences may come your way, not the least, a visit by the law. Consequences are normal and natural, except when someone intercedes, and takes away the consequences, so that learning and fortitude are stripped away from the individual.

Let's make medical care completely free, so that no one has to take responsibility for any of their personal actions. No one asks about the true costs anymore because it's free. The government will pay for it all. However, it's not "they" who pay, but "us." Every time we pay our taxes, we pay for the legislating away of consequences. Our state government is now in the medical care business – and its 'on demand' by people who will not pay one 'red' cent!

When the government takes away the natural consequences of our behaviors through legislation, they are really saying "We don't believe that you can do it on your own so we'll do it for you." This always becomes a self-fulfilling prophecy. If they think we're stupid, inadequate, incapable, or undesirable, they have no idea how *undesirable* we can become.

Consequences for personal actions enable us to grow, struggle, mature, and thrive. The problems begin when this natural scenario is thwarted.

Our nation has sought for far too long to avoid or deny the natural consequences of our actions in the world. The problem for America is that we simply create new and unintended consequences which are no longer recognizable or even manageable.

For example, we have waged war on:

- The War on Poverty
- The War on Drugs
- The War on Lebanon
- The War on Vietnam
- The War on Weapons of Mass Destruction
- The War on Grenada
- The War on Panama
- The War on the Middle Class

The War on the Middle Class started with a 'shot' by Clinton with Nafta and Glass-Steagall, followed by Bush who increased 'fire power' to destroy opportunities, and then, Obama who is still working on getting the slice out of his golf swing. Just for fun, read chapters nine and ten of *The Fruits of Graft* by Jett, and see if you can recognize a similarity to the 'sitting' president!

All of these "wars" have failed miserably. We listened to the experts on international relations, and they told us about the Gulf of Tonkin (Vietnam), the hidden nukes and biological weapons (Iraq), the drug trail through Panama (Noriega), the massive build-up of Cuban missiles on Grenada (a handful of rifles found), the will of the people of Vietnam to stay divided, the unbelievable wealth which would be created for the Middle Class, if we just opened our borders to all comers in trade (anyone want to comment on that). So they were consistently wrong, and there have been consequences for all of us.

Many of these consequences have devolved to the states. States have lost their youngest and finest in war. States have had to pick up the tab for largely unfunded policies and mandates created in Washington. The War on Drugs has cost local communities billions for policing, incarceration and rehabilitation. The War on Poverty drained so many resources from other projects, that much of local progress in education and infrastructure was brushed to the side.

The so-called need for every single one of these wars was based on LIES. Lies have ruined our world. So why are YOU still joining in on the lies, which are documented, which are easily exposed, which are even, potentially, correctable, but only if we face our COMMON Lies and kill them with an assault of truth.

Consequences have turned to unintended consequences because we trusted the experts who acted so arrogantly about what we needed to do. Johnson, McNamara, Nixon, Kissinger, Reagan, Bush, Cheney, Brzezinski, Rumsfeld, Colin Powell, 'Cap' Weinberg, Tenet, Bert Lance, Ed Meese, Karl Rove, all liars. It seems that they are almost always presented to us as self-made men, true individualists, made of true grit, able to leap tall buildings at a single bound, and just full of American patriotic 'hutzpah'. In every case they fooled us, and we paid the price. In a later chapter, we expose the fallacy of these self-made heroes of these lies.

On a business trip to Panama City, Panama, after our invasion and the 'pacification' of that country, we had to be escorted to a local restaurant by armed guards with Uzis at their side. So much for being greeted as liberators. Of course, the press, back home, painted a picture of 'dancing in the streets!'

Many states are now passing Concealed Carry laws. The Gun Lobby is probably the strongest partisan group in the world. After legislators pass these laws and the governors sign them into law, we notice that there are caveats. It seems that our politicians believe that average citizens need to carry deadly weapons for their personal protection. But politicians are no fools, we are. Guns can be carried and concealed everywhere, except where politicians go. Government buildings, courthouses, government parking lots, political meetings, conventions, well, you get the idea. Appease the Lobby, protect only themselves.

Since weapons are almost never used to protect oneself against a stranger and are overwhelmingly used in an offensive posture, then a few rules need to be applied that will deliver consequences for the abuse of these new freedoms.

- All guns must be registered.
- All gun owners must be rigorously screened for criminal or mental defect.
- All gun owners must be trained and certified in their use.
- All gun owners must have proof that their weapons are secure at all times.
- **All gun owners must carry liability insurance on the misuse of their weapons.**
- All gun owners must report the loss or theft of any weapon within twenty-four hours.
- Any gun, used in a crime, creates a financial liability for its registered owner.
- Possession of any unregistered weapon or weapon with a filed down number automatically results in a five year prison sentence.
- No gun is ever an orphan. Every gun must be registered in the name of the manufacturer until it is registered to another person or entity.
- Upon registration every gun will be fired twice and the spent bullets will be kept at a State crime lab.
- No military-grade weapons may be owned by private citizens.
- No gun may cross state lines without previous registration in the visited state.
- No one under the age of 18 may handle a weapon without an adult present.
- An accidental firing of a weapon by a minor will result in the charge of child neglect and child endangerment.
- The use of a weapon in domestic violence is automatically a capital case.
- All registered, certified, insured gun owners may conceal carry everywhere, including the buildings housing government officials. The next chapter exposes people who are smarter than these poor gun carriers. The next group doesn't even have to carry guns. They can steal billions without any physical weapons at all. The government even drives armored vehicles right up to their doors, so they can carry the loot away. It's Wall Street, baby!

Religious lies, government lies, judicial lies, community lies, business lies, and so now, it's time to finally clean out what's left in your wallet. Don't be shy. Turn the page. It won't hurt…much!

One final book to mention. If you've ever wondered what side of the fence that the government is really on, just read: *Little Pink House. A True Story of Defiance and Courage* by Benedict.

CHAPTER 25

The Big LIE of Wall Street

Investing on Wall Street is gambling, *pure and simple.*

The gullible chump who believes that he can beat 10,000 computer programs, 1,000,000 dishonest brokers, thousands of insider trading cheats, brokerage firms who specialize in making money for themselves, elected government officials who get all their money for elections from them, and with all that… will win doing day trading or working closely with their brother-in-law at a local brokerage, then all I can say is 'go for it.'

Here's the problem: You are nobody and the Market doesn't give a damn about you. After you lose your money, there will be no one to tell because no one will be listening.

Wall Street counts on that. Brokerage firms have been stealing from the American public for over eighty years and no one has gone to prison yet. Well, that's not exactly true. Blatant cases that are over ten years old and can no longer be covered up sometimes come to the attention of the public and someone does something about it. There is no greater incestuous group in the world than the vermin that sleep together on Wall Street. The same names keep moving around to all the agencies: SEC, Treasury Secretary, Federal Reserve positions, Attorney Generals, Commerce Secretaries, Brokerage Chairmen, Governors, and on and on. They have all made fortunes by stealing from the American public.

Most of the theft comes **right out of retirement funds**, so they are virtually impossible to detect. The brokerage firm pays a ratings firm to rate a worthless stock as extremely valuable. The retirement fund buys heavily into the purchase of these worthless stocks (or bonds). The brokerage firms make a fortune in fees selling these worthless stocks and then they short the stock secretly and make fortunes on trashing the stock at the same time. These people have damaged our entire country and then testified before Congress that they were completely unaware how this all happened. They testify to these LIES while looking right into the faces of elected officials—who go to lunch with the brokerage firms' lobbyists to discuss campaign contributions. Usually, it occurs on the same day as testimony.

When gambling, remember that the HOUSE always wins. Pensions in the U.S. have lost trillions of dollars over the years for the retirees who they have a fiduciary responsibility to protect. The persons in charge of these pensions—state or company officials or independents—all have greater allegiance to the brokerage houses. These swindlers are dependent upon insider information to show exemplary performance to keep their jobs.

Let's just say that Wall Street weren't corrupt all the way to their offshore accounts. Let's say that if you could know enough about how the stock market works, you could manage to make good calls on stock purchases and make a nice return, if not a fortune.

Stock is not based on the *value* of the asset, in which you believe that you are investing. Companies lie. They put out false audits and false quarterly reports. They spend a lot of time learning creative accounting methods to cover all kinds of illegal activity. You cannot trust anything that a company tells you. You cannot trust any brokerage house because they make their money by selling you the stock of their client and they tell each client a different story. Even when these brokers are actually caught in a lie, they receive no punishment. Just a few of the names of the guilty: Greenspan, Blankfein, Fuld, Shapiro, Rubin, Corzine, and Cox.

Every stock has over 1,000,000 variables in the real world which can affect its value: price of oil, consumer confidence, tsunamis, wars, drought, elected officials, cost of metals, terrorist attacks, debt rating in other sovereign markets, whether the French Prime Minister is fooling around with a local teenager. There are literally millions, almost all of them unknown and totally unknowable until they happen, but by then it will be too late. Remember that your stock broker *has not lost one penny*. He has been collecting fees all along, mostly on the basis of total ignorance of what he is doing. He probably sold out of that stock a long time ago. Brokers have even lost every single penny their parents had foolishly invested in their ability to pick the right stocks.

I lived in a community of about 100,000 and we had dozens of local brokers. None of them are in business anymore. After a while, you can't even convince your own family to believe in you, or to give you their hard earned money.

In the interest of full disclosure, I must tell you that I have never personally chosen a stock to invest in. I have always used professional financial advisors and every one of them has lost money on my behalf. My Pension, 401K, and personal Stock Portfolio have all lost money. And yes, he was a friend of a friend.

Wall Street has stolen over six trillion dollars from the American public over the last five years. But this money didn't just go away. If the news media had anything to do with presenting the truth, they would have reported the giant sucking sound that pulled the wealth of America out of every community, State, Pension Fund, 401k, bank, charity, and orphanage into the hands of the rich on Wall Street. More billionaires were created on Wall Street during this Raping of America than ever before in history. This occurred while the rest of America was being devastated. These supreme thieves were so shameless that they took taxpayer money to bail out their own thievery. After all this, they gave themselves bonuses—some in the hundreds of millions of dollars—out of the bailout money that *we gave them*. They acted as though the 'stock swaps' 'CDO's' and 'sub-prime' mortgages were total news to them.

What did Obama say, "Duh!"

(check the names of his major campaign contributors! Wall Street was heavily invested in getting Obama elected: Rubin, Geitner, Summers, and on and on)

What did Congress say, "Duh!"

(check the names of their major campaign contributors! See list above)

What did SEC Chairman Shapiro say, "DUH!"

(check how she got the appointment! Rubin, Greenspan, Blankfein, Bernanke, Corzine, the same old crowd made sure that she got the job)

The New York Times uncovered minutes from the meetings of the Federal Reserve, which were conducted while all this was going on. They were laughing at us, while at the same time being clueless about their own supposed economic expertise. The Federal Reserve has been at the forefront of lying from the beginning of its theft of the Treasury of the United States, over one hundred years ago. Read: "Inside the Fed in 2006: A Coming Crisis, and Banter" by Benjamin Applebaum, dated January 12, 2012, New York Times. Everything continues to be Top Secret about the Fed and the movement of money between the banks of the world. And they are laughing about how easy it is to continue keeping all of us in the dark.

So, do you still want to give these Con Men your money?

No one who is not an accredited investor should buy stocks on Wall Street. Only those persons who can afford to lose every penny they invest should play this game. The little guy puts his whole life on the line and, quite predictably, gets crushed by this miasma of filth. A few rich persons can afford to take a major hit and still not get hurt that badly. Taking a hit, by the way, is the only way, that a person can win this game. Still many of them have lost everything. Add to all this the fact that over 80% of all the profits on Wall Street go to the top 1% of the richest Americans.

Everyday people invest because no one can really have a secure retirement with just Social Security and a pension. In order to beat what inflation does to the value of money, you have to find a way to make your money work for you to be ahead of the game when you retire. No one has figured out a reasonable way of doing that. For most small investors they would need to regularly have returns that exceed taxes, fees, and inflation. This rarely happens for the little guy. When principle is lost, it is never again restored. The returns on the lesser asset, which is left after investment losses, will never produce enough gains to meet the initial goal.

Wall Street lives on volatility. They make money going up and they make money going down. Fees are a wonderful thing. And 'shorting' stocks is the *NINTH WONDER OF THE WORLD*. Brokers tell their clients that the stock is quite valuable and that it will go up, while at the same time they are privately betting that the stock is really worthless. Their bet 'profits' are only realized if the stock loses value. And it always does because it is usually really worthless. If the markets are calm, Wall Street is not happy because they are not making the big money so they *create* volatility. A few well-placed comments by Wall Street stooges—Talking Heads on business channels and newspapers, a comment by the President, a manufactured oil shortage, a proposed merger of "giants," a credit crisis—are heard by investors because they are played all day on the business channels, just in case you missed them. They then bring in their usual corporate stooges, brokerage heads, and hedge fund pimps to give it the feel of reality. They don't really care about any of their clients; all they need is a steady stream of suckers to buy their Ponzi-based schemes. What usually burns out most brokers is the constant recruiting of new suckers to buy into their schtick.

The Talking Heads on the business channels are so utterly clueless, that they would likely fail a contest of their supposed knowledge of the markets. And yet, they are 'cheer-leaders' every day for the 'buy' position on every stock out there. So, I would like to challenge them to a contest.

Here it is (the Rules for the Talking Head Contest):

- Every person who makes a comment on any matter concerning financial investing on television or the print media will have to

invest $100,000 of their own money, over a six month period, which will commence on the same day for all participants.
- All investments will be made public, instantaneously, on the internet.
- The investor must disclose every name of every person who has given them advice about that investment.
- The goal for these brainiacs who encourage little old retired ladies to invest in the market will be a modest ten percent return after fees, taxes, and inflation.
- If they make less than a ten percent return after fees, taxes, and inflation, they agree to not appear on TV, or print media, for a period of no less than five years.
- If they actually get a return of less than their original principle, after fees, taxes and inflation, then they agree to forfeit the entire investment and the proceeds will go to an organization, which is established to help victims of their fallacious advice.
- Anyone who refuses to enter the contest—corporate leaders, advisors, fund managers, etc.—will be banned from the airways and print media for a period of no less than ten years.

These people will never agree to this. They want to make it clear that their viewers and readers are the suckers, not them. Yet, when they give their never ending "buy" recommendations on the air, they are positively orgasmic about how certain they are that the Market is where you ought to be.

Two cavemen were standing in a cave. "What that line on wall?" "Don't know. But when it go up, everybody happy. And when it go down, everybody sad." "You smart Rocko, what it mean?" "Don't know." "I watch CNBC and get rocks off. I tell you tomorrow." Isn't it amazing that the standard of financial knowledge has stayed fairly consistent through all these years of evolution. Which makes me feel a little more consoled, when I see all the monkeys giving their advice on TV.

You're going to love these books:

News Incorporated: Corporate Media Ownership and Its Threat to Democracy by Cohen.

Media MythMakers: How Journalists, Activists and Advertisers Mislead Us by Radford.

***Griftopia: Bubble Machines, Vampire Squids, and the Long Con that is Breaking America* by Taibbi.**

Corporate Crooks and How Rogue Executives Ripped Off Americans and Congress Helped Them Do It by Farrell.

***Greenspan's Bubbles* by Fleckenstein.**

Fooled by Randomness by Taleb.

In the next chapter we try to understand these titans of the financial, political, and commercial world. They certainly can't be like the rest of us. They have their own set of rules. They have their lofty, hidden, secret towers. They have what seems to be endless access to insider information, which certainly points out that they must be special. Their only vulnerability seems to be the fictional kryptonite because the Justice Department can't get to them. Investors who have lost everything can't seem to get to them either. World governments, about to go into receivership, can't seem to get to them through international forums. When they are fined for misbehaving, the fines usually amount to less than 1%, so they get to keep the rest of the loot and the court decisions are always sealed so that an unsuspecting public can continue to be unsuspecting. If you are not convinced yet, just read back through all the parties—banks, financial houses, rating agencies, brokers, US Gov't, etc.—who were involved in making the Enron fiasco possible. Then make a list of everyone who got punished for stealing billions of dollars from the public. You will only need a sheet two inches by two inches!

You must read the next chapter to see a perfect example of these holier-than-thou people. Talk about living a lie!

Chapter 26

The Lie of the Self-made Man

Is it possible for anyone to be a "self-made" man or woman?

I was acquainted with a pilot for a major airline who touted himself as a person who didn't need anyone else. To protect his identity, I'll refer to him as Mr. B from now on.

Mr. B claimed he was successful because he was a superstar. He attended a military academy where he had received his training. I would have attributed his education to hard work until I learned that he attended this school as a result of his father's connections. His father was a contributor to a Congressman's political campaign. Even though the son's grades were poor, the Congressman secured his admission to the academy. After leaving the military, Mr. B couldn't find a job and ended up working for his father-in-law digging ditches. Despite his circumstances, he thought he was better than anyone else because he was still a pilot.

Mr. B had acute appendicitis when he was young, so his parents rushed him to the hospital and he survived. I asked him how much he paid to have the ambulance service available at all hours of the day. I asked if he had built the hospital, trained the doctors, nurses and staff to be on stand-by for his needs. I asked if he had paid to build and repave all the highways, which were there when they rushed him to the hospital to save his life.

I asked Mr. B if he had received any special advantages just because he had been born into an upper middle class family. I asked if he could think of anyone in his life whose absence would have resulted in a less favorable life for him. He couldn't think of anyone.

I asked if his parents had ever had to bail him out when life wasn't going well. I already knew that they helped with the down payment for his house and provided money for his kids.

Then one day, the airlines experienced a shortage of pilots due to early retirements, so a friend called Mr. B and told him that he had put in a good word for him.

It seems that at important turning-points, Mr. B always had a helping hand so he could become the ultimate *self-made man*.

To hear Mr. B tell it, every advantage was a result of his own doing.

How does one get to be this "self-made" man and enjoy all these benefits?

- Spend time researching before you decide which family to be born into.
- Preferably be born in America.
- Be born Caucasian (or at least look Caucasian).
- Make sure that your family is well-connected.
- Don't worry about grades (Right, Bill Gates?) just make sure that your family can still get you into the right schools.
- Remember: the first letter in 'team' is 'I'.
- Count on family to bail you out of trouble but denigrate less fortunate persons with slurs and distain for having fewer resources.
- When opportunity knocks pretend that you were on both sides of the door.
- Be generous to a fault. Money in the right pocket, money in the left pocket, money in the back pocket, money in the briefs, a little in the socks. Did you think I meant to give anything to others? No, those are fools, not the self-made pioneers of America.

- Sit at the head of the table, stand at the head of the line, and accept no responsibility for error or misjudgment. Blame others when things go wrong and categorize them as liberals, welfare cheats, and lazy bastards—all those losers who never had the advantages you did.
- Use the leverage in society which you were born with to live a self-centered existence that would make King Henry VIII cringe.
- Accept no limits to your arrogance.

When I was a consultant to major corporations, one of the mysteries I often encountered was that of a manager who had no social or management skills. Most had never received training in working with or over others. Most received their college training in engineering, accounting, or business management, but never in liberal arts or humanistic skills. The problem for me was that they were extremely difficult to work with and often totally resistant to change. They were so arrogant that they always wanted me to focus my change efforts on the workers below them.

After several decades and over 100 major clients, I learned that most of the quality, productivity, and profitability problems within these companies were directly the fault of these "self-made" arrogant managers. They couldn't see what they couldn't see, but the problem went beyond blinders. Most of these individuals were born with silver spoons in their mouths; they never had to work for a living. These people were highly disloyal to everyone but themselves. They made a lot of money, and the people who worked for them did not. The people below them were susceptible to being used and abused by their powerful, wealthy managers. The problems within the company mostly dealt with morale. People were not fooled, and the gossip mill was as efficient as the most sophisticated communication system in the world. People tend not to respect a guy who diddles another man's wife. They flaunted their positions by playing golf in the afternoon several days a week. It was even difficult to set up meetings with them because they were so busy at the club.

I tried to unravel these managers' disconnect with humanity. The greatest progress we could make would be in our ability to help these managers humble themselves and mature.

Advantages given to these "self-made" men and women:

- Born into middle to upper-middle income families
- Did not serve in the military
- A college education—more often than not paid for by others
- Start at their companies at approximately three times the salary of their workers and quickly move to four or five times those wages plus benefits and bonuses
- Family connections with someone in the company where they are employed
- Access to mentors who would see to their welfare and promotions and look out for them in general

When downsizing hit companies a decade ago, many of these middle managers were let go, but they had no place to go. I received calls from several of these guys who were having a difficult time adjusting to the new economy. Of course they blamed everyone else, but they still hoped to ride their silver spoons to another cushy job. Unfortunately for these "self-made" men, those jobs were all gone. The fortunate ones had inherited money from their dead parents or received generous severance packages, but for less than you might think. Several men committed suicide.

One former manager, the most arrogant person I had ever met, called to tell me about what a horrible thing his former company had done to him. His old company had been sold and the new owners were taking no prisoners. First, they lowered his pension pay-out and projected that they might not even be able to honor that. Then they told him that they were going to discontinue his medical insurance. This man had never worked an honest day in his life, and he was shocked he couldn't find a company that wanted someone around who would diddle his secretaries and otherwise be totally worthless. His last salary at his old company was $495,000 a year plus a bonus, which usually equated to two thirds of his salary. He wasn't *self-made*, he was *self-deluded*! Last I heard, his house had been foreclosed, his sailboat repossessed, and his fifth wife had left him. All this loss and several years ago I told him about a job which paid just about $200,000 a year. At the time he was miffed at me for even suggesting it.

No man is an island.

No one is self-made in America. Life is too complex. Too many people contribute to the success of everyone who succeeds. People who believe they are self-made often become the most unbearable wretches. They are living a lie…a lie that has very destructive outcomes for many people who will occupy any space near them.

You're probably thinking that Donald Trump fits this image perfectly. Self-made is a lie and the actions that they take lead to companies and communities being forced to try to survive in the middle of their delusional personalities that bring major harm to everyone and everything around them.

Well, we've covered a lot of ground in exposing all the LIES in our lives, which have ruined the world. We have suggested some possible solutions and alternatives. The one solution, which I had held out the greatest hope for, was education. If we teach the facts, the truth and the methods for discovering truth ongoing, then we should be able to create a better, saner world.

Then, I got a copy of the courses, and services, offered at one of the most progressive universities in the world. To my shock, I discovered that it was just 'chock' full of lunacy. 'Alternative medicine' and 'touch therapy' in the Medical School curriculum. 'Naturopathy' and 'organics' offered to Dietician students. Many, many courses on religion offered in the Humanities curriculum. And this was just the beginning. So, I called the University and voiced my dismay. During my conversation, I was reminded that 'university' means 'welcoming' to all ideas. When I asked, whether it mattered or not, whether these courses were based on fact and truth, I was told 'What is truth?'.

I thought that was their job to find out. I'll call again. Next time, I hope that I will be able to talk to a responsible 'adult'.

Read on to see how these non-adults are conducting the other affairs of these otherwise great institutions.

Chapter 27

Institutions of Higher Learning have become a LIE

I question whether there are any mature adults still leading institutions of higher learning in the United States.

One public university announced that they would pay the head coach of their football team over ***thirteen million dollars.*** When you compare that to the sum of all the academic scholarships of the entire entering Freshman Class it is about equal! The president of the university offered this explanation. "We want to teach our students the extreme value of being competitive in a very hostile world. Our main rival was paying that much, so we really had no choice. Besides, it is all covered by TV revenue and advertising sales." That's what really matters: Money.

Money corrupts even the most saintly of little old ladies. What it does to coaches, players, and universities is perfectly pornographic. We condemn the few who are exposed by disgruntled former players, angry boosters, and the parents of kids who were misled by the program. How many violent crimes have to be committed by these athletes before we admit that we are not recruiting genuine students?

Remember that all this misapplication of money is driven by the media, which makes billions beyond the millions that universities collect. Talking Heads now harp about student athletes being abused by the system and not getting paid their due. They do this because the media wants to field the best athletes, so they can deliver the best entertainment to a gambling public.

Depending on the sport, an elite student athlete will receive a full scholarship, a stipend for books, fees, and materials, full room and board payments, access to the best trainers and training equipment, and an allowance. He will be dragged from total obscurity into the limelight and given the opportunity to showcase his talents before the world. Is there any other venue in the entire world, which would afford him the same opportunity? He will have exposure to professional team executives so that he will ultimately be given an ungodly amount of money for his talents. Even though the taxpayers foot the entire bill for this ungrateful kid, he and his colleagues will still be chosen by the National Football League on a ratio of less than one in ten thousand to actually play in the NFL. We paid for these losers to receive this free largesse, but if you listen to the hucksters on ESPN, NBC, CBS, and ABC you would think that this is a reinstitution of slavery.

The leaders of universities listen with bleeding hearts to the supposed woes of student athletes. The total package for most athletes is worth in excess of $500,000, and they are still crying. It is the taxpayers who should be crying. Still, athletic departments give more and more to these kids because they know they'll be out of a job if their team has two losing seasons. Rival schools pay their players, so why shouldn't we?

We have lost control of our colleges and universities, and there are no reasonable adults left to say that "the emperor has no clothes." There is no integrity in the university system anymore, because there are no adults running the show, anymore.

To add to the insanity: Less than 1% of all the top high school athletes in America get a full scholarship. The rest of them have to work, save, scrimp, and do without while the elite whine, whine, and whine. There are even schools that give no football scholarships at all. Many kids who come from poor families never even got to play high school football because the kids had to work to help support their families. I talked to a young man who was setting state records in his sophomore year in high school but had to quit and go to work to support his alcoholic mother and five siblings. The greatest athletes of all time will never play and never be known. Yet our colleges are being destroyed by the most foolish system ever devised. Consider the character of our elite athletes and ask if that is the kind of adult we want our universities to produce.

I believe in the importance of higher education for any progress to be achieved in this world. They say that children are our future, but I add, only if they get a top-flight education.

Universities don't seem to teach students how to think. And maybe that's a good thing for them because if they did the students would see through the massive hypocrisy of universities which have a separate standard for athletes and a different one for serious students. The lies of our modern world will never be confronted when universities take no interest in challenging the indoctrinated lies that incoming students bring with them in their suitcase.

Universities all have the word "truth" somewhere in their Latin logos, but they perceive the truth as optional. They never confront the lies of religion. That topic is off-limits, verboten. The university gives *tax free* space to these idiots. They allow them to teach courses on the LIES of their heritage. They even encourage a diversity of LIES on their faculties, so they are safely within the cultural lies which pay their salaries.

Students enter and leave with the same religious lies, but now they have learned how to make a living. They are safe from ever having to confront the fact that they worship the most heinous creation in all of history: the mass murderer and his goons, who would have put a stop to all education if they could have.

Forget about evolution. I went to three of the best universities in the United States and was never taught the profound truths of Evolution and the progressive ideas, which have shaped our healthier citizens. That was almost fifty years ago. The facts that have accumulated since then in support of evolution can be numbered in the trillions. Sadly, just recently

I looked through a catalogue of courses offered at the great university I attended as an undergraduate and found they still offer dozens of the same courses that highlight but don't challenge the lies of religion. I found no courses listed as exploring the scientific world of discovery, and evolution.

Some potential relief as a way of working toward centering TRUTH as a centerpiece for education:

- Limit all coaches' salaries to less than 60% of the highest paid professor on campus and have the NCAA enforce this rule across all eligible schools. No competition will be allowed by any school which violates this rule.
- Any athlete who attempts to be paid will be expelled from campus, forfeit his scholarship, and must ask for immediate acceptance into the NFL.
- Any athlete who leaves the university before graduation to enter the NFL or NBA must repay their scholarship money and fees in full. A loan agreement must be signed to this affect before entering the university.
- Any athlete who misses over 5% of his classes will lose his scholarship.

There are plenty of deserving students who never even got a chance at this level of education. They would have given anything to be sitting in one of those seats.

- Any athlete who does not maintain a minimum 2.5 GPA will lose his scholarship. Classes specially designed for athletes should make it unbelievably easy to meet this requirement.
- The admissions process will be conducted on an anonymous basis. Admission will be based on merit alone, and all applications will be submitted to a third party with numbered identification only.

This will stop the process of admitting the children of alumni who are less worthy than other applicants. George Bush's affiliation with Harvard Graduate School makes a lie of the entire higher learning process. When the name of a student seated next to you is written in granite at the corner of the building, you can be certain that his admission was handled through the bank, and not the SAT. We have so many brain-dead diplomats, government workers, Federal Reserve presidents, and cabinet officers because their connections bought them an education. We know that intelligence is a random occurrence throughout the whole human family. We also know that admission to elite universities, for children of the top 1% wealthiest Americans is almost a certainty. At the same time, millions of better qualified and more intelligent students are left out in the cold. Eliminate the process of recruiting athletes who have no academic qualification. Eliminate the activities of scouts, boosters, agents, and other nefarious characters who can recede into the shadows. Universities will actually get a higher *quality* athlete, and most certainly, a more serious student.

- Any university which does not use an anonymous admissions process will be denied access to Federal money for any and all purposes. No more research grants, brick and mortar money, grants of financial aid, or student loans until they comply. This will enable the education of the best and the brightest to the great wealth of America.
- A program will be established that guarantees entering freshmen pay no tuition or fees. We want to encourage all of our young people to get a higher education, and this can get them started. They will still be selected based on merit alone. This program will be offered at all taxpayer supported institutions and no private, for-profit, two-year, or religious colleges. The First Year Free Program will be available to every American citizen up to the age of 25.
- Students who maintain a 3.5 GPA or higher during their freshman year (full curriculum) will be funded at 50% of their tuition and fees for their second year.
- A Certified National Security Scholarship program will be set up at all public universities. The Federal Government will determine which majors are 'critical' to the wealth production and security of the United States. It may include physics, math, computer technology, etc. Students of the highest merit will be accepted

into this program. They will pay no tuition or fees through to graduation. Upon graduation they will begin to pay 3% of their gross income for the rest of their lives added to their normal income tax liability. They will graduate debt free and will undoubtedly add tremendously to the wealth production of the nation.
- A mandatory course on evolution will be taught in the freshman year at every state supported school. Any state, which does not have this required course, will not receive Federal funding.
- Every Instructor in state supported schools must receive training and certification in teaching methods and evaluation before being allowed to teach undergraduates.
- Every time tuition increases at any state supported university, the president of the university's salary would be reduced by 3% and no bonuses, raises, or additional benefits will be allowed.
- When a university's athletic programs are sanctioned by the NCAA, the president of the university should resign. Hopefully, they will be replaced by an ethical adult.

How we educate our children. How we demand veracity in every institution. How we fund what should be 'truth' machines of our higher education. How we make demands on ourselves to examine everything we do and say to make sure that the 'truth' is at the core of our being and our activities will build a future of our dreams, or if we fail, the disaster of our nightmares.

Well, I guess that all of this really leaves it up to you and your choices. Lies have ruined the world, so why are you still lying? You have a choice. You can decide that you will live a life based on fact and truth, or you can continue to lie to yourself, your children, and your neighbors. You will be right in someone's eyes, no matter what you do, but there will be consequences.

Truth will conquer the world one person at a time.

I wish you and yours a happy, truth-filled future. Thank you for the time you gave to read my book.

Coming Soon........

.......more LIES!

BIBLIOGRAPHY

Alley, Robert S. *James Madison on Religious Liberty* Amherst, NY: Prometheus Books, 1985.

Angela, Piero, et al *The Extraordinary Story of Human Origins* Buffalo, NY: Prometheus Books, Publishers, 1993.

_____ *The Extraordinary Story of Life on Earth* Buffalo, NY: Prometheus Books, 1996.

Angeles, Peter A. *Critiques of God* Buffalo, NY: Prometheus Books, 1976.

Ariely, Dan et al *Predictably Irrational: The Hidden Forces That Shape Our Decisions* New York, NY: HarperCollins Publishers, 2010.

Baker, Robert A. and Nickell, Joe *Missing Pieces: How to Investigate Ghosts, UFO's, Psychics and other Mysteries* Buffalo NY: Prometheus Books, 1992.

Barrett, Stephen M., M.D. and Hirbert, Victor, M.D., J.D. *The Vitamin Pusher: How the "Health Food" Industry is Selling America a Bill of Goods* Amherst NY: Prometheus Books, 1994.

Benedict, Jeff *Little Pink House, A True Story of Defiance and Courage* New York NY: Grand Central Publishing, 2009.

Bernneman, Richard J. *Deadly Blessings: Faith Healing on Trial* Buffalo, NY: Prometheus Books, 1990.

Blastland, Michael, et al *The Numbers Game: The Commonsense Guide to Understanding Numbers in the News, in Politics, and in Life* New York, NY: Penguin Group (USA) Incorporated, 2010.

Capaldi, Nicholas, et al *The Art of Deception: An Introduction to Critical Thinking* Amherst, NY: Prometheus Books, 1996.

Carroll, Sean B. *The Making of the Fittest: DNA and the Ultimate Forensic Record of Evolution* New York, NY: W.W. Norton Company, Incorporated, 2006.

Cohen, Elliot D., PhD. *News Incorporated: Corporate Media Ownership and Its Threat to Democracy* Amherst, NY: Prometheus Books, 2005.

Darraj, Susan Muaddi, et al *The Universal Declaration of Human Rights* New York, NY: Facts on File, Incorporated, 2010.

Darwin, Charles *The Voyage of the Beagle* Vercelli: White Star; Exeter: Star Book Sales, 2006.

_____ *On the Origin of Species* New York: Oxford University Press, Incorporated, 2009.

Dawkins, Richard *Greatest Show on Earth: the Evidence for Evolution* New York, NY: Free Press, 2009.

_____ *The Blind Watchmaker* New York, NY: W.W. Norton & Company, Inc., 1996.

_____ *The God Delusion* Boston, MA: Houghton Mifflin Company, 2006.

_____ *The Selfish Gene* Oxford; New York: Oxford University Press, 2006.

Deakin, Michael A. B. *Hypatia of Alexandria: Mathematician and Martyr* Amherst, NY: Prometheus Books, 2007.

Doerr, Edd et al *The Case Against School Vouchers* Amherst, NY: Prometheus Books, 1996.

Donald, Graeme *Lies, Damned Lies and History – A Catalogue of Historical Errors and Misunderstandings* Brimscombe: Sproud: Gloucestershire: The History Press Limited, 2009.

Douglass, Frederick *My Bondage and My Freedom* Radford, VA: Wilbur Publishing, 2005.

Doyno, Victor (Editor) *Mark Twain: Selected Writings of an American Skeptic* Amherst, NY: Prometheus Books, 1995.

Engh, Mary Jane *In the Name of Heaven: 3000 Years of Religious Persecution* Amherst, NY: Prometheus Books, 2007.

Evenson, A. Edward *The Telephone Patent Conspiracy of 1876: The Elisha Gray –Alexander Graham Bell Controversy and Its Many Players* Jefferson, NC: McFarland & Company, Incorporated Publishers, 2000.

Evenson, George *The Story of Television: The Life of Philo T. Farnsworth* North Stratford, NH: Ayer Company Publishers, 1978.

Fairbanks, Daniel J. et al *Relics of Eden: The Powerful Evidence of Evolution in Human DNA* Amherst, NY: Prometheus Books, 2010.

Falk, Dean *The Fossil Chronicles: How Two Controversial Discoveries Changed Our View of Human Evolution* Berkeley, CA: University of California Press, 2011.

Farrell, Greg *Corporate Crooks and How Rogue Executives Ripped Off Americans and Congress Helped Them Do It* Amherst, NY: Prometheus Books, 2006.

Fleckenstein, William with Frederick Sheehan *Greenspan's Bubbles* New York, NY: McGraw Hill Companies, 2008.

Francis, Richard C. *Epigenetics: The Ultimate Mystery of Inheritance* New York: W.W. Norton and Company, 2011.

Gardner, Martin *Great Essays in Science* Amherst, NY: Prometheus Books, 1994.

_____ *Science: Good, Bad & Bogus* Amherst, NY: Prometheus Books, 1996.

_____ *The Sacred Beetle and Other Great Essays in Science* New York, NY: Penguin Group (USA) Incorporated, 1986.

_____ *Weird Water and Fuzzy Logic* Amherst NY: Prometheus Books, 1996.

Garrett, Brandon L. et al *Convicting the Innocent: Where Criminal Prosecutions Go Wrong* Cambridge, MA: Harvard University Press, 2011.

Goldberg, Steven *When Wish Replaces Thought: Why So Much of What You Believe is False* Amherst, NY: Prometheus Books, 1990.

Goldstone, Lawrence, et al *Inherently Unequal – The Betrayal of Equal Rights By the Supreme Court 1865-1903* New York, NY: Walker and Company, 2011.

Gordon, Henry *Extraordinary Deception* Buffalo, NY: Prometheus Books, 1987.

Gould, Stephen Jay *Wonderful Life: The Burgess Shale and Nature of History* New York, NY: W.W. Norton, 1989.

Greenblatt, Stephen *The Swerve – How the World Became Modern* New York, NY: W.W. Norton and Company, Incorporated, 2011.

Greenwald, Glenn *With Liberty and Justice for Some – How the Law is Used to Destroy Equality and Protect the Powerful* New York, Metropolitan Books, Henry Holt & Company, 2011.

Gutzman, Kevin R. C. *Politically Incorrect Guide to the Constitution* Washington D.C.: Regnery Publishing, Inc., 2007.

Harris, Sam *The Moral Landscape: How Science Can Determine Human Values* New York: Free Press, 2010.

Harrison, Guy P. *Fifty Popular Beliefs that People Think are True* Amherst, NY: Prometheus Books, 2011.

Harwood, William R. *Mythology's Last Gods: Yahweh and Jesus* Buffalo, NY: Prometheus Books, 1992.

Haught, James A. *2000 Years of Disbelief: Famous People with the Courage to Doubt* Amherst, NY: Prometheus Books, 1996.

Helms, Randel *Gospel Fictions* Amherst, NY: Prometheus Books, 1988.

_____ *The Bible Against Itself* Agawam, MA: Millennium Press, 2006.

_____ *Who Wrote the Gospels?* Millennium Press, 1997.

Hitchens, Christopher *God is Not Great – How Religion Poisons Everything* New York, NY: Grand Central Publishing, 2007.

_____ *The Missionary Position: Mother Teresa in Theory and Practice* Great Britain: Biddle, Ltd., 1995.

Hoffman, P. Joseph, edited by, *Jesus Outside the Gospels* Buffalo, NY: Prometheus Books, 1987.

_____ *Sources of the Jesus Tradition: Separating History from Myth* Amherst, NY: Prometheus Books, 2010.

Houdini, Harry *Miracle Mongers and Their Methods: A Complete Exposition* Fairfield, IA: Akasha Publishing, LLC, 2009.

Ilaiah, Kancha *Why I Am Not a Hindu* Calcutta: Mandura Sen, 2005.

Ingersoll, Robert G. et al *On The Gods: And Other Essays* Buffalo, NY: Prometheus Books, 1990.

Jett, Wayne *The Fruits of Graft: Great Depression Then and Now* California: Launfal Press, 2011.

Joshi, S. T. *In Her Place: A Documentary History of Prejudice Against Women* Amherst, NY: Prometheus Books, 2006.

Korman, Richard I. *Story of Goodyear: An Inventor's Obsession and the Struggles for a Rubber Monopoly* San Francisco, CA: Encounter Books, 2001.

Kurtz, Paul (drafted by) *Humanist Manifesto l and ll* Buffalo, NY: Prometheus Books, 1973.

Secular Humanist Declaration Buffalo, NY: Prometheus Books, 1980.

Kusche, Larry *The Bermuda Triangle Mystery – Solved* New York, NY: Harper & Row, 1975.

Kush, Induskhamit *What They Never Told You In History Class* A & B Distributors & Publishers, 2000.

Lehman, Godfrey *We the Jury…The Impact on Our Basic Freedoms* Amherst, NY: Prometheus Books, 1997.

Lin Zixin et al *Qigong: Chinese Medicine or Pseudoscience?* Darby, MA: Diane Publishing Company, 2003.

Ludemann, Gerd *Jesus After 2000 Years* Amherst, NY: Prometheus Books, 2001.

_____ *Paul: The Founder of Christianity* Amherst, NY: Prometheus Books, 2002.

_____ *The Acts of the Apostles: What Really Happened in the Earliest Days of the Church?* Amherst, NY: Prometheus Books, 2005.

_____ *The Great Deception: And What Jesus Really Said and Did* Amherst, NY: Prometheus Books, 1999.

Madrick, Jeff et al *Age of Greed: The Triumph of Finance and the Decline of America, 1970 to the Present* New York, NY: Knopf Doubleday Publishing Group, 2012.

Magner, George *Chiropractic: The Victims Perspective* Amherst, NY: Prometheus Books, 1995.

McGowan, Christopher *In the Beginning: A Scientist Shows Why the Creationists Are Wrong* Buffalo, NY: Prometheus Books, 1984.

McKinsey, C. Dennis *Biblical Errancy: A Reference Guide* Amherst, NY: Prometheus Books, 2000.

Meister, Kathleen *Cigarettes: What the Warning Label Doesn't Tell You* Morrisville, NC: LuLu Enterprises, Incorporated, 2010.

Mendelson, Robert *A Family Divided: A Divorced Father's Struggle with the Child Custody Industry* Amherst, NY: Prometheus Books, 1997.

Menzies, Gavin *1421: The Year China Discovered America* New York, NY: HarperCollins Publishers, Inc., 2002.

Morgenson, Gretchen and Rosner, Joshua *Reckless Endangerment: How Outsized Ambition, Greed, and Corruption led to Economic Armageddon* New York, NY: Times Books, Henry Holt and Company, LLC, 2011.

Nickell, Joe *Looking for a Miracle: Weeping Icons, Relics, Stigmata, Visions and Healing Cures* Buffalo, NY: Prometheus Books, 1993.

_____ *Psychic Sleuths: ESP and Sensational Cases* Buffalo, NY: Prometheus Books, 1994.

Nietzsche, Frederich *Thus Spake Zarathustra* Charleston, SC: CreateSpace, 2011.

Northcutt, Wendy *The Darwin Awards: Countdown to Extinction* New York, NY: Penguin Group (USA) Incorporated, 2010.

Paine, Thomas *The Age of Reason* Whitefish, MT: Kessinger Publications, LLC, 2010.

_____ *Common Sense* Mineola, NY: Dover Publications, Inc. 2011.

_____ *Rights of Man* New York, NY: USA, Penguin Books, 1985.

Paulos, John Allen *Innumeracy: Mathematical Illiteracy and Its Consequences* New York, NY: Hill and Wang, 1988.

Perakh, Mark, et al *Unintelligent Design* Amherst, NY: Prometheus Books, 2003.

Prakash, Snigdha *All the Justice Money Can Buy: Corporate Greed on Trial* New York, NY: Kaplan Publishing, 2011.

Price, Robert M. *Deconstructing Jesus* Amherst, NY: Prometheus Books, 1986.

Radford, Benjamin *Media MythMakers: How Journalists, Activists and Advertisers Mislead Us* Amherst, NY: Prometheus Books, 2003.

Randi, James *Flim Flam: Psychics, ESP, Unicorns and Other Delusions* Buffalo, NY: Prometheus Books, 1982.

_____ *The Faith Healers* Buffalo, NY: Prometheus Books, 1987.

Reel, Guy *Unequal Justice: Wayne Dumond, Bill Clinton, and the Politics of Rape in Arkansas* Amherst, NY: Prometheus Books, 1990.

Ross, Brian *The Madoff Chronicles: Inside the Secret World of Bernie and Ruth* Darby, PA: Diane Publishing Company, 2011.

Rovelli, Carlo *First Scientist: Anaximander and His Legacy* Yardley, PA: Westholme Publishing, 2011.

Sagan, Carl *Pale Blue Dot: A Vision of the Human Future in Space* New York, NY: Random House, 1994.

_____ *The Demon-haunted World: Science as a Candle in the Dark* New York, NY: Random House, 1995.

Schweizer, Peter *Architects of Ruin: How Big Government Liberals Wrecked the Economy and How They Will Do It Again if No One Stops Them* New York, NY: HarperCollins Publishers, 2007.

Sebald, Hans, PhD. *Witch-Children: From Salem Witch Hunts to Modern Courtrooms* Amherst, NY: Prometheus Books, 1990.

Seckel, Al (Editor) *Bertrand Russell: On God and Religion* Buffalo, NY: Prometheus Books, 1986.

Shoebat, Walid et al *God's War On Terror: Islam, Prophecy and the Bible* Lafayette, LA: Top Executive Media, 2008.

Shubin, Neil *Your Inner Fish: A Journey into 3.5 Billion-Year History of the Human Body* New York, NY: Knopf Doubleday Publishing Group, 2008.

Silvertown, Jonathan (Editor) *99% Ape: How Evolution Adds Up* Chicago: The University of Chicago Press, 2009.

Skloot, Rebecca *The Immortal Life of Henrietta Lacks* New York: Crown Publishers, 2010.

Smith, Cameron M., PhD. et al *The Fact of Evolution* Amherst, NY: Prometheus Books, 2011.

Smith, George H. *Atheism: The Case Against God* Buffalo, NY: Prometheus Books, 1989.

Smith, Morton (Editor) *What the Bible Really Says* Buffalo, NY: Prometheus Books, 1986.

Spector, Michael *Denialism: How Irrational Thinking Hinders Scientific Progress, Harms the Planet, and Threatens Our Lives* New York, NY: Penguin Group (USA) Incorporated, 2009.

Sperry, Paul *The Great American Bank Robbery: The Unauthorized Report About What Really Caused the Great Recession* Nashville, Tennessee: Thomas Nelson Incorporated, 2011.

Stenger, Victor J., PhD. *God the Failed Hypothesis, How Science Shows That God Does Not Exist* Amherst, NY: Prometheus Books, 2008.

Stiebing, William H., Jr. *Out of the Desert? Archaeology and the Exodus/ Conquest Narratives* Buffalo, NY: Prometheus Books, 1989.

Stout, Martha *The Sociopath Next Door: The Ruthless Versus the Rest of Us* New York, NY: Broadway Books, 2005.

Taibbi, Matt *Griftopia: Bubble Machines, Vampire Squids, and the Long Con that is Breaking America* New York, NY: Spiegel & Grau, 2010.

Taleb, Nassim Nicholas *Fooled by Randomness: The Hidden Role of Chance in Life and in the Markets* New York, NY: Random House, 2005.

Taves, Ernest H. *This is the Place: Brigham Young and the New Zion* Buffalo, NY: Prometheus Books, 1990.

Tucker, Holly *Blood Work: A Tale of Medicine and Murder in the Scientific Revolution* New York, NY: W.W. Norton Company, Incorporated, 2011.

Twain, Mark *Christian Science* New York, NY: Oxford University Press, 1996.

Warraq, Ibn *Why I Am Not a Muslim* Amherst, NY: Prometheus Books Publishing, 2003.

Watters, Wendell W., M.D. *Deadly Doctrines: Health, Illness, and Christian God Talk* Buffalo, NY: Prometheus Books, 1992.

Weintraub, David *How Old is the Universe?* Princeton, NJ: Princeton University Press, 2010.

Wells, G. A. *Did Jesus Exist?* Buffalo, NY: Prometheus Books, 1986.

Wisotsky, Steven *Beyond the War on Drugs* Amherst, NY: Prometheus Books Publishers, 1990.

Wolfe, Nathan *The Viral Storm: The Dawn of a New Pandemic Age* New York, NY: Henry Holt & Company, 2011.

Yant, Martin *Presumed Guilty: Why Innocent People are Wrongly Convicted* Amherst, NY: Prometheus Books, 1990.

www.ingramcontent.com/pod-product-compliance
Lightning Source LLC
LaVergne TN
LVHW091534060526
838200LV00036B/603